T0355706

The Public Insult Playbook

The publisher and the University of California Press Foundation gratefully acknowledge the generous support of the Barbara S. Isgur Endowment Fund in Public Affairs.

The Public
Insult Playbook

HOW ABUSERS IN POWER
UNDERMINE CIVIL
RIGHTS REFORM

Ruth Colker

UNIVERSITY OF CALIFORNIA PRESS

University of California Press
Oakland, California

© 2021 by Ruth Colker

Library of Congress Cataloging-in-Publication Data

Names: Colker, Ruth, author.
Title: The public insult playbook : how abusers in power undermine civil
  rights reform / Ruth Colker.
Description: Oakland, California : University of California Press, [2021] |
  Includes bibliographical references and index.
Identifiers: LCCN 2021006469 (print) | LCCN 2021006470 (ebook) |
  ISBN 9780520343818 (cloth) | ISBN 9780520975187 (epub)
Subjects: LCSH: Invective—Political aspects—United States. | Civil
  rights—United States.
Classification: LCC BF463.I58 C65 2021 (print) | LCC BF463.I58 (ebook) |
  DDC 179—dc23
LC record available at https://lccn.loc.gov/2021006469
LC ebook record available at https://lccn.loc.gov/2021006470

Manufactured in the United States of America

30 29 28 27 26 25 24 23 22 21
10 9 8 7 6 5 4 3 2 1

In memory of James Colker, 1928–2019; may others follow his example of public service and compassion

Contents

Acknowledgments

Many people have contributed to this book coming to fruition, although of course its weaknesses are attributable to me alone.

This book began as a consideration of the role of public insults in impeding disability advocacy. I thank Amy Robertson, Co-Executive Director of the Civil Rights Education and Enforcement Center, for initially bringing this issue to my attention through her blogging and discussions. Amy also helped give me access to a database that she was compiling, to help me document the scope of this problem. A sabbatical from teaching at the Moritz College of Law then provided me with the time necessary to share earlier versions of this work at the AALS Conference in New Orleans, Louisiana; a faculty workshop at Berkeley Law School hosted by the Center for the Study of Law and Society; a faculty workshop at University of New South Wales in Sydney, Australia; and a faculty workshop at U.C. Davis Law School in Davis, California.

Many research assistants also helped with this project. Stacey Dettwiller, Emily Durell, Kelsie Hendren, and Lindsey Woods helped with the initial disability research in 2018. MacKenzie Boyd then helped me take the project to a broader level as it grew from an article to a book with her careful editing eye in 2019. Finally, research assistants John Coming and Jaclyn

Serpico helped me expand the scope and depth of the work in the summer of 2020. Jaclyn assisted with my abortion research; John checked all the citations, did a very careful proofread, and helped with the research for chapter 8. I very much appreciate the Moritz College of Law's generous research budget, which made this support possible.

Moritz law librarian Stephanie Ziegler helped me with research at every stage of this project, and office associate Allyson Hennelly helped me resolve various technical issues with the manuscript.

Senior editor Maura Roessner at University of California Press encouraged me to develop these ideas into a book project and helped me think about how I could broaden my audience to include other political junkies like myself. It has been fun to find a voice that may not be boringly legalistic.

Finally, many people read versions of the manuscript in its early stages and offered me constructive suggestions. They include Amna Akbar, Amy Cohen, Rosalind Dixon, Doron Dorfman, Jasmine Harris, Arlene Mayerson, Courtlyn Roser-Jones, and Dan Tokaji. While I am responsible for the books' weaknesses and errors, everyone helped improve the quality of the final product with their constructive, positive attitudes. In particular, David Levine's careful word-by-word and macro-editing suggestions greatly improved the book, and I am especially grateful for his generous donation of his time to make this book stronger.

Introduction

Sticks and stones will break your bones, but words will never hurt you.

Unfortunately, that is not true, which is why I need to start this book with a "trigger warning." The reader will feel pain, anxiety, anger, depression, and indignation as I remind us of the pervasive insults that have been thrown at disadvantaged members of our society forever.

. . . . .

More than thirty years ago, on July 26, 1990, on a bright and sunny day, many hard-working members of the disability rights movement celebrated during an outdoor ceremony in the wheelchair-accessible Rose Garden when President George H. W. Bush signed into law the Americans with Disabilities Act (ADA). In an unprecedented moment, Reverend Harold Wilke accepted one of the signatory pens from President Bush with his left foot. Disability activists Evan J. Kemp Jr., Justin Dart, and Sandra Swift Parrino were elevated onto the national stage in a moment of bipartisan support. The ADA created broad-ranging reform that protected people with disabilities from discrimination in both the private and public sectors in both employment and access to public spaces.

Congress enacted those reforms at a time when it was still politically commonplace to demonize people with disabilities. The term "retard" could be heard on the playground as an accepted epithet to utter at another child. But disability epithets were not limited to the playground. For example, Senator William Armstrong (R-Colo.) felt comfortable complaining on the Senate floor that the proposed ADA would cover those with "alcohol withdrawal, delirium, hallucinosis, dementia with alcoholism, marijuana, delusional disorder, cocaine intoxication, cocaine delirium, [and] disillusional disorder."[1] Conflating the term "disability" with demonized patterns of behavior, Congress insisted that homosexuality, bisexuality, transvestism, transsexualism, pedophilia, exhibitionism, voyeurism, gender identity disorders, compulsive gambling, kleptomania, and pyromania be specifically listed as disorders that would not be covered by the statute.[2]

In response to these insulting characterizations of the people who would be assisted by the statute, Congress agreed to certain compromises. One, to ensure passage of the accessibility provisions, was to limit plaintiffs to injunctive relief (without monetary damages) through a private (rather than public) enforcement model.[3] In other words, a disabled person who could not access a public space had to find a private lawyer who would bring a lawsuit, in which the only available relief was an order to make the facility accessible. Even so, when private lawyers used these limited mechanisms to enforce the statute, the media and defense counsel attacked them for "gaming" or "plaguing" the system, "abusive" tactics, and "shakedown" litigation, merely because they would seek attorney's fees *after* demonstrating that the facility was inaccessible. An entire *60 Minutes* segment was devoted to criticizing these so-called abusive plaintiffs and their lawyers in December 2016,[4] even though they were enforcing the statute with exactly the limited scope of relief that Congress provided.

In the framework of this book, the public insult campaign at the time that the ADA was enacted in 1990 acted as a headwind to effective reform. Advocates were forced to accept bizarre exemptions and an ineffectual enforcement scheme. And the public insult campaign that proceeded in the postenactment era served as a dead weight to effective enforcement of the limited rights provided by Congress. As Jasmine Harris has argued, the ADA may have been better able to obtain effective relief in the first place if a stronger public media campaign had acted as a headwind during its journey through Congress.[5] With hindsight, we can also see that a public, rather than private, enforcement scheme may have blunted the dead weight effect of public insults in undermining ADA enforcement. Without an effective public media campaign, the public insult campaign has gone largely unanswered.

I argue in this book that the political left needs to account for the power of public insults when it crafts a theory of social and political change. Through many examples—ranging from disability accessibility to immigration reform—I argue that the political left has failed to account for the power of public insults when it designs its strategies to attain progressive reform. Rather than being overly concerned with what counts or doesn't count as an insult, I focus on the *impact* that people whom I characterize as "power bullies," through their deployment of public insults, have had on the ability of the political left to achieve structural reform, particularly in the civil rights arena. I broaden C. Wright Mill's phrase "power elite"[6] to the term "power bullies" to capture the way that the military, economic, political, and media elites, irrespective of their political views, can use their power to undermine structural reform. Public insults act as a headwind and dead weight to the sustained achievement of civil rights advances. As a headwind, they make the achievement of effective reforms quite difficult and then, after such reforms have been crafted into law, they act as a dead weight to preclude their effective enforcement. They can also be an important deflecting strategy by moving attention to the question of whether someone was insulted and away from a structural civil right being undermined.

This book provides a detailed cataloging of the way public insults have been used against people with disabilities, immigrants, women seeking abortions, individuals who are sexually harassed, members of the LGBTQ community, and of course, African American people. Every chapter requires a trigger warning because every chapter repeats these demeaning public insults. I do not convey these insults to cause discomfort or pain to the reader, but so that so we can better understand their comprehensive power. They are a tactic. They are fundamental to the power bullies' playbook. Hence, we need to think deeply about their impact in order to develop an equally powerful response.

In cataloging the power of insults to undermine civil rights reform, this book owes tribute to other scholars who have documented the power of words to wound. In 1993, Charles Lawrence, Mari Matsuda, Richard Delgado, and Kimberlè Crenshaw coauthored a groundbreaking book called *Words That Wound: Critical Race Theory, Assaultive Speech, and the First Amendment.* Like many young scholars at the time, I was mesmerized by this book because it challenged the traditional understanding of the First Amendment and reflected what Matsuda so aptly called "outsider jurisprudence." Rather than seeking to offer a balanced view of the First Amendment, they sought to "present a dissenting view grounded in our experiences as people of color and ask how those experiences lead to different understandings of racism and law."[7] Their work was grounded in the emerging movement called "critical race theory."

They placed their book in their experiences on college campuses and elsewhere of assaultive speech being used to injure racial minorities as a group. For example, Lawrence was alarmed when a Stanford University poster was defaced with the word "niggers" and the university responded that the students who defaced the poster and engaged in other hateful speech could not be disciplined under university discipline rules because their actions constituted protected speech. Lawrence, however, argued that the students' hate speech was not for the purpose of advancing debate. It was an example of speech being used to intimidate and stifle intellectual exchange. Taking Lawrence's storytelling in a new direction and foreshadowing the #MeToo movement that was decades away, Matsuda emphasized the importance of first listening to the voice of the victims of hate speech in developing an appropriate response.

By the time their book was published, Lawrence had helped to push Stanford to adopt a regulation that provided sanctions for some kinds of derogatory student speech that the regulation described as "harassment by vilification." While Lawrence recognized that some people thought this kind of regulation constituted the work of the "thought police," he defended it as regulating speech that lies outside of the First Amendment.[8] In a later chapter, Delgado tried to craft remedies against this kind of hate speech by arguing that there should be a tort action for racial insults, epithets, and name calling.[9]

Their work is very important in reminding us that the problem of racist and other injurious speech is nothing new in the public domain. Delgado recalled that many people in the village of Skokie, Illinois, found the demonstration by the National Socialist Party of America in 1977 with its Nazi uniforms and swastikas inflicted significant psychological trauma, especially because of the large number of Holocaust survivors who lived in that community.[10] Like Lawrence, Delgado tried to use conventional legal tools to obtain remedies for that kind of trauma or enjoin it from occurring in the first place. In 1978, the American Civil Liberties Union (ACLU) defended the right of the white nationalists to engage in hate speech as part of their First Amendment rights.

A lot has happened since that book was published in 1993, although much has remained the same regarding the presence of what this book calls public insults in the political domain. Echoing Skokie, white nationalists held a rally in Emancipation Park in Charlottesville, Virginia, on August 12, 2017, and the ACLU defended their right to march. Counterprotesters also exercised their right to free speech by protesting the white nationalists' racist message. The situation turned deadly when a protester on the side of the white nationalists accelerated his car into the crowd of counterprotesters, killing thirty-two-year-old Heather Heyer and injuring nineteen other people.

But unlike its response to criticism of its First Amendment position in 1978, the ACLU of 2017 did some soul-searching after the Charlottesville protest.[11] It invited Jameel Jaffer, Charles Lawrence, and Mary Frances Berry, prominent scholars on the First Amendment, to its biennial meeting on September 16, 2017, to discuss the ACLU's proper role in representing proponents of hate speech. The work of Lawrence, Delgado, Crenshaw, and Matsuda, along with others, made it possible for Lawrence's ideas to be considered important enough to be part of the ACLU's consideration of how to defend the First Amendment *and* racial equality. Following the 2017 discussion of its role in Charlottesville, the ACLU revised its case selection guidelines to help local affiliates resolve conflicts between competing values or priorities. While not changing its fundamental position that it should defend hateful speech, it also emphasized two important factors that might cause a local affiliate to choose not to defend a particular speaker: "whether the speaker seeks to engage in or promote violence" and "whether the speakers seek to carry weapons."[12] With hindsight, it is possible to argue that the Charlottesville protesters were in the category of those whom the ACLU affiliate could have chosen not to represent even if it had the resources to engage in that representation. The issuance of these selection guidelines caused free speech advocates, such as Wendy Kaminer, to publish an op-ed in the *Wall Street Journal* arguing that the ACLU had retreated from its protection of free speech.[13]

While benefiting enormously from this lively debate about the proper role of the First Amendment in the face of hateful speech, I seek to reframe the consideration of such speech. I accept the reality that hate speech will continue to be a part of the American political landscape and that the First Amendment will preclude us from enjoining such speech or creating strong remedies for the emotional harm that it may cause. Instead, I ask how we can be better prepared to deal with the reality of hate speech, or what I more broadly call "public insults," by anticipating their use by the power bullies.

I seek to take the discussion of public insults in a new direction. I argue that the phenomenon of public insults is undertheorized. The power of public insults goes much further than suggested by Lawrence and his colleagues. Public insults have the ability to systematically deflect civil rights advances in many areas of the law. We need to understand public insults as a *tool* or *weapon* of the power bullies, which is very effective in undermining statutory and civil rights advances. I argue that this tool has the power to act as a headwind to deflect or impede attempts to attain structural reform and then act as a dead weight to frustrate efforts to effectively implement whatever reform is attained. In this book, I use five case studies from different areas of the law—disability, immigration, marriage equality, abortion, and sexual harassment—to concretely examine the power of public insults in practice.

I write this book in the context of my lifelong work seeking to construct tools to advance structural reform rather than to advance reform through one-person-at-a-time remedies. The latter remedy is part of the neoliberal approach to reform, which privileges private, market-based solutions over systemic governmental answers. This book provides a comprehensive critique of this approach. For example, while it is important for an individual woman in the workplace to obtain relief when she is a victim of sexual harassment, we will never attain a fair workplace until we eliminate the structural rules that facilitate sexual harassment. As discussed in chapter 7, we need to think of the phenomenon of sexual harassment as tied to the larger problem of low wages, inflexible work schedules, differential workplace expectations based on gender, inadequate pregnancy leaves, and sexist dress codes. A man's harassment of a woman in the workplace is a reflection of the gender-based power imbalance in the workplace rather than an isolated incident of rude behavior. An appropriate remedy needs to understand the full scope of the nature of the harm. The law's neoliberal approach to the problem of insults rarely asks those structural, systematic questions.

I expect that many readers will want to know what I propose as a grand solution to the enormous power of public insults that this book painstakingly portrays. Unfortunately, there is no one-size-fits-all answer. Solutions can only be developed in context. My broad argument is that it is important that civil rights advocates *anticipate* the power of insults when we craft legislative or constitutional law solutions to important problems like disability discrimination (chapter 3), immigration reform (chapter 4), marriage equality (chapter 5), abortion rights (chapter 6), and sexual harassment (chapter 7) so that we try to build some defensive protection into the civil rights framework. For example, in chapter 4 I show how Obama-era executive orders to help advance immigration reform could not withstand the anti-Muslim onslaught of the Trump administration, because such reforms could be deleted with the stroke of a pen by a new administration. Even when the US Congress enacts reforms into law, it is difficult to withstand both headwinds and dead weights. As discussed in chapter 7, Congress's willingness to amend Title VII after Anita Hill brought attention to the problem of sexual harassment could not withstand the enduring dead weight against effective enforcement. Despite the conceptual promise of the legal tool of sanctions against sexual harassment, Title VII often seems stuck in assisting only a small cross-section of women who are harmed by public insults in the workplace. In chapter 8, I end the book by considering how public campaigns like #BlackLivesMatter (BLM) can help to directly challenge the public insult narrative by elevating the lives of Black people and seeking structural reform.

Nonetheless, we must also recognize that even those public campaigns can backfire. Considering, for example, the impact of the #MeToo movement, Aya Gruber cautions us to remember that the "criminal law causes real injuries" and that one should examine "feminist participation in the penal system with a jaundiced eye."[14] She urges feminists to look "ahead to how the laws will operate in the world as it exists: a world of racialized overpolicing and overimprisonment." She argues that criminal law should be "a last, not first, resort." In the framework of this book, the dead weight of the power bullies' penchant for solving many problems with a heavy criminal hand is undermining the attempts of these various social movements to attain justice. It is easier to throw Harvey Weinstein or Derek Chauvin in jail than to fundamentally change society so that *all* people can live and work in an environment of dignity and respect. We need to measure success through structural change rather than through isolated examples of bad actors being imprisoned. Thus, the BLM movement provides an important road map, because it has refused to declare success on the basis of indictments of police officers. Instead, it continues to strive for structural reform with hashtags like #DefundThePolice.

We should never underestimate the power of insults, especially in the hands of the power bullies. Words are weapons. They can hurt us. They have. I hope this book helps us better understand the ways in which power bullies can harness public insults to undermine civil rights reform, and how we might fight back. Our lives depend on it.

1 Insults

INSULTS IN HISTORICAL CONTEXT

The use of public insults by politicians is nothing new.

Since the founding of our republic, politicians have engaged in vociferous, insulting behavior to attain and retain power in society. "When John Adams ran against Thomas Jefferson, [b]oth candidates suffered personal attacks; Adams, for his perceived lack of masculine virtues, Jefferson for rumors that he had fathered children with one of his slaves and, enamored with French revolutionary ideas, had plans to install a Bonaparte-like dictatorship in America. His heterodox Christianity also raised charges of atheism."[1]

In the late eighteenth and early nineteenth centuries, politicians would respond to perceived insults, such as being called "a worthless scoundrel, a poltroon and a coward"[2] or a "bowl of skimmed milk,"[3] by seeking a duel.[4] "Raised by an immigrant mother on a subsistence farm on the Carolina frontier,"[5] Andrew Jackson, for example, was taught that he needed to establish and prove his status as a gentleman by dueling. "A gentleman dueled only with other gentlemen. If insulted by an underling, a gentleman responded by thrashing the upstart with a cane or horsewhip."[6]

9

The deployment of and response to insults has always been class based. Upper-class society tolerates and uses it in the political sphere. In the early nineteenth century, "[e]verywhere, dueling was considered the prerogative of upper class gentlemen, who decreed that the unwashed rabble had no honor to defend and thus were ineligible to spill blood on the sacred field of honor."[7] The deployment of base insults was an important arsenal of the power elite to maintain their control in society, including the support of slavery. Historian Joanne Freeman documented how southern members of Congress, in particular, who were loyal to a violent code of masculine honor, often bullied and beat their northern colleagues to silence their opposition to slavery.[8]

Insults continued to play an important role in public life as the United States entered the modern era. Although the use of insults for political purposes spans social classes and political ideology, I demonstrate here that those in positions of power based on class, race, sex, gender, and disability status, whom I call "power bullies," have been able to deploy insults to greater effect than others. The purveyors of insults include politicians, corporate lawyers, media personalities, judges, and police officials. Whether they are barring immigrants from entering the United States, engaging in sexual harassment, demeaning people with disabilities, or devaluing Black lives, actors who possess political, economic, and social advantages have relied on insults to undermine the civil rights of historically subordinated groups.

Insults have been power tools for power bullies. These insults need to be understood not merely as a personal attack on a discrete individual or group of individuals but as a tool that helps undermine the attainment of structural, progressive policies. As Owen Fiss has argued, "[s]tructural reform is premised on the notion that the quality of social life is affected in important ways by the operation of large-scale organizations, not just by individuals acting either beyond or within these organizations."[9] Thus, this book captures three important ways that public insults can be effective: (1) by *deflecting* attention away from the erosion of or need for structural reform, (2) by acting as a *headwind* to impede attempts to attain structural reform, and (3) by acting as a *dead weight* to impede people from exercising their statutory or constitutional rights.

Deflection

A well-known example of deflection was the public response to the shooting of Michael Brown in Ferguson, Missouri, on August 9, 2014. Even though witnesses claimed that Michael Brown had his hands up when approached by police, conservative news sources immediately emphasized Brown's purported criminal record for minor shoplifting.[10] Officer Darren Wilson, who was charged with the shooting, was not indicted; the issue of whether Michael Brown was a "good person" should have been irrelevant to the issue of whether the shooting was justified. As Ezra Klein has said: "But this is a sick conversation. The Good Ones don't deserve to be shot when they're surrendering. But neither does anyone else. It doesn't matter that Michael Brown was starting college on Monday. And it doesn't matter if he was involved in a robbery on Saturday. What matters is the precise circumstance in which Officer Darren Wilson shot Brown."[11] Office Wilson was never indicted; the power bullies succeeded in their campaign of insults.

But the murder of George Floyd shows us how public protests can challenge this power bully deflection strategy. Predictably, after Floyd's murder on May 25, 2020, the power bullies started posting that Floyd had a criminal history and was accused of passing counterfeit bills. President Donald Trump called the Minneapolis protesters "thugs," raged against the media for "doing everything within their power to foment hatred and anarchy," and criticized Democratic officials for letting the protests spin out of control. He quoted a 1960s southern sheriff's threat to shoot looters in Black neighborhoods and threatened to bring in the army if "liberal governors and mayors" don't get tougher on demonstrators.[12] Trump's strongest tactic of deflection was to pose for a photo in front of a Catholic Church, holding a Bible, in defiance of the protesters.

The national and international protests that followed the murder of Floyd, however, served to control the narrative. British newspapers proclaimed that Trump's response "inflames America's injustice." The largest German newspaper announced: "Trump declares War on America." India's second-largest English daily wrote that Trump's tactics, if conducted by the Indian government, would have caused "the U.S. State Department . . .

[to] condemn[] the government, and call[] for respecting human rights." The Chinese Communist Party's flagship newspaper published a cartoon featuring a police officer's uniform beneath the cracked façade of the Statue of Liberty with the tagline "Beneath human rights." Pakistan's paper of record ran the headline "Trump on the Warpath." One of Mexico's leading daily newspapers proclaimed that the United States "seems to be on the edge of an abyss with incalculable consequences for its own population, but also for the rest of the world."[13] The attempts to insult George Floyd and the protesters were drowned out by the worldwide protesters who spoke out against police brutality.

It took many years of murders of Black people for Black Lives Matter to begin to control the narrative. After each senseless killing, as I discuss further in chapter 8, the police spun out a fabric of lies to make it look like the murder was justified. But the shooting and murder of unarmed Laquan McDonald, a Black male, in the back as he was moving away from the numerous officers who surrounded him was so outrageous that even white America could no longer look the other way. Multiracial crowds began to fill US streets, and streets around the world, with radical calls to "defund police." Their success shows both that deflection is penetrable and the high cost in deaths that must occur before those deflections can be beaten back. Further, as I discuss in chapter 8, it provides us with an example of how to control the narrative to seek *structural* change rather than merely justice for one family of a murder victim.

Deflection with Headwinds

Deflections often occur with headwinds. That combination can be seen in the well-known example of candidate Donald Trump mocking reporter Serge Kovaleski. In November 2015, Trump mocked reporter Kovaleski at a campaign rally by flapping his arms to imitate Kovaleski's congenital joint condition, arthrogryposis.[14] Trump's behavior led to public discussion about whether his campaign could survive such boorish behavior.[15]

But not many can recall why Trump was mocking Kovaleski. When I have talked about this book's thesis, few audience members have indicated that they remember why Trump mocked the reporter. So let me remind the reader of the sequence of events that led to Trump mocking him. On November 21, 2015, Trump made a false claim that Arab Americans cheered the 9/11 attacks from rooftops in New Jersey. At a campaign rally in Birmingham, Alabama, Trump said: "I watched when the World Trade Center came tumbling down. . . . And I watched in Jersey City, N.J., where thousands and thousands of people were cheering as that building was coming down. Thousands of people were cheering." [16] He made that claim to support his campaign position that the United States needed to curtail Muslim immigration and reverse the immigration reform that had occurred under President Barack Obama.[17] When his claim was challenged, he repeated: "People over in New Jersey that were watching it, a heavy Arab population, that were cheering as the buildings came down."[18] A couple of days later, Trump defended his false claim by citing a 2001 *Washington Post* article by Kovaleski.[19] Trump wanted to curtail Muslim immigration into the United States; he was inventing a false narrative to justify that step.

When Kovaleski heard that Trump was citing his news reporting to support this false claim about people cheering the 9/11 attacks, he responded to correct the record. Rather than respond to Kovaleski with facts, Trump responded with ridicule. He mocked and imitated Kovaleski's arm gestures.[20] Trump then doubled down on this insult by saying that he was "showing that the reporter was groveling when he totally changed a 16 year old story that he had written in order to make me look bad. Just more very dishonest media!"[21]

What did this insult accomplish? It deflected attention from the inaccuracy of Trump's original assertion that people in New Jersey were cheering the 9/11 attacks. It allowed Trump to continue his anti-Muslim vendetta, which arguably helped him win the presidential election. A deflecting insult was a tool to undermine some immigration reforms that had been achieved during the Obama presidency.

Notice the dynamic of the insults. A wealthy, celebrity, political candidate made an unsubstantiated and insulting claim. It was part of his anti-immigrant rhetoric to support banning Muslims from entering the United States and curtail immigration from Mexico.[22] The purpose of those proposals was to undermine the immigration reform that had occurred under President Obama. Trump's ten-point immigration plan included terminating "President Obama's two illegal executive amnesties."[23] Within three days of Trump making this false claim, which itself was deeply insulting to Muslims and Arabs, the media turned its attention to whether Trump had mocked Kovaleski. Trump supported this diversion by saying that Kovaleski was "groveling."[24]

By the time Meryl Streep, during her Golden Globes speech, repeated the allegation that Trump had insulted Kovaleski, the *New York Times* reported that Trump had "appeared"[25] to mock Kovaleski and made no mention of the underlying anti-immigrant stance of Trump that spurred the insulting behavior. The insult helped transform the immigration debate from whether American Muslims had actually cheered the 9/11 attack to whether Trump had insulted Kovaleski.[26] Trump's ten-point immigration plan included the following: "Immediately terminate President Obama's two illegal executive amnesties (Deferred Action for Parents of Americans and Lawful Permanent Residents and Deferred Action for Childhood Arrivals). All immigration laws will be enforced—we will triple the number of ICE agents. Anyone who enters the U.S. illegally is subject to deportation. That is what it means to have laws and to have a country."[27] The details of that immigration plan received little public discussion while people dissected Trump's gestures and words in mocking Koveleski. The eventual implementation of that immigration plan had a devastating impact on the progressive change that was attained during the Obama administration.

As this example reveals, insults can be highly effective against disadvantaged individuals and groups in society to deflect public attention from harmful public policies and act as a headwind to undermine existing civil rights reform. In this example, the insult was directed at a person with a disability; the reform was in the area of immigration law. But diversionary insults are not limited to deflecting public attention away from the need for immigration reform. In fact, one should understand public insults to be an important tool of the financial and political power elite to undermine or overturn nearly all areas of civil rights reform.

Another interactive example comes from the area of LGBT rights.

As discussed further in chapter 5, the LGBT* community has faced decades and decades of horrible public insults. Lesbians were characterized

---

* I am deliberately using the term "LGBT" rather than "LGBTQ+" because I am describing a moment in political history when the primary focus of the gay rights movement was the

as man-haters. Gay men were considered to be pedophiles. Transgender people were largely invisible, but when they began to be more public, they faced horrific slander and violence. Until the Supreme Court decision in *Lawrence v. Texas* in 2003, many states still had enforceable laws that made gay men and lesbians face long prison sentences if they were convicted of engaging in sodomy. It is difficult to think of a group that the political right more openly despised and castigated. Public insults seemed to impose a nearly insurmountable barrier to reform, not merely a headwind.

The LGBT community certainly understood that it was the victim of such public insults, given the lack of subtlety in the expression of those insults. They had to engage in a massive public relations campaign to humanize their experience and make society more tolerant of their right to live in a respectful environment.

The LGBT community had a number of aspirations for how to attain a more just society. The general view was that the sodomy laws needed to be overturned, then a national nondiscrimination statute needed to be passed, and finally, same-sex marriage should be made possible through litigation. The general view was that it would not make sense to obtain the right to marry if the members of the married couple could be fired the next day for getting married. Nondiscrimination had to precede the right to marry.

But guess what? It didn't happen that way. The Supreme Court did invalidate sodomy statutes in 2003. But it also invalidated bans on same-sex marriage in 2014, *before* a national statute was passed that protected the LGBT community from discrimination. (As I write this book in June 2020, the Supreme Court has just interpreted Title VII to cover sexual orientation and transgender discrimination.) What went wrong with the predictions about the needed sequence of events?

As I argue in chapter 5, the political strategy failed to account for the power of insults not only to make political reform difficult but also to narrow the ultimate type of victory that the LGBT community could attain.

---

rights of lesbians and gay men. Concern for other issues arose later. I have written elsewhere about the invisibility of bisexuality. So I am really talking about the "LG" movement but, because the movement self-identified as "LGBT," I am using that shorthand.

Even though the LGBT community was able to persuade a bare majority of the US Supreme Court to invalidate sodomy laws and bans on same-sex marriage, it has not been able to persuade a majority of the US Congress to affirmatively protect the well-being of the LGBT community. Further, as I argue in chapter 5, same-sex marriage is a much more *conservative* victory than the attainment of antidiscrimination laws, because marriage itself is a highly conservative institution, whereas legislative nondiscrimination laws reflect more radical change. If one understands that individualistic, conservative goals are the easiest to attain, then the jump from judicially overturning sodomy statutes to overturning bans on same-sex marriage through the use of the conservative judicial system, while skipping legislative nondiscrimination statutes, makes sense and is even predictable. And oddly, as I discuss in chapter 5, federal nondiscrimination protection was achieved by the Supreme Court interpreting the already-existing Title VII to ban LGBT discrimination rather than by Congress passing a freestanding statute on the subject. While that result was also not predicted by LGBT activists, it will likely lead to narrower protection than a freestanding statute would provide because, as I discuss in chapter 5, the Court avoided some of the more controversial aspects of nondiscrimination protection.

These roles are therefore interactive. In acting as a headwind, the power of insults often helps cause political change to be narrow and individualistic. If one recognizes that civil rights activists are likely to achieve narrow and individualistic victories, then one can also better anticipate that the power elite is likely to narrow these victories further as they go into effect. While some of the scholarly work on civil rights reform recognizes that the powerful can undermine or impede advances,[28] none of this scholarship considers the *interaction* between the headwind and dead weight effects of public insults. These tools limit the scope of victory at every step of the process of seeking progressive reform from enactment to implementation.

Dead Weight

The biggest dead weight to structural reform is the US Constitution. It enshrined slavery while counting slaves as three-fifths of a person for the purpose of southern voting strength. In *Dred Scott v. Sanford*, 60 U.S. 393

(1857), the Supreme Court declared that a freed Black man was not even a "citizen" of the United States and therefore could not take advantage of the rights and privileges conferred on US citizens. It was not until the Civil War was over and the Fourteenth Amendment was ratified in 1868 that the Constitution guaranteed citizenship to all persons born or naturalized in the United States.

The enshrinement of slavery with disproportionate electoral power given to the southern states is built on the very premise that Black lives don't matter. As conservative Virginian George Fitzhugh said in the mid-nineteenth century: "Subordination, difference of caste and classes, difference of sex, age, and slavery beget peace and good will."[29] Although slavery was eventually abolished, we have not abolished the electoral system that gives disproportionate power to the former slaveholding states. From the electoral college to the design of the US Senate, southern states have more power than northern states. When Black citizens won the right to vote and tried to exercise it in the 1960s, southern states created obstacles like literacy tests, which they could justify through the stereotype of Black people as being stupid and uneducated (while they also insisted on segregating and underfunding schools for Black children). As I discuss further in chapter 2, this constitutional design makes it exceedingly difficult to attain structural reform that advances civil rights because the slaveholding mentality still controls the voting behavior of most of the southern states. The Constitution is designed to promote one-person-at-a-time remedies rather than structural remedies that can genuinely make Black lives matter. But in understanding the creation and permanency of this constitutional design, I urge the reader to remember that it was predicated on the view of Black people as having a proper role as slaves and not being entitled to US citizenship. As Fitzhugh famously said: "The negro slaves of the South are the happiest, and, in some sense, the freest people in the world."[30] We may scoff at that idea today as ridiculous, but we should remember that the constitutional design embodied that premise.

But the dead weight effect is not limited to the area of racial equality. It can also be seen, for example, in the abortion context, discussed more fully in chapter 6. The antiabortion movement has done a masterful job of hurling insults at pregnant women to harass and demonize them so that they will be intimidated from exercising their constitutional right to choose to terminate their pregnancies. These insults act as a dead weight to impede the exercise of constitutional rights. While the antiabortion movement has not yet succeeded in overturning *Roe v. Wade*, it has managed to use the force of the state to harass and intimidate women in the hope they will not terminate their pregnancies. This state-sponsored strategy, which has included requiring women to view enlarged images of fetuses and being told that they face certain depression and suicide if they terminate their pregnancies, has resulted in the terrorization of pregnant women. This strategy has successfully chipped away at the supposed right of pregnant women to make autonomous decisions about whether to terminate their pregnancies. In the abortion context, as discussed in chapter 6, the Supreme Court has removed the requirement that the state stay neutral. It has allowed the state to use its power to impose its moral view that the fetus is a person and a pregnant woman's only proper role is as a mother. This book argues that it is helpful to understand the state as using the tool of public insults to terrorize women from exercising their constitutional right to terminate their pregnancies.

INSULTS WITHIN THEIR STRUCTURAL AND SOCIAL CONTEXT

We can best understand the power of insults if we assess them within their structural and social context. In the abortion context, for example, the state does not simply use billboards or public service announcements to announce its antiabortion perspective. It imposes itself into the life of a pregnant woman by handing her a booklet with distorted images of fetuses and inaccurate medical facts, which are intended to scare, harass, and terrorize her so that she will not exercise her constitutional right to terminate her pregnancy. Through its so-called informed consent requirements, it imposes a view of the pregnant woman as a dithering emotional creature who is too immature to exercise her right to bodily autonomy. Similarly, in the drive-by litigant example discussed in chapter 3, the corporate power elite tries to avoid complying with the requirements of the ADA by deflecting attention from its own blatant violation of accessibility standards. It portrays the wheelchair user who cannot even get into the local pharmacy to pick up a prescription as a greedy gold digger who is unconcerned about the broader needs of the disability community. And these examples of the use of public insults to terrorize and deflect are not unique. As shown in the later chapters of this book, this is a systematic strategy deployed by the power elite to undermine civil rights advances by the political left.

For the purposes of this book, I am using the definition of insults offered by psychologist Michele Wellsby and her coauthors: "a verbal expression that conveys a negative (e.g., offensive, degrading) meaning."[31] Linguists José Mateo and Francisco Ramos Yus add a vital element to my definition by underscoring the element of intentionality, defining insults as "utterances with which speakers intend to offend their interlocutors, by saying or doing something rude or insensitive that offends them."[32] Insults, of course, can be largely private in nature. The insults that I analyze, although at times directed at people who are not public figures, have the larger aims of broadly impacting public discourse and accomplishing legal and policy goals.

Work by psychologists, communication theorists, and others can help us understand the complex definition of insults and their potential effects on others. We learn that insults can be especially effective when they are innovative and that they might have a strongly negative effect on one or more groups in society, while others consider them to be harmless. There is no objective definition of insults. Their impact must be understood in context. The important point that I seek to illuminate in this book is that the deployment of public insults by power bullies has existed for hundreds of years and in recent years has been an effective tool to help dismantle the effectiveness of civil rights advances. What I have learned as I have examined various political and legal events in American history is that it is helpful to add a new question to our analysis: How have public insults been part of the strategy that led to a particular result that took civil rights issues in a conservative or limiting direction? Some examples are straightforward; others are more subtle, but I have found this tool to be very useful in better understanding a particular historical phenomenon. Obviously, examination of the use of public insults is not the only tool we need to use in understanding retrenchment on civil rights issues, but it is an important one that we need to add to our analytical framework.

Let us walk back through the annals of history to see this effective use of public insults by the powerful. In 1991, Anita Hill offered graphic testimony accusing Clarence Thomas of sexual harassment that included discussion of "penis sizes, breasts, pubic hairs and pornography."[33] Before she offered this testimony before the US Senate, Thomas spoke angrily, turning the tables on his Senate accusers and insulting them and the process in stark terms:

> This is a circus. It is a national disgrace. And from my standpoint, as a black American, as far as I am concerned, it is a high-tech lynching for uppity-blacks who in any way deign to think for themselves, to do for themselves, to have different ideas, and it is a message that, unless you kow-tow to an old order, this is what will happen to you, you will be lynched, destroyed, caricatured by a committee of the U.S. Senate, rather than hung from a tree.[34]

Communication experts William Benoit and Dawn Nill published a critical analysis of Thomas's statements before the Senate Judiciary Committee. They argue that "Hill's allegations, while providing a salacious spectacle and temporarily impeding his confirmation, might have ultimately aided his nomination by distracting the Senate's attention from the critical questions about Thomas' judicial qualifications."[35] Thomas was quite clever in how he responded to the Hill allegations. Although he denied them and suggested they were not credible, because she had followed him to the Equal Employment Opportunity Commission (EEOC) (after these episodes had reportedly occurred) and did not complain about his behavior to others at the time, he did not attack her directly. Benoit and Nill describe this strategic choice as an "extremely wise decision," because a verbal attack on Hill "would place Thomas in the role of aggressor and Hill in the role of victim."[36] A verbal attack on Hill might create an "*impression* which was congruent with Hill's accusations, not with his defense."[37]

Rather than attack Hill, Thomas attacked the senators who were accusing him of sexual misconduct. He called the confirmation process an "ordeal" and an "obstacle" that was "Kafka-esque." He said that the process was destroying his life, his accomplishments, and his family. He refused to "provide rope for my own lynching or for further humiliation." He accused the senators of engaging in that lynching. Benoit and Nill point out that these "remarks might seem out of place in a speech designed to restore his reputation. In fact, one might think their intent was to antagonize the very people who would decide whether he ought to become a Supreme Court Justice."[38] But the strategy worked because it placed the senators voting against him in position of appearing to be "racists and bigots." Benoit and Nill argue that "Thomas' decision to attack his accusers (in the Senate) deflected attention away from charges of sexual harassment (Thomas allegedly victimizing Hill) to charges of racism (the Senators victimizing Thomas)."[39]

While it is clear that Thomas powerfully used insults to deflect attention, Benoit and Nill have understated the scope of that deflection. Before the Hill allegations were brought forward, there were serious questions raised about Thomas's judicial qualifications and his positions on civil liberties issues. Those concerns about his qualifications and potential impact on civil liberties cases had resulted in a deadlocked vote in the Senate Judiciary Committee before Hill's allegations arose. No previous Supreme Court nominee had been confirmed by the Senate without a positive recommendation from the Judiciary Committee. Thus, Thomas had a steep hill to climb even before the Hill allegations were put forward. Rather than hurting his chances to be confirmed, Thomas's ability to powerfully invoke public insults arguably helped his candidacy succeed. By marshaling such a strong attack against the senators, he put them in a defensive posture of having to worry that they would be considered racists if they voted against Thomas.

Given the closeness of the vote, Thomas needed to convince only one potential fence-sitter, such as Arlen Specter, to be confirmed. At the time of the Thomas hearings, Specter grilled Hill and accused her of "flat-out perjury." He told the press that her "credibility has been demolished."[40] As a pro-choice Republican who had helped block the nomination of Robert Bork to the Supreme Court three years earlier, Specter was arguably an unlikely ally of Clarence Thomas. But it appears that Thomas fooled Specter, who did not fully grapple with his record. In a *Washington Post* interview in 1994, Specter said that his "greatest disappointment" was that Thomas turned out to "be anything but a moderate." He had naively hoped that Thomas's "life experience as an African American, going from poverty to success, [would] ultimately take hold."[41]

But why would Specter have that view, in light of Thomas's record at the EEOC? Thomas opposed affirmative action and had deliberately allowed age discrimination claims to lapse through inaction at the EEOC. He was accused of transforming the "EEOC into a claims adjustment bureau" rather than an "instrument of social change."[42] There was little reason to think that Thomas was a "moderate." By lashing out at the Senate judiciary committee in stark racialized terms, Thomas was able to cloak himself as an African American man who was being attacked by the white lynch mob. In that context, Specter came forward as a strong proponent, beating back what he perceived to be Hill's role in this lynch mob. Hill somehow became the aggressor instead of the victim. Her race and gender status was erased in the context of Thomas's pummeling insults.

Specter's susceptibility to Thomas's powerful invocation of insults in 1991, when the country had not yet begun to understand the harm imposed by sexual harassment, may be understandable. What may be more surprising is that Brett Kavanaugh was able to take a page from Thomas's playbook and be equally successful at attacking the Senate to obtain confirmation to the US Supreme Court in 2018. Unlike Thomas, Kavanaugh could not invoke the image of the lynched Black man, but he and his surrogates did invoke the image of an angry mob.

Like Thomas, Kavanaugh denounced the process, saying it was a "national disgrace" and a "circus," vowing: "You may defeat me in the final vote, but you'll never get me to quit, ever."[43] Like Thomas, who refrained from attacking Hill, Kavanaugh was careful not to attack his accuser, Christine Blasey Ford, personally, saying: "I'm not questioning that Dr. Ford may have been sexually assaulted by some person in some place at some time, but I have never done this to her or to anyone."[44]

Senator John Cornyn, a Republican from Texas, called the opposition to Kavanaugh an example of "mob rule," and Senator Mitch McConnell of Kentucky said that "the virtual mob that has assaulted all of us in this process has turned our base on fire."[45] Senator Lindsey Graham of South Carolina went the furthest in defending Kavanaugh, denouncing anyone who would oppose his confirmation. He said: "To my Republican colleagues, if you vote no, you're legitimizing the most despicable thing I have seen in my time in politics." Then, gesturing to the Democrats, he said: "You want this seat? I hope you never get it."[46]

These two examples from recent US history show a particularly inventive use of public insults. Both Thomas and Kavanaugh insulted the Senate Democrats for creating a so-called sham process. Republican senators indirectly demeaned the women (Hill and Ford) as liars, playing into the stereotype that women fabricate claims of sexual harassment and sexual assault while directly demeaning the senators who pursued these charges and found them credible. This powerful use of insults helped two men gain positions of enormous power in American society. Clarence Thomas replaced civil rights icon Thurgood Marshall, and Brett Kavanaugh replaced the swing vote of Anthony Kennedy. Ideologically, their selection to the Court would have a huge impact on the Supreme Court's jurisprudence for decades to come. For both men, their confirmation was not assured in light of the serious allegations brought against them. Thomas survived a 52–48 roll-call vote, with eleven Democrats voting yes and two Republicans voting no.[47] Kavanaugh survived a 50–48 vote. It would appear that the clever hurling of public insults by the nominees and their supporters helped stem the bleeding so they could get confirmed. Public attention was drawn to the issue of whether these men had been unfairly accused of sexual misconduct rather than to the arguably more important issue of how their legacy might transform the US Supreme Court.

The Thomas and Kavanaugh cases are not isolated examples of power bullies being able to use insults to undermine civil rights reform. They and their supporters were able to deploy public insults to help them climb the ladder of success, where they would then have additional power to undermine civil rights advances.

Another important aspect of the Thomas and Kavanaugh episodes is understanding the narrow range of discourse available to Hill and Ford. While Thomas and Kavanaugh engaged in explosive, angry testimony, Hill and Ford were comparatively composed. The *New York Times* described Ford as offering "cautious testimony laced with a scientific description of how neurotransmitters code 'memories into the hippocampus' to lock trauma-related experiences in the brain."[48] Similarly, the *New York Times* described Hill as "speaking in a calm, even tone."[49] Although Kavanaugh and Thomas were certainly insulted by the allegations leveled against them, it is important to remember the somber and calm tone that Hill and Ford used to recount their experiences. Although they arguably tried to use the platform of the US Senate to offer an insulting account of Kavanaugh's and Thomas's behavior, these attempts were not successful in derailing these nominations. In understanding the effectiveness of insults, we must remember that the power bullies have more muscle to hurl effective insults than those from disadvantaged communities. Neither Ford nor Hill could use the angry posture deployed by Thomas and Kavanaugh to offer their accusations. They could not "hurl" insults; they could merely recite the facts which, if believed, would be very insulting toward Thomas and Kavanaugh.

While there have been times in US history when the political left could hurl insults to maintain its own grip on power, this book canvasses recent US events in which that tool has been an effective part of the political right's arsenal to undermine civil rights reform. The tool of public insults is most effective in the hands of the power bullies.

2 Headwinds, Deflections, and Dead Weights in Action

Community organizers, sociologists, and contemporary constitutional theorists agree that civil rights activists need cultural, political, and legal tools to attain effective structural reform, although they differ about how those tools should work together. Sociologists argue over the relative efficacy of local grassroots organizing, the role of national campaigns and organizations, nonviolent action, and more mainstream advocacy efforts.[1] Legal scholars disagree on how effective courts can be in promoting progressive change and what factors advance or impede meaningful reforms effectuated through the legal system. These scholars have a lot to teach us about how to achieve effective change. However, I believe that their insights could be deepened if they gave more robust consideration to how the power of insults often has a deep impact on the struggle to attain and maintain effective structural reforms.

Sociologists and legal theorists need to incorporate how public insults act as deflections, headwinds, and dead weights in the struggle for social and political change. By focusing on the work of two sociologists, I hope

25

to show how such incorporation could strengthen their theory of social change. In the next section I look closely at some legal theorists.

In their book *This Is an Uprising: How Nonviolent Revolt Is Shaping the Twenty-First Century*, sociologists Mark Engler and Paul Engler have effectively drawn on the work of others in their field to try to understand how effective change can occur. They tell the story of how what they call "nonviolent revolt" by the political left has helped shape successful civil rights movements.[2] They describe many successful civil rights struggles, showing how seemingly polarizing tactics, when deployed by the political left, combined with community activism, can help change public attitudes and lay the groundwork for successful civil rights reforms. Like my work, they seemingly understand the power of insults and emphasize the need to combat anti-immigrant vitriol to achieve progressive reform. In other words, they provide some evidence for how the political left can overcome the dead weight of public insults. But I believe their work would be even stronger if they also considered the headwind effect of public insults.

Engler and Engler describe the transformation from a time of anti-immigrant vitriol to the embrace of the so-called DREAMers staying in the United States during the Obama administration. Their story begins with a description of the power of insults to prevent reform. In 2005, Representative James Sensebrenner proposed "a reactionary piece of immigration legislation that would have instated harsh penalties for unauthorized presence in the United States, erected a seven-hundred-mile fence along the border . . . and criminalized those assisting undocumented immigrants in obtaining food, housing, or medical services."[3] The story continues with Minuteman Project volunteers in 2005 bragging to a reporter that they wanted to kill all immigrants who crossed the border illegally. "You break into my country, you die," they reportedly said.[4] The cascade of anti-immigration insults continued when Fox News's Lou Dobbs "warned that hordes of unwashed immigrants would bring plagues of tuberculosis, malaria, and even leprosy" to the United States.[5]

Focusing on the power of polarizing tactics, Engler and Engler then explain how immigration rights activists effectively responded. They argue that huge mass protests by immigrant rights activists brought about a political sea change. Right-wing candidates entered the general elections "facing down an energized bloc of the immigrant rights movement's active public supporters."[6] Immigration activists staged a hunger strike at the Denver office of Obama for America, pushing President Obama to issue executive orders in favor of the DREAMers.[7] "Polarization," they argued, paid "dividends."[8] They end their chapter with the hope that Sensebrenner will reverse himself and say "I'm sorry" to the DREAM Act students.[9] Further, they suggest that "it is possible that the polarized extremism of the Minutemen may soon look just as archaic and bigoted as the White Citizens' Councils that thrived, for a brief moment, thanks to the 'unwise and untimely' clashes generated by the civil rights movement."[10]

But Engler and Engler's predictions have not come to pass. Obama's executive orders could not survive the onslaught of public insults by the political right. Those insults were not merely a dead weight; they resulted in a virtual reversal of the Obama-era reform. In 2018 Sensenbrenner's web page proclaimed his strong support for many of the measures he first supported in 2005.[11] In an interview in 2016, Minuteman cofounder Jim Gilchrist, "insists that it was his group's actions that led to the conservative fervor over cracking down on illegal immigration. He traces the current Republican discourse on the issue—Donald Trump's infamous wall, the renewed interest in revoking birthright citizenship, and the calls for mass deportations back to his movement."[12] And in November 2018, in response to Trump's warning about US security being threatened by Central American caravans of migrants, the Texas Minutemen announced that they were going to the border to stop the caravans from moving through Mexico.[13] In 2019, the leader of an armed militia held migrants against their will at the New Mexico border, apparently fortified by Trump's anti-immigrant rhetoric. The armed militias were reportedly emboldened by Trump's "assertion that the arrivals constitute an 'invasion.'"[14]

Although Engler and Engler's account gave astute emphasis to the impact of anti-immigrant rhetoric, they underplayed the power of insults to act as a headwind and undermine enduring immigration reform. Possibly, Engler and Engler should have foreseen how the political right would use the strategies that they claimed could be effective against them. The political left does not have a monopoly on the use of disruptive tactics. Engler and Engler argued that conflict and disruption are important tools for change. They argued that "successful movements are often celebrated as heroic and noble" but "while they are still active, their tactics are never beloved by all. Accepting that reality is part of using conflict and disruption as tools for change."[15] Thus, Trump garnered free publicity during the presidential campaign in 2016 with statements that promoted conflict and disruption. His lack of civility received constant criticism. As predicted by Engler and Engler, he made "people uncomfortable."[16] Some people talked about holding their noses while voting for him due to his lack of civility. But at the end of the day, he beat the more conventional candidates (in both the primary and general elections in 2016) who "prefer[red] to look moderate and reasonable."[17] One should understand Trump's success as being part of a broader social movement, with goals for structural change that were reflected by the Minutemen in 2005. The Minutemen were not just a bunch of vigilantes. They wanted a wall, they wanted immigrants deported, they even wanted immigrants to be executed at the border.[18] Although their desire to execute immigrants at the border may remain unfulfilled, their desire for a wall and mass deportation achieved some success.

The political right's recent success at social disruption illustrates that insults can become more powerful when marshaled by actors in positions of prestige and power. I argue that it is often possible for the power bullies to disrupt civil rights progress through the power of insults, because civil rights progress hangs by a narrow thread. What Engler and Engler describe as immigration victories were merely a couple of executive orders signed by President Obama that could quickly be erased by President Trump. "Some programs were created through guidance memoranda, agency policy, or operational changes that can be easily revoked or changed by the new administration."[19] The immigration rights community was not able to attain lasting immigration legislation during the eight years of the Obama presidency. While it took years for Obama to sign a pro-immigrant executive order, it only took about a week for the Trump administration to sign its first immigration executive order banning many refugees from entering the United States.[20] Had immigration reform been achieved through legislation, it would have been more difficult for Trump to reverse course. The dead weight would have been lighter.

But I do not want to overstate my point about the difficulties for the political left of achieving reform in light of the dead weight and headwinds of public insults. There is evidence that political and social media campaigns, such as #Dreamers, have increased public support for these issues. Their social media campaign helped overcome the dead weight of negative portrayals of immigrants that make immigration reform difficult. Activism by DREAMers, including the shutting down of one of President Obama's reelection campaign offices in 2012, likely influenced Obama's decision to implement DACA as an executive order. Further, in nineteen states, DREAMers have won the right to go to public university at in-state rates.[21] DREAMer groups have also given a voice to the hundreds of thousands of undocumented students across the country who felt isolated and alone before being connected to the many students who share their position.[22] My point is simply that our understanding of any success must also take into account the way the headwinds of public insults can undermine any gains that are seemingly attained. While the DREAMers have helped move public opinion to broaden support for DACA,[23] the Fox News network will reliably continue to spread lies that DACA recipients are connected to gang violence and high crime rates even though a felony conviction automatically ends a person's DACA status.[24]

My point is simple. Reexamine the work of any sociologist who explains how to achieve structural reform and ask yourself: Could that scholar's theory of social change be strengthened by considering the power of insults to act as deflection, headwinds, or dead weights? I suspect the answer is yes.

CONTEMPORARY CONSTITUTIONAL THEORISTS

In addition to sociologists, constitutional theorists also try to account for the importance of cultural forces in achieving successful legal transformations. Reva Siegel, for example, argues that cultural forces work alongside the law to help transform the Supreme Court's understandings of the US Constitution. She tells a compelling story of how the social and political activism of the feminist movement helped propel the Supreme Court to recognize sex as a quasi-suspect class under the Constitution despite the failure of the states to amend the Constitution by ratifying the Equal Rights Amendment (ERA).[25] Her work, however, does not provide an adequate explanation of why the political right was so successful in planting fear of women being drafted or being raped in gender-neutral bathrooms if the ERA were to be ratified. The power bullies' cultural disruptions were an important headwind against attaining gender equity.

Further, not everyone accepts this account of constitutional litigation working in lockstep with cultural forces to achieve long-term legal and political success. In her response to Siegel, Robin West argues that the recognition of gender as a quasi-suspect class has not resulted in the kind of broad structural reform that feminists have long sought.[26] The state still does not subsidize childcare, paid pregnancy leave is not a legal right, reproductive choices are increasingly limited and under attack, and the wage gap between women and men stubbornly persists as comparable worth cases continue to not be recognized by the courts. Sociologists would likely not be surprised at West's account of the difficulties of attaining success in this area, because they would not expect a top-down litigation approach to be successful at achieving lasting reform.[27] West embraces the importance of more ground-up cultural work to create lasting reform but does not fully account for the difficulty of responding to the power bullies' use of public insults to influence the mainstream cultural mindset. In the context of the struggle to pass the ERA, an important power bully was a white woman, Phyllis Schlafly, who masterfully created the STOP ERA campaign ("Stop Taking Our Privileges") in the 1970s. Joan Williams argues that the "ERA was defeated when Schlafly turned it into a war among women over gender roles."[28] But Schlafly's ability to gain access to the media to push against the ERA by scaring women into thinking they would be drafted and have to abandon their role as homemakers should have been a totally predictable headwind under my book's thesis. Rather than consider Schlafly's role unexpected or exceptional, we should have anticipated such use of the public airways to scare voters away from ERA ratification.

While some sociologists and legal scholars helpfully emphasize the importance of ground-level disruptions to help attain political and legal changes, their theories fail to account for some additional insights offered by this book. They fail to understand how it is easier for the power bullies than the political left to create social disruptions. One reason that litigation is insufficiently effective is that the US legal system has built-in rules and policies that heavily favor narrow, individualistic remedies rather than structural reform. Further, and equally important, is that these built-in headwinds to civil rights victories make it especially easy for the power bullies to harness public insults to derail whatever victories may be achieved. It is the *intersection* of narrow political/legal rules and power bullies' public insults that undermines the efforts of the civil rights community. Thus, West appreciates the importance of ground-level work by the political left but does not consider the importance of that work in fighting against the public insult headwinds. And Siegel may be correct about the important victories achieved by constitutional litigation, but she overstates these successes because she fails to account for the dead weight effect of power bullies undermining narrowly crafted victories.

This observation is critically important to understanding the Trump era. Many people were aghast at Trump's use of public insults to derail civil rights reform and have suggested that the political left should engage in similar tactics.[29] Yet during the Kavanaugh hearing, when civil rights activists descended on the US Senate to hold senators accountable for their failure to respect a woman's claim of sexual assault, they were minimized as an "angry mob."[30] Grassroots organizers who opposed Kavanaugh were characterized as "un-American" or needing to "grow up."[31] At the same time, Republicans were able to use the antidemocratic structure of the US Constitution to ram through Supreme Court candidates whose views were well outside the mainstream of US society.[32] The president nominates Supreme Court justices, who are confirmed with the "advice and consent" of a mere majority of the US Senate.[33] The Senate is a nondemocratic institution crafted to give disproportionate power to southern, former slaveholding states. The Constitution has always been crafted to keep white, propertied men in power;[34] it is not based on the democratic principles reflected in grassroots organizing. Thus, the power bullies have on their side a Constitution that was deliberately crafted to allow a minority of the country's population to decide who sits on the Supreme Court and prevent a "radical left-wing mob"[35] from attaining power and voice. This minority can call grassroots activists "un-American" while they use every tool in their playbook to ram through justices committed to undermining civil rights. There are likely those in the US Senate and in the country at large who still endorse the nineteenth-century view that "subordination, difference of caste and classes, difference of sex, age, and slavery beget peace and good will."[36]

Kavanaugh's confirmation is just one example of the Constitution's built-in limitations making structural reform exceedingly difficult. The Constitution is often interpreted to reflect a narrow conception of formal equality and state action, which are difficult to use if activists are seeking, for example, to create structural reform in areas of sex discrimination or race discrimination. Regarding sex discrimination, before joining the Supreme Court, Ruth Bader Ginsburg argued that abortion rights would be better protected under a substantive equality model rather than a privacy model.[37] A substantive equality model would recognize that reproductive freedom is essential to a woman's ability to act as an equal citizen in society. As a Supreme Court justice, however, Ginsburg was not able to use her power and authority to broaden our understanding of reproductive freedom. The Court continues to use a conception of reproductive freedom narrowly premised on the *Roe v. Wade* privacy theory.

In the race context, a substantive equality model would more broadly recognize the societal conditions that are necessary to remediate a history of racial subjugation in the United States, stemming in part from slavery. The Supreme Court, however, has largely embraced a narrow formal equality model that failed, for example, to require effective structural remedies such as busing to eliminate urban/suburban boundaries, thereby allowing white flight to resegregate our nation's public schools. In *Milliken v. Bradley*,[38] the Supreme Court refused to require interdistrict remedies to promote racial integration.

Similarly, a narrow state action doctrine has precluded an effective structural argument in both gender and race discrimination, because constitutional litigation can only be brought when the state itself has directly imposed the barrier that is being challenged. In the abortion rights area, for example, the Court has declined to rule that a state violates the equal protection clause when it fails to fund abortions for poor women, because a lack of funding is not considered to be unconstitutional state "action." Hence, in *Harris v. McRae*,[39] the Supreme Court refused to require government to fund abortions under Medicaid even though the privacy-based *Roe v. Wade* decision precluded government from banning abortions altogether. Professors Isaac Saidel-Goley and Joseph Singer have described the state action doctrine as "born of overt racial discrimination,"[40] because it leaves the state free to maintain broad swaths of inequality that are tied to discrimination in the private sector. While it may be true that genuine racial equality in the United States requires the state to fund health care, housing, and education for everyone, it is highly unlikely that the US individual-rights-based constitutional law system will help progressives attain that kind of substantive equality, because a failure to fund is not constitutionally actionable. Obviously, public insults cannot be blamed for the creation of all these barriers to substantive equality even if their original creation can be tied to a devaluation of Black lives. The many concrete examples of the use of public insults by power bullies, however, illustrate that the public insult playbook continues to act as a dead weight and headwind to effective structural reform.

One response to the headwind and dead weight problems is to say that political and cultural transformations not only need to precede legal changes but also must *follow* such changes. Thus, after *Brown v. Board of Education* (1954), it was more important than ever for parents to work hard to fund public schools and ensure a high-quality education for their children, as well as to fight privatization of education. After *Roe*, it became more important than ever for activists to make sure that doctors are trained in how to perform abortions and legislation is passed to fund abortion services, as well as to fight antiabortion efforts. The individualistic nature of the constitutional right does not preclude progressives from finding other forums for pushing for an extension of that right to attain structural reform. And when pushing for those further reforms, we need to be aware of the power of insults to act as a headwind and then as a dead weight after we make those advances.

The present political moment can help us see the power of insults in derailing attempts to provide a high-quality public education for all children. Public school teachers perceive that structural barriers outside the classroom walls, such as housing instability, food insecurity, violence, and lack of health care, impede their students' education.[41] Yet as Kevin Kumashiro has argued in *Bad Teacher! How Blaming Teachers Distorts the Bigger Picture*, scapegoating teachers blurs the reality of what is really happening in education. "Rather than focus on education as a broken system, the debate becomes about fixing individual teachers."[42] Teachers are scapegoated or insulted on an individual basis to obfuscate the larger need for structural reform. The public insults deflect attention from the core of the actual problem and thereby serve as a headwind against discovering appropriate progressive reforms.

Similarly, public insults have played a significant role in moving the abortion debate away from the need for structural reform to further the substantive equality of women. The extensive discourse on women's right to make reproductive health decisions never takes into account the onslaught of public insults that the political right has leveled against women who terminate their pregnancies and the doctors who assist them in acting on that choice. Chapter 6 details the visual and verbal campaign against pregnant women and their doctors to help us better understand how and why women's reproductive rights have eroded in the last several decades.

While states act to strip all reproductive freedom from women by fighting the availability of both contraception and abortions, the public debate has largely demonized pregnant women and ignored the consequences for women of losing their ability to make reproductive decisions. Following the passage of brutal "heartbeat bills" that stripped women of all reproductive freedom after conception, for example, the media often centered its discussion on whether there needed to be a rape or incest exception in those laws. The fact that we are even arguing about whether there needs to be such an exception to a law that otherwise eviscerates a woman's right to reproductive freedom demonstrates the enormous success that the political right has had in demonizing women for terminating their pregnancies. Abortion opponents have turned the conversation away from what reproductive freedom means to a woman's basic access to equality in society. The rape or incest discussion is just a distraction from the core problems of how sexual abuse occurs and the consequences of lack of access to reproductive choice. Ironically, many of the states that were rushing to pass a fetal heartbeat bill with some kind of highly limited (or no) rape or incest exception had *no* statute of limitation for reporting rape or incest. Why was that? Because the legal system used to understand that rape and incest are such traumatizing events that a woman may not quickly (or ever) rush to the police to report an incident. The absurd debate about whether there should even be a rape or incest exception presupposed that girls or women who are raped or are victims of incest routinely consider going to the police to report these violations *before* there might be a fetal heartbeat. It is just a deflection, and a highly successful one. But it is a deflection that is part of an attempt to demonize *all* women who seek to terminate a pregnancy by essentially creating no legitimate reasons whatsoever for doing so.

In 1992, when the Supreme Court reaffirmed *Roe v. Wade* in *Planned Parenthood v. Casey*,[43] the Court seemingly understood the connection between reproductive freedom and women's status in society. Further, it seemed to understand that whether there was a rape or incest exception was not an important issue in deciding whether women's reproductive freedom was protected.[44] In elegant language, the plurality opinion (which included Justice Kennedy) said:

> The mother who carries a child to full term is subject to anxieties, to physical constraints, to pain that only she must bear. That these sacrifices have from the beginning of the human race been endured by woman with a pride that ennobles her in the eyes of others and gives to the infant a bond of love cannot alone be grounds for the State to insist she make the sacrifice. Her suffering is too intimate and personal for the State to insist, without more, upon its own vision of the woman's role, however dominant that vision has been in the course of our history and our culture. The destiny of the woman must be shaped to a large extent on her own conception of her spiritual imperatives and her place in society.[45]

Nonetheless, by 2019, as a result of an effective public relations campaign by the political right, the abortion debate started to focus on the so-called reprehensible decisions that women make in terminating their pregnancies. In an extreme example of a contribution to that debate, Justice Thomas accused women who chose contraception or abortion of contributing to eugenics to secure the "elimination of the unfit."[46] Although more subtle in his jabs against women who chose to have abortions in their second trimester of pregnancy, Justice Kennedy (who joined the 1992 *Casey* plurality opinion quoted previously) voted to uphold a ban on a particular second-term abortion procedure in 2007 with the comment: "While we find no reliable data to measure the phenomenon, it seems unexceptionable to conclude that some women come to regret their choice to abort the infant life they once created and sustained."[47]

It is hard to understand how Kennedy could agree to the language in *Casey* about the imperatives of women deciding their own destiny and the language in *Gonzales* banning a procedure for all women because of the fear that some women are unable to make good choices. Kennedy's insulting claim that women need to be protected from an inability to make a reasoned decision ignored the conditions of structural inequality that lead a state to ban women's choices altogether. Even *Business Insider* observed in May 2019 that a "state legislature [Alabama] that is 85% male passed the most extreme abortion ban in the United States since *Roe v. Wade*."[48] But Justice Kennedy was seemingly unable to see the underlying structural elements of inequality in various state abortion bans because he was so moved by the amicus briefs filled with stories of some women who purportedly regretted their abortion decision. The public insults worked, as reflected in his seeming change in position from 1992 to 2007.

These examples provide insight into how the power of insults can stall the development of structural constitutional law remedies. A theory of change needs to account for the predictable onslaught of public insults both before and after change is effectuated. But insults are just as powerful in the statutory arena, which this chapter tackles next.

APPLICATION TO STATUTORY REFORM

Much of the literature on the difficulties of civil rights reform has focused on constitutional law. This chapter ends with consideration of the challenges of *statutory* reform. Like constitutional law, civil rights legislation often has not had a strong enough foundation to obtain effective remedies in the face of public insult headwinds. And after legislation is enacted that is inherently limited in its ability to achieve structural reform, it may be even easier for power bullies to further limit that legislation through cultural, political, and legal tools, including public insults. That is the dead weight effect. While the specific mechanisms that make statutory litigation a limited avenue for structural change are often different from the mechanisms that make constitutional litigation a limited vehicle, they share many of the same fundamental challenges in seeking broad-based, effective remedies. Thus, it is easy to find examples that reflect the fact that civil rights advocacy has led to narrow civil rights advances, helping, for example, only the African American plaintiff who "acts white."[49]

The enactment of the Americans with Disabilities Act (ADA), discussed more extensively in chapter 3, provides a good example of how a limited statutory right, when combined with a vociferous campaign of public insults, can greatly limit what appeared to be a significant civil rights victory. In response to a broad-based political campaign, Congress and administrative agencies enacted a statute and promulgated regulations that, on paper, should create a more accessible society. Beginning in 1992, the ADA required all new construction and significantly altered facilities to meet stringent accessibility requirements.[50] Although these requirements have arguably changed the default rules regarding expectations of accessibility, it is also easy to find violations of these simple rules everywhere. Curb cuts, while typically installed, are also often in disrepair. For example, in 2017, 80 percent of New York City sidewalks were reportedly not ADA compliant.[51] Voting facilities are often inaccessible, and many voting machines do not permit individuals with visual impairments to vote independently.[52] When disabled people make hotel reservations, they can only hope that the hotel meets their request for an accessible room, and that the room is genuinely accessible.[53] It continues to be impossible to make a reservation at a restaurant on the assumption that one can actually enter the front door and use the restroom if one uses a wheelchair, crutches, or a cane.[54]

Accessibility opponents have been tremendously successful at harnessing cultural, political, and legal tools to undermine this attempt to create structural change. While one *might* have thought that the point of making a hotel accessible to its guests was so that everyone could have an expectation of visiting that hotel and enjoying its facilities, the courts have interpreted that right as only applying to the lone guest who has been denied access and wants to return when the particular impediment to entry has been eliminated. In other words, a potential structural right has been transformed into a highly individualistic right. How could that happen? It happened because accessibility opponents mobilized cultural, political, and legal tools to synergistically block change. Their efforts were greatly facilitated by the inherent bias toward limited, individualistic rights built into the legal system in both statutory and constitutional law. Their obstruction was also effective because of the willingness of the popular press to accept the master narrative that insulted and branded disabled people as greedy and undeserving of access.

Like other groups in civil rights struggles, the affected community has not just sat on its hands and accepted the public insults. Building on the tactics of community organizer Saul Alinsky,[55] the disability rights community held a twenty-eight-day sit-in at a San Francisco federal building to force the federal government to issue regulations to enforce Section 504 of the Rehabilitation Act;[56] engaged in many public demonstrations through ACT UP in support of people with AIDs to change public policy on available medication;[57] and in 2017, engaged in mass demonstrations to stop Congress from repealing important aspects of the Affordable Care Act.[58] The disability rights community has been active and even belligerent, although its history has long been absent from most school curriculums and is often little known outside of disability circles.[59]

The disability rights community's belligerent activism has not been effective at maintaining a positive image of the importance of accessibility reform. "Drive-by litigation" is the dominant theme covered by the media in response to attempts by disability advocates to make public facilities more accessible without any attempt to even interrogate the slur. Even liberal media often accept the use of the term "drive-by lawsuits."[60] The phrase drive-by litigation invokes the image of a gang member fatally shooting an innocent bystander from an automobile. Lawsuits brought against corporations that are still inaccessible decades after the enactment of the ADA can hardly be put in that category, yet that phrase has stuck with little resistance. And the story of disability activism is largely absent from the many books and articles written about civil rights work. One explanation, which is consistent with an argument made by Michael Waterstone,[61] is that the success of the disability rights community in enacting the ADA may also explain its failure to achieve effective structural reform that could resist the onslaught of insults. Waterstone argues that there was insufficient political activism to press for the ADA, so that it passed by "flying under the radar." He argues that "society cannot be transformed if it is not paying sufficient attention"[62] to the need for disability rights. While recognizing that no civil rights community is monolithic, he argues that disability is especially diffuse because it is made up of different communities with different impairments who "have not had much in common and have not worked together (or even gotten along) as a social or political matter."[63]

Waterstone's "flying under the radar" observation was made in the context of the employment discrimination provisions of the ADA, but his argument would be equally helpful in understanding the lack of public commitment to the physical changes to structures that would be necessary to implement ADA Title III. He argues that because disability is a more "amorphous group identity than that found in other civil rights movements," it may be especially difficult for those who "are not necessarily natural allies" to forcefully support a particular vision of what might constitute equality.[64] Drawing on Siegel's work, Waterstone argues that the passage of the ADA failed to be the result of the kinds of civil rights conflict that Siegel argued was essential to the attainment of civil rights transformations.[65] If Waterstone is correct, then disability activists have an especially difficult challenge to enact and then enforce legislation that creates broad structural changes to society. Their own community, with its diffuseness, is an additional impediment to structural reform.

The structural impediments to reform, especially in the disability context, may make it especially difficult for the civil rights community to withstand verbal onslaughts from the power bullies. To understand these challenges, we need to better understand how limited statutory civil rights structures can combine with public insults to undermine civil rights reform, as discussed in the next four chapters of this book.

I am not suggesting that it is hopeless to seek to use the legal system to effectuate change. In chapter 7, I examine the ways in which Title VII has been amended and interpreted to protect victims of workplace sexual harassment. Not surprisingly, the remedy provided by Congress is limited in that it only provides an individual remedy to one woman at a time. But the availability of that remedy may encourage businesses to provide a more equal workplace. And of course we can expect some members of the business community to resist the reforms required by Title VII. But chapter 7 suggests that the #MeToo movement may be putting pressure on the judiciary to broaden its understanding of the scope of the problem of sexual harassment. Alinsky-style organizing can make inroads on the social conscience if we also remember the difficulty and scope of the challenges of progressive reform. Similarly, chapter 8 asks what we can learn from the recent inroads made by the Black Lives Matter movement in restructuring policing rather than merely seeking justice for individual victims of police violence. Headwinds and dead weights may be everywhere, but we do have some effective tools of resistance if we work together and refuse to give up.

3   Drive-By Litigators
or Accessibility Heroes?

Disability slurs by public figures are often visible. In chapter 1, I reminded the reader of candidate Donald Trump's mocking reporter Serge Kovaleski's physical impairment as a way to deflect attention from Trump's lies about the supposed cheering from New Jersey rooftops after 9/11. Trump has also reportedly called Jeff Sessions "mentally retarded"[1] and Representative Maxine Waters an "extraordinary low IQ person."[2] The political left has also tried to slur President Trump by suggesting he is disabled when his hands shake or he moves slowly down a ramp, as if his possible disability status has a bearing on his competency. These ableist insults deflect public attention from actual government policies and do nothing to advance reform. As Rebecca Cokley said in a *Washington Post* op-ed: "[T]he answer to Trump's ableism can't be to outdo him. Ableism hurts people with disabilities regardless of who pushes it."[3]

Trump is not the only public figure to use insults against people with disabilities with seeming impunity. In February 2015, Jay Ruderman published an opinion piece in *Huffington Post* in which he listed some recent, bipartisan public insults.

- A source in the Obama administration referred to Israeli prime minister Benjamin Netanyahu as "Aspergery."
- Former CNN senior anchorman Jim Clancy called a critic a "cripple."
- Kentucky senator Rand Paul declared that "over half the people on disabilities are anxious or have back pain—join the club."[4]

In each of these examples, insults were used to undermine a political figure or a policy position rather than respond to the underlying issue on the merits. Insults are a powerful form of deflection, routinely and sometimes unconsciously used against people with disabilities. As this chapter reveals, they have also been a successful strategy in Americans with Disabilities Act (ADA) litigation.

This chapter tells the dead weight story of the use of public insults within ADA litigation. I show how a criticized method of enforcement—often dubbed a "bounty hunter" method—was embedded in the ADA. Then, when lawyers tried to use this mode of enforcement for the benefit of their clients, further insults were leveled to restrict their efforts.

DEFENSE INSULT STRATEGY

Amy Robertson is one of the premier ADA litigators in the country and Co-Executive Director of the nonprofit Civil Rights Education and Enforcement Center.[5] She inspired the public insult thesis in this book through her vivid and powerful blog entries about their use in ADA litigation. In July 2013, she posted an entry on her thoughsnax.com blog about Craig Yates's case against Popeyes. The point of the story, recounted in the following paragraphs, is that the defendant knew it was in violation of the law. Rather than correct the obvious problem, defendant Popeyes decided to impugn Yates's motives as a supposed serial litigator. Further, it tried to keep the judge from hearing any sympathetic evidence about the challenges that Yates faces on a day-to-day basis when he cannot get through front doors or park in accessible locations. Because the defendant had no cognizable legal defense, it tried to win through the strategy of insults.

This is the story.

Yates uses a wheelchair and, beginning in 2011, wanted to get into the front door at his local Popeyes. Rather than installing a power door to make his entry possible, Popeyes put a bell on the front door that one could ring in the hope that an employee would come out and open the door. At the time that Yates brought suit, his expert stated that a power door could be installed for $3,500. At trial, the defendant testified that its gross revenue each year at that facility was about $750,000, making the purchase of a power door easily within the ADA legal standard for modifying an existing structure "without much difficulty or expense." This was an easy fix, and in fact, after losing at trial, the defendant installed the power door, on November 14, 2014, several years after Yates first brought this problem to its attention.[6] Rather than install the power door and resolve the case quickly, the defendant decided to insult Yates as an untrustworthy, serial litigant. Litigation in this case dragged on until September 21, 2017, while Popeyes wasted Yates's time with frivolous motions.

In the judge's words:

> Defendant alleges that Plaintiff and his counsel are vexatious litigants who have filed hundreds of similar lawsuits against small businesses, making the same type of boilerplate allegations, in an effort to "extort" settlements from them. In particular, Defendant alleges—and Plaintiff does not dispute—that since 2007, Plaintiff has filed over 168 disability access lawsuits throughout California using the same cut-and-pasted allegations with identical claims of injury.[7]

Some readers might read the judge's description of Yates's lawsuits and agree with the characterization of him as a "serial litigant." But notice the nature of this argument. It assumes the claims are frivolous because the plaintiff filed 168 access cases over a four-year period. Robertson effectively addressed the weakness of that assumption:

> If people who use wheelchairs filed a lawsuit challenging every illegal barrier they encountered each day, most would file—I'm guessing—five to ten lawsuits each day. Instead, most people go about their days, swearing at the illegal and thoughtless barriers, but without the time or resources to file those tens and eventually hundreds of lawsuits. A brave and energetic few take the time to bring the lawsuits that remain necessary—twenty years after the effective date of the ADA's architectural provisions and thirty years

after California's—to achieve a modicum of compliance. For their trouble, these people are dubbed—in the press and in court—"serial litigators."[8]

But the defendant did not stop at accusing the plaintiff of being an inappropriate serial litigator. Popeyes also sought to exclude any "sympathy-inducing evidence or testimony regarding Plaintiff's disability that is not relevant to prove or disprove disputed facts that are of consequence to the determination of this action."[9]

Given the serial litigator allegation—which was at the heart of the defendant's legal strategy—one can understand why the plaintiff would want to respond with evidence of how these kinds of accessibility problems are routine in the lives of people with disabilities. Maybe a judge or a jury would be tempted to overlook the clear legal requirement of having an accessible front entrance unless they were educated about the meaning of inaccessibility in people's lives. Because of routine misunderstanding about the lives of people with disabilities, such evidence is essential to countering unconscious biases on the part of judges or juries.

The judge in this case, however, caved to the power of public insults and took no steps to assist the plaintiff in countering negative stereotypes. First, the judge ruled that "the prejudicial effect of evidence relating to Plaintiff's general day-to-day hardships attributable to his disability substantially outweighs its probative value." Second, the court *granted* the defendant's motion to admit evidence of the plaintiff's prior litigation history because those lawsuits bore "directly upon his credibility."[10]

Yates had to go forward with his lawsuit in a courtroom in which his credibility was brought into question by the large number of accessibility lawsuits that he had filed, without the opportunity to explain why someone in a wheelchair might find it necessary to bring repeated lawsuits about similar situations. He did not have an opportunity to explain how the weak injunctive relief mode of law enforcement enacted by Congress under the ADA makes it difficult to force compliance *without* litigation. In other words, the public insults were piled on as a dead weight to limit his use of the narrow, neoliberal method of law enforcement, making the method of law enforcement even more narrow or unavailable. Amazingly, he had hired lawyers who were willing to pursue litigation for several years and insist that a remedy be crafted for this obvious violation of the legal standard. But many plaintiffs would not be able to find lawyers who would act with such perseverance. They would have felt overwhelmed by such hurdles to litigation. I have had many plaintiff lawyers tell me that they will not sue big chains because they do not have the resources to respond to the dozens of frivolous defense obstacles that will be placed in their way.

As someone who practices disability law, Robertson knew that the challenges Yates faced in bringing a lawsuit to gain entry to a restaurant were not unique. She soon published another blog entry on a different ADA case, against Steak 'N Shake,[11] in which once again the plaintiff faced what Robertson called "defense lawyer abuse." The National Association of Convenience Stores and other trade associations filed an amicus brief to accuse the plaintiff of being part of "drive-by" litigation and using "non-disabled law firm-paid detectives taking measurements." Citing an alleged uptick in the number of ADA lawsuits being filed, they argued (without citation) that these lawsuits existed "not because restaurants, convenience stores, and grocery stores in these states ignore their legal obligations."[12] Specifically, they cited a different case against Cracker Barrel as evidence of this so-called abusive litigation by plaintiffs.

Robertson decided to look more closely at the case brought against Cracker Barrel to see if it actually supported their thesis. She found eighteen unsuccessful motions that Cracker Barrel's seven lawyers had filed during the course of litigation, which padded their bill to the client and delayed the litigation even though they acknowledged that the identified barriers to access had not been fixed.[13] In this case, justice delayed was justice denied for the many people with mobility impairments who still could not gain access to Cracker Barrel by parking at the store. Rather than serving as evidence of litigation abuse by the plaintiffs, the Cracker Barrel case was an example of defendants who tried to demean and exhaust the plaintiffs so they would not seek justice. They were using public insults as a dead weight to try to impede recovery under the limited source of remedies made available by the statute.

As discussed later in this chapter, not all ADA plaintiffs have the resources to withstand such concerted attacks on their right to seek an accessible society. The depth of this problem, I argue, is attributable to the power of insults. As we will see, the power of insults was a factor in the civil rights community having to accept an enforcement regime under ADA Title III that was inherently limited: the private attorney general mode of enforcement. That was the headwind that the political right was able to insert into the law when it was enacted in 1990. But then, as enforcement proceeded over the next several decades, the power of insults became even stronger. The media and defense bar attacked plaintiffs, as shown in the preceding two examples, for using exactly the enforcement mechanism that Congress had created. That is the dead weight problem.

Because the dead weight on the ADA enforcement mechanism is so profound, its nature and impact deserve detailed consideration.

PRIVATE ATTORNEY GENERAL MODE OF ENFORCEMENT

The ADA, like many other civil rights statutes, contains what is called the private attorney general mode of enforcement, whereby private lawyers bring cases on behalf of clients and can obtain attorney's fees from the defendant if they are successful.[14] In this context, a private attorney serves a public enforcement role that government might otherwise be expected to fill.

While many legal and political devices can help undermine effective structural reform, the private attorney general model of enforcement is among the most important limitations and deserves focused attention. Because the clients of the lawyers in these cases are often poor and may not be entitled to large financial remedial awards, this model, in theory, benefits low-income plaintiffs. Although contingency fees may work in some areas of the law, where large awards are possible, they are not viable in many civil rights cases, especially areas of the law like ADA accessibility cases, where the statute only provides for injunctive relief and does not provide for monetary damages.[15] Without this model, government would need to play a much larger role in the enforcement of rights, especially for low-income clients. The awarding of attorney's fees overturns the "American rule," under which all sides bear their own legal expenses.[16]

The private attorney general model of law enforcement for civil rights violations has been around since the enactment of the Civil Rights Act of 1964, but it did not receive much critical attention until John Coffee published his 1983 article "Rescuing the Private Attorney General: Why the Model of the Lawyer as Bounty Hunter Is Not Working."[17] His focus was on antitrust litigation, but he suggested that the problems caused in that arena by using private attorneys general could eventually extend to civil rights litigation. In many ways, he predicted how courts would cut back on the ability of lawyers to earn a living as private attorneys general because of the perceived sense that they were "bounty hunters" rather than high-minded public interest lawyers. "Bounty hunters" was a powerful slur that would undermine the otherwise positive image of private lawyers using litigation to further the public good.

Professor Coffee gave Judge Jerome Frank credit for coining the term "private attorney general" in 1943.[18] "[H]is felicitous phrase conferred an intellectual legitimacy on practices that otherwise were scorned by the established bar as champerty and maintenance,"[19] which are illegal agreements to file lawsuits for monetary gain. Coffee recognized the importance of the characterization of the lawyer's role in such work. "Much can hang on the choice of words, and the phrase 'private attorney general' is as value-loaded in an affirmative sense as the term 'bounty hunter' is in a negative one. Both terms, however, represent only different sides of the same legal coin."[20] Not surprisingly, Coffee's work was soon cited in cases in which courts considered whether so-called private attorney general lawsuits should be able to move forward and the appropriate size of attorney's fees awarded to plaintiff's counsel for their successful work.[21]

In 2003, Michael Selmi used Coffee's work to argue that the private attorney general model in class action lawsuits has enriched lawyers while not producing meaningful change for their clients.[22] Then, in 2007, Michael Waterstone wrote an article entitled "A New Vision of Public Enforcement"[23] in which he looked at whether the private attorney general model is effective in ADA litigation. He observed that the private attorney general model, which was incorporated in the early civil rights laws, had support from both liberals and conservatives. "Conservatives championed the role of the private attorney general because it privatized enforcement, thus shrinking the role of the federal government, and liberals supported private actors enforcing civil rights because it freed up civil rights enforcement from any conservative political agenda or administration."[24] In other words, the private attorney general model was a neoliberal conception of law reform under which economic incentives in a private marketplace would be used to obtain civil rights remedies.

At the time these rules were embedded in federal law, public interest lawyers could use the class action procedural device while working for the federally funded Legal Services Corporation (LSC), which provides free legal services to low-income clients.[25] Although the private attorney general model may not have made civil rights enforcement dependent on the political views of the executive branch, it did make them dependent on the continued funding of LSC and the viability of the class action lawsuit by LSC lawyers. But that rule soon changed; since 1996, LSC may no longer bring class action litigation.[26]

Waterstone argues that the cure for this problem of underenforcement through the private attorney general model is to have more public enforcement.[27] He argues that there needs to be a "public commitment to systemic litigation," especially in areas, like disability accessibility, where "the profit motive for plaintiffs and private attorneys is low, noncompliance appears to be systemic, there is an absence of case development, and individual plaintiffs will have standing difficulties in challenging various forms of discrimination."[28]

While Waterstone's argument has much appeal, it suffers from the problem of seeing public enforcement through the executive branch as immune from cultural and political problems. As Samuel Bagenstos has argued, the public enforcement model is dependent on an executive branch that wants to enforce the civil rights laws.[29] During the Trump presidency, when the Department of Justice used its systemic enforcement authority to threaten the rights of voters, reverse affirmative action, and place children who cross the border into detention centers,[30] it was hard to see public enforcement as a panacea. In the affirmative action context, for example, the Trump administration said "it was abandoning Obama administration policies that called on universities to consider race as a factor in diversifying their campuses, signaling that the administration will champion race-blind admissions standards."[31] "On the eve of the 2018 midterm elections, President Donald Trump said he ordered law enforcement officials to monitor the virtually nonexistent problem of voter fraud, warning that 'maximum criminal penalties' would be leveled against anyone found attempting to cast a ballot illegally."[32] The same forces that shrunk the effectiveness of the private attorney general model captured the executive branch. Civil rights advocates cannot escape to another branch of government when one seems to be closed, because the same cultural and political forces that have closed one branch have infected the other branch. In fact, when the government is most closed to civil rights concerns, and enforcement is most needed, a public enforcement model would be weakest. This problem permeates not just new cases that might be brought but also existing litigation that has not yet been resolved.[33]

Nonetheless, it is important, as well documented in Waterstone's work, to recognize that Coffee's initial "bounty hunter" charge in 1983 has now permeated the public's conception of the private attorney general model of enforcement, including in the civil rights arena. In statutory schemes that permit prevailing parties to obtain attorney's fees, plaintiffs' lawyers often battle against a conception of them as greedy bounty hunters. Under state law, courts have explicitly referred to the possibility that private attorneys general would be "bounty hunters" in refusing to recognize a right to attorney's fees for prevailing parties.[34] The bounty hunter insult has become a dead weight hanging on the necks of lawyers as they seek to pursue relief for their clients.

This "bounty hunter" metaphor reflects a theme that was discussed in chapters 1 and 2. Insults are used against disadvantaged groups for conduct that is praiseworthy when engaged in by the power bullies. The private attorney general model of enforcement is a way to privatize the enforcement of civil rights. It was developed as a compromise remedy in light of the headwinds stalling passage of the ADA. Civil rights advocates do not favor this model of enforcement, because it requires a plaintiff to find a lawyer to take a case that is not likely to generate significant attorney's fees for the lawyer. Private enforcement is part of the neoliberal model to hand over public tasks to the private sector. Power bullies praise profit maximization when it furthers their financial interests but castigate it when it is sought by disadvantaged people. Hence, candidate Trump could brag about his wealth as part of his qualifications to become president, but when private attorneys take advantage of the opportunity to earn a living by enforcing the civil rights laws, they are accused of being "bounty hunters." This use of insults is to be expected; what is good for the goose is not good for the gander. Political headwinds force the civil rights community to accept the narrow remedy of a private attorney general mode of enforcement, and then insults are hurled as a dead weight against lawyers to further narrow that mode of enforcement, as discussed in the next section.

ADA'S PRIVATE ATTORNEY GENERAL
MODEL OF ENFORCEMENT

When ADA Title III was introduced as a bill in 1988,[35] it provided for compensatory damages for accessibility violations. Disability rights advocates argued that Congress should adopt the compensatory damages model available under the Fair Housing Act (FHA),[36] which prohibits discrimination in the sale or rental of housing to any buyer or renter and permits compensatory and punitive damages through public enforcement.[37] Nonetheless, Congress ultimately enacted injunctive relief[38] through suits brought by private lawyers in exchange for a broad list of covered entities. As Senator Thomas Harkin acknowledged on the floor of the Senate, the ADA cosponsors agreed "to cutback the remedies included in the original bill in exchange for a broad scope of coverage . . . in other words to extend protections to most commercial establishments large and small open to the public."[39] He characterized this decision as a "fragile compromise."[40]

Although the ADA requires enforcement by private lawyers, who can collect attorney's fees if they obtain relief, the media and defense bar have been very successful at criticizing plaintiffs' lawyers for using this mode of enforcement. Plaintiff's attorneys are often wary of bringing ADA accessibility cases for fear that they will be vilified as "drive-by litigators."[41]

The media largely furthers this tale of insults, likely creating implicit bias at all stages of the judicial process. Anderson Cooper ran a story for CBS's *60 Minutes* on December 4, 2016, criticizing so-called drive-by lawsuits.[42] Cooper's piece was largely devoted to interviewing business owners who complained about being coerced into complying with the ADA's accessibility rules. A few sentences were offered by retired Department of Justice section chief of the Disabilities Rights Section John Wodatch, who tried to explain why the requirements in the law are important. However, in an attempt to seem reasonable, he conceded that some lawsuits might be "shakedowns or frivolous."[43] Cooper emphasized that aspect of

Wodatch's comments instead of his statement that businesses have had twenty-five years' notice to comply with the ADA but still maintain many inaccessible features.[44]

Although Cooper spent hours interviewing disability rights attorney Lainey Feingold and Ingrid Tisher, a woman with muscular dystrophy, who offered a very strong defense of ADA accessibility lawsuits, Cooper did not use that footage or air their remarks. Tischer was especially incensed because Cooper used her image in the coverage without using her words. She complained: "60 Minutes came to OUR house, used us, and told the world people with disabilities are either dupes, greedy, or both."[45] Rather than offer balanced coverage, CBS merely responded to complaints about the biased story with a brief statement that "disabled viewers criticize 60 Minutes story," with a handful of links to tweets they had received, one of which supported the original story (and was not from a self-identified disabled viewer).[46] Senator Jeff Flake used the CBS story to push a bill that would make it even more difficult to bring accessibility lawsuits.[47]

The Hill ran an opinion piece on November 13, 2017, entitled "'Drive-By' Lawsuits under Disabilities Statute Costing Economy."[48] *Forbes Magazine* published a guest post by Ken Barnes in December 14, 2017, entitled "Congress Should Take Action on ADA 'Drive-By' Lawsuits." Barnes is described as the executive director of Citizens Against Lawsuit Abuse.[49] The media onslaught against accessibility litigation permeated the mainstream, financial, and political media. Rather than understand that private attorneys are the primary mechanism for enforcing ADA Title III and that rampant noncompliance makes it reasonable for lawyers to sue multiple businesses for violations, these media accounts criticize lawyers for being effective at using the ADA's enforcement mechanism. Playing on the notion that people with disabilities are incompetent to assess their own needs, the news stories advance the trope that these lawyers are taking advantage of disabled plaintiffs purely for their own financial gain through attorney's fees. Lost in these stories is the dead weight put in place by Congress when it decided *not* to permit compensatory and punitive damage awards for the disabled plaintiffs, so that only their lawyers could obtain financial awards.

The responses to this onslaught of insults cannot be found in widely available media networks. Instead, one has to look for blog entries from the Equal Rights Center[50] or attend a distance education event sponsored by the ADA National Network.[51] One would have to look in obscure media outlets like the *Times Herald-Record*[52] to find quotes from disability activists who focus on the importance of such lawsuits.

The media onslaught against the ADA's accessibility requirements is a perfect example of how public insults are especially effective when a legal rule hangs by a narrow thread. The Cooper segment emphasized that a few states allow plaintiffs in accessibility lawsuits to seek modest compensatory damages and ignored the overwhelming majority of states where only injunctive relief is available.[53] And the reaction of many members of Congress to such adverse publicity is to seek passage of a bill misleadingly called the ADA Education and Reform Act.[54] This bill passed the House of Representatives in 2018 by a 225–192 vote, with 12 Democrats voting in favor of the bill.[55]

The proposed accessibility statute would add a notice requirement to ADA Title III that would make such lawsuits virtually impossible in the future because private plaintiffs' lawyers would have no way to obtain fees for bringing such lawsuits if the business decided to remedy its accessibility problems within 180 days of receiving specific notice of the accessibility barriers (even though Congress put businesses on notice in 1990 of the need to remove such barriers).[56] Businesses would be exempt from an ADA lawsuit if they could show they were making "substantial progress" in remedying the specific defects alleged by the plaintiffs. The statute would encourage businesses to fail to be accessible until they are sued, and even then, the disabled plaintiffs would have to wait as long as six months to get the right to possibly enter the business. As the ACLU said in its analysis of the bill: "Businesses have had more than enough 'notification' to comply with disability rights law. People with disabilities deserve equal access today—civil rights should not be delayed or tied up in bureaucratic red tape."[57] The fragile thread that continues to require businesses to be accessible was therefore at risk of pulling apart entirely if this proposed statute had become law. The pattern of public insults overwhelms the ability of the disability rights community to defend a statute that can determine whether they have the ability to leave their homes and go to a local supermarket or restaurant.

One key factor in the defeat of the proposed accessibility statute was Senator Tammy Duckworth's eloquent op-ed opposing this measure in the *Washington Post*. Duckworth said: "This offensive legislation would segregate the disability community, making it the only protected class under civil rights law that must rely on 'education'—rather than strong enforcement—to guarantee access to public spaces."[58] As a well-respected member of the Senate who "lost [her] legs when an RPG tore through the cockpit of the Black Hawk helicopter [she] was flying over Iraq," she was able to counter comments from other politicians that ADA violations are not "significant."[59] It is hard to know if grassroots efforts to defeat the proposed legislation would have been successful without the additional support of a well-respected and disabled politician who is also a veteran. Duckworth's role shows the importance of civil rights activists also having access to politically powerful allies to sustain their hard-won structural reforms. Duckworth was able to counter Democratic representative Jackie Speier's description of the ADA Title III litigation as merely "gotcha stuff."[60]

It is no surprise that this pattern of public insults has also permeated ADA accessibility litigation. While not always successful at causing a judge to rule in favor of a defendant (where the accessibility violations are blatant), these attacks increase the costs of litigation and make it more difficult for lawyers to obtain reasonable attorney's fees for their work. In some cases, however, the insults cause judges to deny class action certification, limit standing, and create inappropriate notice requirements. Public insults act as an important dead weight given their breadth and intensity even when they do not always achieve a complete victory by the defendant. In assessing the power of these public insults, it is important to remember that courts virtually never conclude that the plaintiff's complaints are nonmeritorious. Further, the courts have available Rule 11 sanctions, and even attorney's fee awards to defendants as the prevailing party, if plaintiffs' litigation is truly abusive.[61]

Inaccessibility is still so widespread that it is possible some lawyers and plaintiffs will file numerous lawsuits. Yet these lawyers and their clients are described as the villains for pointing out the continued pattern of egregious violations. As Samuel Bagenstos has said, it is "inaccurate to say that 'legitimate ADA advocates' should want to get accessibility problems fixed without worrying about whether they will get paid."[62] "Attorneys who handle serial ADA litigation are thus likely to be among the few lawyers for whom public accommodation cases are cheap enough and lucrative enough to be economically worthwhile."[63] They develop expertise, have expert witnesses on hand to provide necessary documentation, and have good relations with potential client communities. These lawyers are put in this position by Congress and the courts, not by their unreasonably needy determination to get paid for their work, yet the media casts them as villains. What the media and some courts characterize as serial litigation could more properly be described as litigation based on expertise. These lawyers and their clients should be considered heroes rather than bounty hunters.

BOILER PLATE LITIGATION BY INSULT

Building on the media blitz against ADA plaintiffs, it is common for defendants to try to accuse all plaintiffs of being serial litigators, even when the facts do not support that allegation. For example, Daniel Sharp brought five legal actions using the law firm of Barbosa, Metz & Harrison.[64] Three complaints were against restaurants and one was against a nursing home where he stayed for an extended period of time. Sharp uses a wheelchair, and each complaint appears to be based on obvious, important problems such as inaccessible tables, lack of accessible parking, inaccessible path of travel, and inaccessible restrooms. At the initial stages of these cases, the defendants used Gregory Francis Hurley,[65] who works for the law firm of Greenberg, Traurig, and would aggressively proceed through insult by litigation to have all of the plaintiffs' claims dismissed.

The language below reflects the typical kind of broad and unsubstantiated insults hurled by the defendant's law firm in these kinds of accessibility cases:

> Unfortunately, there are increasingly widespread reports of vexatious ADA litigation. Courts have described these disability access lawsuits as "shakedown schemes" for statutory damages and attorney's fees. . . . "The abuse is a kind of legal shakedown scheme . . . the unscrupulous law firm sends a disabled individual to as many businesses as possible in order to have him or her aggressively seek out all violations of the ADA." . . . Of course, "this type of shotgun litigation undermines both the spirit and purpose of the ADA," *id.*, and "brings into disrepute the important objectives of the ADA by instead focusing public attention on the injustices suffered by defendants

forced to expend large sums to amount defenses to groundless or hyper-technical claims."[66]

After arguing that the plaintiff was part of an unethical takedown scheme, the defendant specifically argued that the plaintiff did not have standing because he " is a serial ADA plaintiff who has at least 4 ADA law-suits currently pending. Plaintiff's counsel specializes in these drive-by law-suits and has brought a myriad of them on behalf of a flock of plaintiffs."[67]

The defendant's lawyer cut and pasted that same sentence in another case against different defendants, again suggesting that it is inappropriate "serial litigation" for a law firm to bring four or five accessibility cases.[68] The defendant found no need to justify why bringing four or five cases is unethical, because the foundation laid by the power of insults seemed to be all the justification it needed. The defendant then piled on the insults by saying that Sharp was not disabled because "he admitted that he could stand with parallel bars, and within the past six months was able to walk approximately 22 feet with the aid of a walker."[69]

The defendant also criticized Sharp for excessive drinking, as if his alleged drinking habits somehow made the defendant's establishment accessible. While the defendant did not succeed in persuading the court to grant its motion for summary judgment on every claim, the frivolous and insulting arguments did require the plaintiff's lawyer to waste valu-able resources to persuade the court that Sharp's need to rely on a walker and parallel bars to ambulate clearly made him disabled for the purposes of the ADA. As the court said: "The Court is at a complete loss as to how this testimony supports Defendants' contention that he can stand and/or walk *independently*. The only inference that could reasonably be drawn is that in order to stand or walk, Sharp requires the use of the parallel bars or a walker."[70]

One might respond to these observations by noting that lawyers are supposed to be assertive and aggressive on behalf of their clients. None-theless, claiming that a plaintiff's lawyer who is enforcing a law through the mechanisms established by Congress is engaging in a "take-down scheme" goes beyond merely aggressive lawyering. Further, this norm of aggressive lawyering overlooks the underlying power imbalance in many civil rights cases. The firm representing the plaintiff in these cases is listed as Metz & Harrison. Their website indicates they have one partner, one of-counsel lawyer, and one senior associate.[71] By contrast, the defendants in these cases are represented by Greenberg Traurig; their website lists them as having two thousand attorneys on three continents.[72] This is a typical setup in civil rights suits: the plaintiffs' firms are small, sometimes one-person firms, while the defendants' firms are significantly larger, with significantly more resources and expertise at their disposal. While one could imagine government lawyers with government resources litigating against a large law firm, that kind of work is much more difficult for a small firm. Thus, litigation by insult is much more likely to be effective when deployed by defendants in litigation because of the disproportionate financial resources at their disposal.

LITIGATION BY INSULT PREVAILS

Litigation by insult is often tied to specific legal arguments that make it difficult for plaintiffs to prevail in civil rights cases. They create dead weights by blocking plaintiff's lawyers from obtaining attorney's fees, having cases dismissed for not meeting rigorous pleading requirements, and having plaintiffs' cases thrown out due to technical standing problems. None of these strategies have anything to do with whether the plaintiffs have meritorious complaints about inaccessible buildings. If government lawyers were allowed to bring these kinds of cases, few of these arguments would be available. In other words, litigation by insult builds on the challenges and inequities underlying civil rights litigation.

Race to Correct

A successful tactic used by defendants is to rush to correct alleged violations and then argue that the plaintiffs' lawyers should not get any attorney's fees for bringing these problems to the defendants' attention.[73] The most favorable precedent on this issue for plaintiffs is the Eleventh Circuit decision in *Sheely v. MR Radiology Network*,[74] in which the court found that a defendant's voluntary cessation of a challenged practice did not deprive a federal court of its power to determine the legality of the practice.

Nonetheless, even in the Eleventh Circuit, where *Sheely* was decided, district courts have routinely found ADA accessibility cases to be moot and denied attorney's fees, especially in cases against large corporate defendants who can quickly marshal resources to try to solve any accessibility issues alleged in a complaint, then ask for sympathy for their decades-long failure to comply.[75] One good example is an accessibility lawsuit filed against Walgreens's Lake City, Florida, store by the National Alliance for Accessibility.[76] The plaintiffs alleged that the store had numerous architectural barriers such as inaccessible parking spaces, entrance access, paths of travel, and restroom facilities.[77] All of these accessibility problems were visible. In fact, Walgreens hired an expert shortly after the suit was filed who submitted a report that detailed instances of noncompliance.[78] As the court noted (as a factor in Walgreens's favor), the defendant never claimed that it was originally in compliance.[79]

Citing *Sheely*, the district court examined whether the conduct was isolated or unintentional, whether cessation of the offending conduct reflected a "genuine change of heart or timed to anticipate suit," and whether the defendant had acknowledged liability, to determine whether to dismiss the case as moot.[80] Even though Walgreens had had a duty since the ADA was enacted in 1990 to ensure that such apparent accessibility defects were not present and readily found the violations once a lawsuit was commenced, the court concluded that Walgreens's violations were "unknowing and unintentional."[81] It found that the company's expenditure of "substantial resources to makes its store ADA-compliant" showed that it "genuinely attempted to comply with the law"[82] rather than being a ploy to avoid attorney's fees and costs.

Although ignorance of the law is usually not considered to be a valid defense, Walgreens convinced the court that its conduct was unknowing and unintentional because it simply had not bothered to look for obvious violations (until the company was sued). Further, the court concluded the defendant would be vigilant to ensure that violations did not occur in the future even though these modifications might deteriorate and need updating. One of the modifications was "fixing cracks in a curb ramp."[83] Anyone who has walked around outside knows how common it is for curb ramps to be in disrepair and how important safe curb ramps are for someone who uses a wheelchair or a cane. While prior decisions purportedly put the burden of proof on the defendants to demonstrate that they are unlikely to be out of compliance in the future under the *Friends of the Earth* precedent,[84] the court bent over backwards to accept the defendant's mea culpa explanations and determine the case was moot (and therefore not eligible for attorney's fees). This case reflected unwarranted sympathy for the corporation and little appreciation of the importance of having a court enter an injunction to prevent repeat violations as well as allow lawyers to be paid for their work. This kind of sympathy is likely the result of repeated public insults against those who seek to use litigation to attain a more accessible society.

Specific Pleading Requirements

ADA defendants also couple litigation by insult with narrow pleading requirements for filing lawsuits. This strategy is particularly effective because of the "rush to repair" problem just described.

For example, in *Oliver v. Ralphs Grocery Company*,[85] A. J. Oliver sued Ralphs Grocery Company and Cypress Creek Company alleging that a Food 4 Less grocery store was not ADA compliant. In his complaint, Oliver indicated that he used a motorized wheelchair and found eighteen separate architectural barriers to using the facility.[86] Seeking to avoid paying attorney's fees as a result of this successful litigation, Ralphs began eliminating many of these architectural barriers.[87] Four months after the deadline had passed to file an amended complaint, Oliver filed an expert report identifying approximately twenty architectural barriers at the Food 4 Less store. The plaintiff's lawyer openly explained "that his delays in identifying the barriers at the facility were part of his legal strategy: he purposely 'forces the defense to wait until expert disclosures (or discovery) before revealing a complete list of barriers,' because otherwise a defendant could remove all the barriers prior to trial and moot the entire case."[88] Given that the defendant had had notice since 1990 of the need to create an accessible structure, the plaintiff's lawyer did not want to risk mooting the case by listing every accessibility problem with specificity well before trial.

The defendant's strategy succeeded. The district court refused to consider the new barriers listed in the expert's report and mooted the barriers that were already remedied.[89] The court of appeals affirmed these rulings.[90] Defense counsel used litigation by insult to persuade the courts to grant its motion for summary judgment. The defense accused the plaintiff's lawyer of using a "common ploy" of attempting "to thwart defendants from fixing all alleged barriers and mooting his ADA claims."[91] Further, the defense counsel criticized the plaintiff's counsel for filing "over a thousand ADA cases in the Southern District of California alone[; he] is frequently reprimanded for not sufficiently identifying alleged barriers, misleading the court regarding applicable case law, lying about his client's disability, and coaching his clients to lie."[92]

In support of the argument that the plaintiff's counsel was "frequently reprimanded," the motion cited one example of a court awarding the defendant attorney's fees in a case involving a different plaintiff.[93] Considering that, as the defendant stated, the plaintiff's counsel had filed over a thousand cases, this can hardly qualify as "frequent." Further, there was no suggestion in this case that the newly alleged defects were erroneous; the expert report was allegedly not timely. The passage of ADA Title III in 1990 was not considered sufficient notice to defendants of the need to conduct their *own* accessibility audit to determine if they were in compliance with federal law. Instead, the plaintiff's case was dismissed for waiting four months to conduct an accessibility audit of the defendant's business after filing suit.

These arguments were possible (and successful) because of the limited relief available under ADA Title III due to problems stemming from rigid pleading rules,[94] attorney's fee restrictions under *Buckhannon*[95] that limit such fees to cases that proceed to court-ordered remedies rather than private settlements, and the limited availability of only injunctive relief under federal law. It is impossible to obtain injunctive relief if a problem is cured, but if the plaintiff does not detail all the barriers that need to be cured at the time of filing suit, then the plaintiff fails to meet the required pleading rules. In other words, the success of litigation by insult depends on the preexisting procedural rules that make accessibility cases very difficult to bring. Without narrow pleading rules and strict attorney's fee requirements, a court may be able to fend off the insults as scurrilous and irrelevant. Instead, the court supports the defendant's arguments.

Standing Arguments

Defendants also ridicule so-called serial litigants by suggesting that they could not possibly be interested in visiting many businesses in their neighborhood. For example, in *Coleman v. Chin Ju Pritchett d.b.a. New Star Restaurant*, Glen Coleman openly acknowledged that he was a plaintiff who had filed numerous barriers to access lawsuits under the ADA. In seeking to have his case dismissed, the defendant restaurant argued that it was implausible that Coleman might want to return to fourteen different establishments, including five eating establishments "and even a funeral home."[96] The defendant also insisted that the plaintiff's status as a "serial ADA litigant" meant that he should have to prove "more than an intent to return to places previously visited."[97]

Although that strategy did not result in the claim against the restaurant being dismissed, it has worked in many other lawsuits.[98] In *Rosenkrantz v. Markapoulos*,[99] the court insisted that the plaintiff must detail concrete plans for when he might want to return to the defendant hotel. Unlike what it would have assumed about nondisabled individuals, the district court was not willing to entertain the likelihood that he might travel "hundreds of miles" to visit the defendant's hotel.[100] Because the court saw the purpose of the litigation as making it possible for only the listed plaintiff to visit the hotel (rather than the disability community generally), it was not willing to let the plaintiff's case withstand a motion to dismiss.

Similarly, the court dismissed Steven Brother's lawsuit against a hotel chain because he lived several hundred miles away from the hotel chain and could only allege a general intent to return to the facility.[101] The court found it appropriate in its statement of facts to mention the plaintiff's low income and receipt of social security checks and food stamps.[102] The Florida court was so disturbed by Mr. Brother's attempt to use the ADA to make hotels accessible that it offered these extensive remarks after dismissing his case:

> If history is any guide, then William Charouhis [Steven Brother's lawyer] and his clients will adjust to this ruling so that their future filings satisfy Article III's standing requirements. When that occurs, this Court (respect-

ing the separation of powers) will be obligated to allow such cases to proceed.

This being said, it should be emphasized that the system for adjudicating disputes under the ADA cries out for a legislative solution. Only Congress can respond to vexatious litigation tactics that otherwise comply with its statutory frameworks. Instead of promoting "conciliation and voluntary compliance[,]" the existing law encourages massive litigation. . . . "[P]re-suit settlements[,]" after all, "do not vest plaintiffs' counsel with an entitlement to attorney's fees" under the ADA. . . . Moreover, the means for enforcing the ADA (attorney's fees) have become more important and desirable than the end (accessibility for disabled individuals). *See Id.* at 1285 (finding a litigious ADA Plaintiff represented by William Charouhis "merely a professional pawn in an ongoing scheme to bilk attorney's fees from the Defendant"). This is particularly the case in the Middle District of Florida where the same plaintiffs file hundreds of lawsuits against establishments they purportedly visit regularly. This type of shotgun litigation undermines both the spirit and purpose of the ADA.[103]

This example illustrates how highly resourced law firms can function as interconnected strongholds that undermine effective civil rights reform. The defense bar does not even need to engage in litigation by insult when the courts, themselves, fail to see the value in private attorneys collaborating with disabled plaintiffs to make facilities more accessible. The district court's diatribe against the plaintiff's lawyer by name is symptomatic of the broader failure to understand how the ADA's accessibility standards are enforced. There is no governmental entity making sure that hotels, for example, have adequately accessible rooms. These problems are only discovered one plaintiff at a time. Rather than be castigated as a serial plaintiff, Steven Brother and his lawyer, William Charouhis, should be thanked for their willingness to investigate and determine which hotels are not accessible. But instead, suits like theirs are often dismissed because the disabled plaintiff does not have a credible claim of an interest to revisit the facility.[104]

The requirement that plaintiffs visit every facility owned by a defendant provides yet another dead weight to accessibility litigation. In *Campbell v. Moon Palace, Inc.*,[105] the defendant's motion for summary judgment argued that the plaintiff was an improper "serial plaintiff" and requested that the entire case be dismissed on that theory. Although the defendant did not obtain a dismissal, the stringent legal standard developed in that case then caused the dismissal of other accessibility cases. For example, in *Access 4 All v. Starbucks Corp.*,[106] the plaintiffs alleged ADA violations in 18 Starbucks locations within the Southern District of Florida, but also listed approximately 300 other locations within Florida as having similar violations. The defendant contended that the plaintiffs lacked standing because they had no evidence to substantiate their contention that they had personally encountered any barriers to access at any of the 304 locations identified in the complaint. In this case, Starbucks claimed to have a policy of requesting patrons to move from a wheelchair accessible table when someone needed access to such a table. At the stores that the plaintiffs visited, they also found other violations such as sloped parking, a transaction counter that was too high, lack of accessible tables, a bathroom door opening the wrong way, and a too-narrow bathroom corridor.

The court refused to find that the plaintiffs had standing at any location they had not visited despite an expert report that documented lack of accessibility at numerous locations. Their list of violations was criticized for being "exhaustive and overbroad."[107] The court cited *Campbell v. Moon Palace* for the proposition that the plaintiffs needed to identify and produce evidence of each and every barrier they had personally encountered. An expert report was not a sufficient basis for proceeding with the lawsuit. That kind of impossible hurdle shut down what the court considered to be improper serial litigation. Again, this example reflects the limitations of a private mode of enforcement; only a government entity can pursue that kind of systemic theory.

The economic power of large corporations and law firms discourages disability lawyers from filing meritorious suits, because they know they will be drowned in frivolous and insulting defense pleadings. Ironically, they may instead agree to take cases against small businesses that may be less likely to respond aggressively in litigation. This, in turn, feeds the media account of "drive-by litigation" against helpless, sympathetic defendants when, in fact, it is the plaintiffs' lawyers who are in the disadvantageous position.

When I talk about this work at workshops and conferences, I am always asked to acknowledge sympathy with the notion that there is vexatious

Title III litigation. My answer is that Rule 11, which gives judges the discretion to fine lawyers and their clients who bring meritless cases, is designed to deal with frivolous litigation. The so-called vexatious litigation is virtually never frivolous. The ADA violations do exist, which is why the plaintiffs are often able to obtain settlements. Further, there is a benefit to defendants genuinely having to worry about being sued for ADA violations, because such concerns might increase voluntary compliance. In the absence of monetary relief being available, corporations need some financial reason to engage in compliance. Fear of litigation can act as such an incentive.

If public enforcement of accessibility problems existed, then government entities might prioritize bringing lawsuits against major corporations that have the largest impact on people with disabilities. The private mode of enforcement may therefore have the consequence of affecting only the weakest defendants. This makes sense, of course, when one understands that business owners may have agreed to precisely this mode of enforcement, knowing they would have the strength to push back against solo practitioners who sought to sue them. It should be no surprise that plaintiffs' lawyers would seek to sue the defendants who are least likely to have the resources to aggressively fight back, just as the defense bar is most likely to use its resources to fight large-scale structural reform. Both sides are merely working under the neoliberal, one-plaintiff-at-a-time framework that Congress created. Yet it is the plaintiffs' lawyers who are criticized for taking advantage of the very system that Congress created to avoid broad public, structural enforcement of these rights.

Exhaustion and Delay

While one can find instances in which the litigation by insult strategy has not succeeded, this strategy still serves to exhaust and delay the attainment of justice. Lengthy lawsuits or appeals are needed to remedy simple accessibility violations, sending the message to plaintiffs' attorneys that this kind of litigation is rarely worth the effort.

When defendants have allegedly remedied the defects raised in the plaintiffs' lawsuits before trial, plaintiffs may find themselves needing to endure years of litigation merely to overcome the mootness argument. For example, in *Pereira v. Ralph's Grocery*,[108] on January 17, 2007, a plaintiff sued twenty-three grocery stores in Southern California that allegedly did not provide sufficient access to persons who use wheelchairs or scooters for mobility. The parties agreed that the defendant had corrected all of the accessibility issues raised in the plaintiff's complaint, yet the plaintiff argued the case was not moot because the challenged conduct could be expected to recur. The plaintiff argued that "over time parking lots will need to be restriped and handicapped and accessible signage will need to be repaired and/or replaced."[109] The defendant argued that the case should be mooted because the court could readily believe that Ralph's intended to fully comply with the ADA in the future.[110]

The district court accepted the mootness argument, finding: "Plaintiffs allege ADA violations that are of a physical nature, not due to an ineffective policy. For example, Plaintiffs alleged that the placement of toilets and the disabled parking signage violate the ADA, not that Defendant failed to enforce a policy to keep an accessible grocery store check-out line staffed."[111] The argument that the facility *may* fall out of compliance was not considered sufficient to overcome the mootness problem. Thus, the court concluded, the plaintiff could not establish that the inaccessibility could reasonably be expected to recur, even though the *Friends of the Earth* court[112] had said that the burden was on the *defendant*, not the plaintiff, to show that it was unlikely to fall out of compliance in the future.

In an unpublished, 2–1 decision, the Ninth Circuit reversed the district court.[113] Writing for the majority, Judge Alex Kozinski found that the "defendant's 'voluntary cessation of allegedly illegal conduct' did not moot this case" and that the plaintiff had standing to challenge all the disability-related barriers.[114]

Although the court of appeals reversed the district court in *Pereira*, many other courts have ruled for defendants in similar ADA cases, thereby precluding plaintiffs' lawyers from obtaining any attorney's fees for their work in bringing accessibility violations to the attention of various defendants.[115]

Defendants also use litigation by insult to seek to impose a backdoor notice requirement. A good example is *Rudder v. Costco Wholesale Corporation*,[116] in which the defendant was partially successful in having issues dismissed that were resolved after the case was filed. The law firm of Metz & Harrison represented Christie Rudder in this case. Rudder is an individual with a disability who sustained various injuries in an automobile accident. She is not able to stand independently and uses a wheelchair for mobility. She appears to have been involved in six lawsuits involving accessibility problems that she has experienced: lack of accessibility at a supermarket,[117] drug store,[118] a local restaurant,[119] a hotel,[120] and a nearby transportation facility.[121]

The *Costco* case was a suit against many businesses at a local shopping center, with Costco being the anchor store and primary defendant.[122] Rudder made two allegations that related to the site itself: lack of accessible parking and lack of accessible path of travel. The other allegations were specific to Costco. Because the parking and path of travel problems were common to all the stores at the facility, she had to name them all as defendants in the lawsuit.

Rather than acknowledge that the shopping center was out of compliance with basic rules about parking and site accessibility, the defendant attacked the right of the plaintiff to name so many defendants in a lawsuit about access to a shopping center, accusing the plaintiff's counsel of "extort[ing] separate nuisance settlements from each of the multiple defendants."[123] Further, the defendant argued that the case against Costco should be dismissed "for failure to adequately provide notice to Costco" and by pulling a "bait and switch by filing a complaint and then go[ing] fishing for additional violations with her expert in tow."[124]

Despite the defendant's arguments about lack of notice, the original complaint alleged many violations that were still found to exist when the court resolved the defendant's summary judgment motion on September 20, 2013, more than a year after Rudder filed the original lawsuit.[125] Although the defendant did not succeed in having the entire case dismissed, its strategy was partially successful, because the plaintiff was able to obtain only very narrow relief.

The notice strategy is tied to a mootness strategy. Defendants seek to insist that plaintiffs name every ADA violation at the time they file lawsuits so that they can rush to cure each of those violations before trial and then argue mootness. Even when a plaintiff cannot get into a facility, due to an accessibility violation, the defendant seeks to argue that the plaintiff needed to name all potential defects in the initial lawsuit. As the Ninth Circuit has said, "it would be ironic if not perverse to charge that the natural consequence of this deterrence, the inability to personally discover additional facts about the defendant's violations, would defeat that plaintiff's standing to challenge other violations at the same location that subsequently come to light."[126] Nonetheless, not all circuits accept this rule; as the previous section indicated, plaintiffs are often found not to have standing when they cannot allege repeated exposure to a defendant's inaccessible facilities.

After vigorously attacking the plaintiffs' standing and ability to represent a class, defendants then challenge plaintiffs' claims for attorney's fees. The size of the attorney's fee bill, of course, is related to the number of objections thrown at attorneys by opposing counsel. Again, litigation by insult is used as a dead weight to lower the attorney's fee petition.

A case in which a plaintiff successfully deflected this strategy is *Charlebois v. Angels Baseball, LP*.[127] Paul Charlebois filed a complaint against Angels Baseball after he sought to attend a baseball game and have a good line of sight in the Club level, where there is also portable food service.[128] The plaintiff sought to certify a class of wheelchair users who have sought or would seek in the future to attend a game at the stadium. The defendants did not apparently dispute that they had an insufficient number of wheelchair-accessible seats and, in particular, had very few accessible seats in the Club section of the stadium.

This should not have been a difficult claim to certify as a class.[129] People who use wheelchairs, like much of the general public, might enjoy viewing a professional baseball game. And like the general public, those people might want to sit in seats where venders sell food. In fact, one might speculate that their need to use a wheelchair to travel, combined with the apparent inaccessibility of the newly renovated stadium, might make them more likely than the general public to seek to purchase food from a vender who walks around the stadium. Despite the obviousness of the plaintiff's ability to meet these requirements, the defendants strongly opposed class certification and required the plaintiff to engage in extensive surveys and data analysis to certify the class.

In opposing class certification, the defendants argued that the plaintiff could only establish that there were thirty-one potential class members who had suffered or would suffer harm from the inaccessible stadium design, even though thousands of individuals attend baseball games at the stadium. After extensive litigation and fact gathering by both sides, the court ruled: "This Court believes that attending a baseball game is more akin to attending a movie than it is to going to a golf course. Baseball is often referenced as America's favorite past-time, and given that Plaintiff's class includes future attendees, it is reasonable to presume that many wheelchair-using baseball fans will emerge as future class members based on the statistical evidence provided by Plaintiff through the shared survey and, to a limited extent, Plaintiff's supplemental data."[130]

The class certification skirmish was typical of the heated nature of this litigation. Thus, not surprisingly, the defendants then attacked the plaintiff's request for attorney's fees after this case finally settled. The defendants unsuccessfully argued that attorneys at large, prestigious firms were not an appropriate comparator,[131] that one lawyer's fees should be reduced because another judge in another case more than four years earlier had reduced his fees,[132] that the fees should be reduced because they were more than the defendants paid their lawyers,[133] that one lawyer's fees should not be included because he was not counsel of record,[134] that the hours the lawyers worked on the complaint and motion for summary judgment were excessive,[135] and that some work was duplicative.[136] The court observed: "If Defendants had wished not to pay Class Counsel's fees, Defendants could have settled earlier."[137]

Nonetheless, the attorney's fee petition shows how difficult and time consuming it can be to win a relatively straightforward accessibility case about stadium seating. The plaintiff's request for attorney's fees showed that the lawyers had devoted 1,709 hours to this case even though it settled without litigation.[138] Further, as the court noted, this kind of private enforcement is essential because there is little public enforcement of disability access.[139] And, as noted by defendants, this strategy had been partially successful against one of the lawyers in another civil rights case, in which his attorney's fees were somewhat reduced.[140]

Even when plaintiffs are successful in these kinds of cases, the defendants' tactics often involve enormous delays in the attainment of an accessible facility. This chapter ends with a discussion of one of the earlier examples in this chapter. As discussed in the opening paragraphs, attorney Amy Robertson has documented the impact of these kinds of tactics in a case challenging the inaccessibility of Cracker Barrel's parking lot.[141] She chose this example because the amicus brief filed in the Third Circuit by an industry trade group[142] described the Cracker Barrel case[143] with the kind of public insults that this chapter has amply documented. The Cracker Barrel plaintiffs were described as "clients [who] often identify a particular type of accessibility issue, and then bring the same claim over and over against different businesses,"[144] even though the plaintiffs eventually *prevailed* in this litigation.[145]

Robertson documented that rather than being an example of abusive litigation by the *plaintiffs*, it was the *defendants* that used every available stalling tactic to delay the implementation of an accessible parking lot in the Cracker Barrel litigation. Cracker Barrel's lawyers filed twenty-one separate briefs over a two-and-a-half-year period, while people with mobility impairments continued not to have access to their parking lots.[146] The amicus brief criticized plaintiffs who bring numerous lawsuits against the same defendant for "excessive slopes or other accessibility issues in parking lots"[147] without considering why these claims are almost always successful due to the underlying inaccessible design of the parking lots at these stores. The implicit message of the amicus brief is that the inaccessibility of parking lots is a trivial issue that does not merit litigation. Senator Duckworth argued otherwise in her powerful *Washington Post* editorial, in which she explained how disability access was not a luxury for someone with profound mobility impairments.

The amicus brief reflected the strength of the power bullies. The brief was funded by three trade associations representing various convenience stores and supermarkets.[148] The corporate and political elite have combined to weaken the ADA by trivializing the rights protected by this statute and creating caricatures of those who try to vindicate those rights. They point out that "the class action mechanism and the prospect of attorneys' fees under federal law provide alternative incentive to bring such litigation" and then argue that such mechanisms should be disfavored.[149] They do not hide their direct attempt to undermine the statute's underlying enforcement mechanism. They simply do not want plaintiffs to be able to use this statute effectively to force their corporate interests to modify their facilities to make them accessible.[150]

CONCLUSION

The scope and power of public insults as a litigation strategy are far reaching, and this chapter could not possibly catalog all such cases, even in the disability context alone. We have seen public insults often succeed when civil rights hang by a weak thread.

But the power bullies do not always win. In 2017, the US Senate was poised to repeal the Affordable Care Act (ACA), which would have had a devastating impact on many people with disabilities. Disability rights activists worked tirelessly to defeat the ACA's repeal, keeping "vigils day and night, sleeping in wheelchairs when necessary." John Nichols's column in *The Nation* described disability activists as the "real heroes" in the fight against the ACA's repeal.[151] But what most Americans remember is that, at 2:00 a.m. on July 27, 2017, Senator John McCain, who had returned to the Senate to cast a vote after receiving a diagnosis of brain cancer, voted "no" on the bill, causing it to lose by a slim 49–51 margin.[152] Although there is no way to know exactly why Senator McCain saved the ACA by a single vote in the Senate, one might wonder if it was his response to both the groundwork of disability activists and the bully Trump. Douglas Holtz-Eakin, McCain's chief domestic policy adviser, described McCain as a person who will "punch the bully for you."[153] The collaboration of ground-level activists with a politician who wielded power delivered an effective punch against the bullies who were trying to dismantle the ACA.

It is also important to remember that progressive change *can* happen without resort to public insults. Michelle Alexander's best-selling, poignant, and fact-based account of mass incarceration in the United States[154] brought important attention to this problem in 2010, with an initial print run of only three thousand copies from the New Press.[155] With enormous grassroots support from community organizers[156] and civil rights organizations,[157] important structural changes have occurred since 2010, including "banning the box" initiatives,[158] mass bailouts of inmates,[159] the curtailment of money bonds,[160] and the reinstatement of voting rights for convicted felons.[161] Following the gruesome murder of George Floyd, Black Lives Matter was able to build on that work even as President Trump tried to bring them down through public insults.[162] While the reforms that Alexander and Black Lives Matter have helped spur are just a start, they show that the political left can overcome the politics of demonization to achieve structural change. But as Alexander also warns,[163] efforts to undermine those reforms will be immediate and need to be resisted through effective mobilization and steadfast movement building.

One needs to be cautious in suggesting a one-size-fits-all response to the public insult playbook. Insults themselves are contextual, so the appropriate response is likely contextual as well. Looking for a universal response, Michelle Obama has said, "When they go low, we go high"; by contrast, Eric Holder has said, "When they go low, we kick them!"[164] Neither universal response is likely to work in every situation. Further, by the time the insults start flying, the response may be irrelevant. This chapter has shown how insults can be especially effective when the underlying right has significant preexisting weaknesses. Thus, it is important to have a fortress *before* the fighting begins. The better analogy may be the Three Little Pigs. In the accessibility provisions of the ADA, the disability community has a straw house that cannot withstand even a slight puff of air by the power bullies. The civil rights community needs a brick house rather than a "fragile compromise."[165] Then it would not have to hold its breath while waiting to see if someone like Senator McCain will display a thumbs up or a thumbs down.[166]

4 Immigrants as Murderers and Rapists

Although Donald Trump's deployment of insults against immigrants marked a striking degradation of our national discourse, the role of insults in shaping anti-immigrant conduct and legislation long predates his presidential campaign. For example, during the nineteenth century, Irish immigrants were disparaged as a "race of savages" and were the subject of such aphorisms as "It's as natural for a Hibernarian [Irish person] to tipple as it is for a pig to grunt."[1] Throughout US history, immigrants of various ethnic backgrounds have endured an onslaught of insults that reflected hostile and often highly racialized stereotypes.

This chapter illustrates the way insults have been historically deployed against immigrants as a headwind to curtail structural reform. This is an example of a direct attack on a group, not a use of subtlety or deflection. Further, this chapter recounts how public insults sometimes act as a dead weight by nullifying long-standing constitutional doctrine. We saw a version of this problem in the disability context (see chapter 3) when defendants and politicians insulted disability plaintiffs and their lawyers to convince the courts to overlook well-settled legal principles. In the immigration context, this problem extends to the realm of constitutional law.

IMMIGRATION RESTRICTIONS
IN THE NAME OF WHITENESS

"America for Americans"

The 1790 Census reported that there were about 700,000 African slaves in the early United States, which had a total population of nearly four million.[2] Government officials and slave owners considered these slaves to be property; slaves were not eligible for citizenship. The nation's first immigration law stated that only a "free white person" of "good moral character" was eligible for naturalization.[3]

But people from Africa were not the only group broadly disparaged as nonwhite in the early days of the United States. "German immigrants were not considered 'White' until the 1840s to 1860s, Irish immigrants until the 1850s to 1880s and eastern and southern European immigrants until the 1900s to 1920s."[4] African people involuntarily came to the United States as slaves; many Irish immigrants entered as indentured servants or were forcibly shipped overseas by the English government due its fear of Catholic influence in Ireland.[5] Many Italian immigrants also came to the United States between 1880 and 1920 and were met with much racial animosity despite their seeming whiteness; the stereotypical linking of them to criminal involvement still lingers today.[6]

Elite members of society often feared immigrants as a source of political subversion. For example, one member of Congress argued for the passage of the Alien and Sedition Acts of 1798 because he did "not wish to invite hoards of wild Irishmen, nor the turbulent and disorderly of all parts of the world, to come here with a view to disturb our tranquility, after having succeeded in the overthrow of their own governments."[7]

Other elite figures welcomed immigrants as a group whose degraded status made them ripe for exploitation. One southern plantation owner considered Irish immigrants preferable to slaves for construction projects, because "[i]f the [slur used to describe Irish deleted] are knocked overboard, or get their backs broke, nobody loses anything."[8] Entrapment in onerous and low-paying labor was evidenced by widespread posting of "No Irish Need Apply" signs in northern cities.[9]

Fear of subversion and job competition, augmented by anti-Catholic sentiment, led to the creation of the Know-Nothing Party in 1854, which espoused nativist, anti-Irish, and anti-German sentiments. Even after the decline of the Know-Nothing Party, union leaders often expressed their distaste for immigrants as unwanted economic competition. In 1904, the president of the United Mine Workers argued:

> No matter how decent and self-respecting and hard working the aliens who are flooding this country may be, they are invading the land of Americans and whether they know it or not, are helping to take the bread out of their mouths. America for Americans should be the motto of every citizen, whether he be a working man or a capitalist.[10]

However, this period of American history also reveals how a castigated group can successfully fight back against a campaign of public insults. Although hostility toward Catholicism and Irish laborers engendered barriers for Irish immigrants, the growth of the US Catholic Church and Irish involvement in unions became paths to higher status. Irish immigrants embraced the union movement; Noel Ignatiev argued that "[e]arly labor unions . . . should be regarded not so much as Irish institutions, in the way they later became, but as institutions for assimilating the Irish into white America."[11] The Catholic Church, which was understood to be Irish dominated, helped improve the public image of Irish people by establishing well-respected parochial schools and hospitals. In the 1870s, for example, St. Patrick's Cathedral in New York City "symbolized the Irish-dominated Catholic Church's increasing solvency and self-confidence."[12] It should come as no surprise that a group is better able to overcome a campaign of public insults when it gains some access to the power structure itself.

It is also important to understand that castigated groups unfortunately sometimes overcome the power of insults by turning on other disadvantaged groups. In his pathbreaking book *How the Irish Became White* (1996), Noel Ignatiev closely examined how the Irish became "white" and pitted themselves against African Americans.[13] He suggested: "Imagine how history might have been different had the Irish, the unskilled labor force of the north, and the slaves, the unskilled labor force of the South, been unified."[14] In 1967 he composed a letter to the Progressive Labor Party positing that true class solidarity would not be possible unless working-class people were willing to reject their whiteness. They "have more to lose than their chains; they have also to 'lose' their white-skin privileges, the perquisites that separate them from the rest of the working class, that act as the material base for the split in the ranks of labor."[15]

It is impossible to rewind history to see how society would have unfolded had the Irish not worked so hard to become recognized as "white," but we can certainly see that the notion of white privilege is nothing new and will continue to harm those who are considered nonwhite. The very fact that we have to utter "Black Lives Matter" reflects the success that some groups have had in acquiring the mantle of privilege by being considered "white."

Sickly and Grasping Jews

Many Eastern European Jews began to immigrate to the United States in the late 1880s, often to escape Tsarist Russia. Their arrival was met with "virulent anti-Semitism."[16] For example, author Henry Adams (who was a descendant of two US presidents) castigated Jews as "agents of international finance who polluted the American landscape" and expressed a desire to "put every moneylender to death."[17]

Ivy League universities took steps in the early twentieth century to restrict the admission of Jews. Harvard University's president, A. Lawrence Lowell, famously noted in the 1920s that "the summer hotel that is ruined by admitting Jews meets its fate . . . because they drive away the Gentiles, and then after the Gentiles [have] left, they leave also."[18] Similarly, Columbia College's dean Herbert Hawkes explained, in justifying the use of the SAT for admissions: "[B]ecause the typical Jewish student was simply a 'grind,' who excelled on the Regents Exam because he worked so hard, a test of innate intelligence would put him back in his place."[19]

The infamous Immigration Act of 1924 set strict quotas on immigration using figures from 1890, before there was large-scale immigration from Eastern and Southern Europe (or any immigration from China or Japan).[20] Congress saw no reason to hide its hostility, stating that it was reducing immigration to avoid charging "our institutions for the care of the socially inadequate."[21] A House report openly stated that the immigration quota system "is used in an effort to preserve, as nearly as possibly, the racial status quo in the United States. It is hoped to guarantee, as best as we can at this late date, racial homogeneity."[22]

Public expression of anti-Semitism continued in the United States in the 1930s, when many Jews found it difficult to immigrate to the United States.[23] Father Charles Coughlin, who reached millions of people each week through his radio religious services, "preached antisemitism, accusing the Jews of manipulating financial institutions and conspiring to control the world."[24]

Industrialist Henry Ford was another prominent voice spreading anti-Semitism. In 1918, he purchased the *Dearborn Independent* and published a series of articles that described a vast Jewish conspiracy infecting the United States. He "attribute[d] all evil to Jews or to the Jewish capitalists. . . . The Jews caused the war, the Jews caused the outbreak of thieving and robbery all over the country, the Jews caused the inefficiency of the navy."[25]

While Eleanor Roosevelt tried to influence US refugee policy to assist Jews trying to escape Nazi Germany in the 1930s, she was largely unsuccessful. Breckinridge Long, the State Department official largely responsible for US refugee policy, created difficult hurdles for those seeking refugee status, arguing that the State Department was "the first line of defense" against those who would "make America vulnerable to enemies for the sake of humanitarianism."[26] A State Department document said that America faced an inundation of "abnormally twisted" and "unassimilable" Jews: "filthy un-American, and often dangerous in their habits."[27]

These kinds of structural barriers, which were justified by resort to public insults, had enormous human consequences. Public opinion was a significant hurdle for Jews seeking to enter the United States, with 83 percent of Americans reportedly opposing their admission as refugees in 1939.[28] In one well-known incident, the United States refused entry to a German ocean liner in May 1939, forcing many of the passengers to return to Germany, where they later perished in the Holocaust. Adolf Hitler correctly predicted the power of insults to act as a headwind against resistance to his campaign of terror and destruction. He reportedly counted on worldwide anti-Semitism to allow his extermination project to succeed. He correctly described the attitude at the time: "Nobody wants these criminals."[29]

In the current era, most "see Jews not as a separate race, but as White Americans. . . . While anti-Semitism still exists, it does not define

American life as it did in the early part of the twentieth century."[30] Nonetheless, the Anti-Defamation League (ADL) reported in 2018 that anti-Semitic incidents have risen dramatically since 2016.[31] In 2017, the ADL reported a 57 percent increase over the previous year in anti-Semitic incidents, and in 2018, a 105 percent increase in anti-Semitic assault incidents, including the murder of eleven Jewish worshippers on October 27, 2018.[32]

Public insults against Jews today can be a continued attempt to act as a dead weight on their ability to be successful, even if those insults are hurled by what might be considered fringe groups. For example, the ADL reported that there was a spike in anti-Semitic propaganda in October 2018, including "35 separate distributions of a flier that blamed Jews for the fraught confirmation process of Justice Brett Kavanaugh to the Supreme Court."[33]

The following transcript of a robocall made by supporters of California Senate primary candidate Patrick Little shows the explicit use of anti-Semitism to challenge Diane Feinstein:

MAN: Diane Feinstein isn't just a Jew, she's an Israeli citizen.

WOMAN: Wait, that can't be legal right? I mean she's a citizen of Israel but gets to vote as a US senator from California to send billions of our dollars away every year to her real country, Israel?

MAN: It used to be illegal but the Jews of our country got rid of that law.

WOMAN: Not only that, but she gets to vote America into Middle East wars based on lies so that Israel can eventually expand its borders like it always planned.

MAN: To rid America of traitorous Jews like Dianne Feinstein, vote for Patrick Little. . . . He's going to get rid of all the nation-wrecking Jews from our country starting with Israeli citizen, Diane Feinstein.

"Goodbye Jews, goodbye Jews, goodbye Jews" (from *Schindler's List* clip).[34]

This robocall made clear that Little was a fervent anti-Semite. *Newsweek* reported in 2018 that he told them that he "admires Adolf Hitler and would prefer to see Jewish Americans deported to Israel."[35]

Although the Republican Party condemned Little, he finished twelfth (with 1.2 percent of votes) in California's primary for the US Senate, after placing second in an early statewide poll.[36] This attempt to hurl public insults was unsuccessful but shows that the tactic is still being deployed to further anti-Semitism, and that some voters are responsive to that message. And unlike in the early twentieth century, well-respected public figures, like the presidents or deans of colleges, are not the ones making these public statements. Fringe groups have taken up the banner of anti-Semitism; when their arguments coalesce with some members of the power elite, they may have traction in acting as a dead weight on the work of Jews in society. While there is no way to prove that public insults, like those found in the robocalls, helped cause violent incidents like the 2018 shooting at the Pittsburgh synagogue, the speaker certainly supported getting "rid of all the nation-wrecking Jews." Acceptance of such public insults can serve as a headwind against progressive reforms but also, as reflected in the massacre in Pittsburgh, can lead to the outright murder of people in the name of anti-Semitism.

Groups like the ADL exist to fight such anti-Semitism, but as in the story of Irish Americans, we can also see a troubling history of one group pitting itself against another disadvantaged group to get access to power. The ADL has been repeatedly criticized for considering any condemnations of Israel's treatment of Palestinians as anti-Semitism. Unlike Jewish leftist organizations, it has "evinced a strong allegiance with the U.S. State."[37] It was able to raise $11 million when neo-Nazis marched in Charlottesville while also heavily criticizing Minnesota representative Ilhan Omar for her purported anti-Semitism.[38] Thus, Emmaia Gelman reported: "This was a well-worn pattern: the ADL's calls to action have successfully mobilized public opinion against Black leadership for decades, from the Student Nonviolent Coordinating Committee (SNCC) and Ocean Hill-Brownsville parents in the New York City teacher strikes of 1968, to the Movement for Black Lives and Marc Lamont Hill."[39]

As Noel Ignatiev might have asked: How would public policy be different if the ADL had joined *with* Black Muslims rather than worked against them, to help defeat racial and religious hatred in the world? Unfortunately and predictably, as groups climb the political and social ladder in the United States, they find it useful to also draw a page from the public insult playbook and castigate those left behind.

The Yellow Peril

Disparaged as "chinks," "slants," "Japs," and the "Yellow Peril," Asian immigrants faced even sharper dehumanization than their European counterparts. While the culmination of those insults in the internment of Japanese Americans during World War II is obvious, one needs to find the roots of those negative attitudes in the treatment of Chinese immigrants in the late nineteenth and early twentieth centuries. A shocking example of the second-class treatment of Chinese immigrants to California occurred in 1854. A "free white citizen" of the state of California was convicted of murder upon the testimony of Chinese witnesses.[40] The defendant argued that Chinese people should not be permitted to testify as witnesses in any action in which a white person is a party, based on a California statute that read: "No Black, or Mulatto person, or Indian, shall be allowed to give evidence in favor of, or against a white man."[41] The California Supreme Court construed that language to apply to Chinese people. The court justified its decision to uphold the application of that statute by openly denigrating them:

> The anomalous spectacle of a distinct people, living in our community, recognizing no laws of this State except through necessity, bringing with them their prejudices and national feuds, in which they indulge in open violation of law; whose mendacity is proverbial; a race of people whom nature has marked as inferior, and who are incapable of progress or intellectual development beyond a certain point, as their history has shown; differing in language, opinions, color, and physical conformation; between whom and ourselves nature has placed an impassable difference, is now presented, and for them is claimed, not only the right to swear away the life of a citizen, but the further privilege of participating with us in administering the affairs of our Government.[42]

In context, this language is astonishing because it was a white person who was accused of murdering a Chinese person. It was a white person who acted contrary to the laws of society. The Chinese person was simply testifying to seek justice for someone in their community. "This ruling proved especially damaging to the Chinese community because Chinese residents often served as the sole witnesses to violence perpetrated by White Americans against Chinese residents."[43] Again, we see

public insults used to justify an important aspect of structural inequality: that Chinese immigrants could not testify in criminal cases against
white people who might be committing crimes against people in their
community. The public insults acted as a dead weight against the courts
applying basic equality principles to protect Chinese immigrants from
murder.

Further demonization of Asian people was codified with the Page Act
of 1875, which prevented the immigration of women from "China, Japan
or any other Oriental country" who were suspected of prostitution.[44] This
statute effectively brought immigration of Chinese women to a halt, result-
ing in Chinese immigrants being largely single, unskilled, and uneducated
male laborers. "This form of cheap labor engendered deep-seated hostility
toward Chinese immigrant laborers among labor organizers and unions in
cities such as San Francisco."[45]

The deep prejudice against Chinese people can also be found in the
pages of US judicial opinions. In 1878, the California legislature requested
that Congress enact legislation to exclude Chinese laborers, asserting that

> the presence of Chinese laborers had a baneful effect upon the material
> interests of the state, and upon public morals; that their immigration was in
> numbers approaching the character of an Oriental invasion, and was a men-
> ace to our civilization; that the discontent from this cause was not confined
> to any political party, or to any class or nationality, but was well nigh univer-
> sal; that they retained the habits and customs of their own country, and in
> fact constituted a Chinese settlement within the state, without any interest
> in our country or its institutions; and praying congress to take measures to
> prevent their further immigration.[46]

In response to this openly prejudiced request, Congress passed a series
of statutes to prevent immigration by Chinese laborers. The Chinese
Exclusion Act of 1882 suspended Chinese immigration for ten years and
made Chinese immigrants ineligible for naturalization. Congress renewed
the statute in 1892 and made it permanent in 1902.[47] The hardships of
the Chinese Exclusion Act were especially harsh on women, when coupled
with a law passed in 1907 stating that "any American woman who mar-
ries a foreigner shall take the nationality of her husband."[48] American-
born women who married Chinese men were forced to move to China and

then, upon the death of their husbands, were not allowed to return to the United States.

In theory, these laws were supposed to merely exclude new Chinese immigrants but not force any Chinese people currently residing in the United States to leave. Frustrated, however, that its attempt to create a safe harbor for Chinese people who were already residing in the United States to visit China and then return to the United States had failed, Congress tightened the statute to declare that no Chinese laborer could return to the United States after the passage of the 1888 act. This rule caused Chae Chan Ping to be excluded from the United States when he sought to return in 1888 with a certificate issued by the US government, pursuant to the Immigration Act of 1882, which stated that he was entitled to return. The Supreme Court upheld the right of the United States to exclude Ping despite a treaty with China that purportedly banned such exclusions and the obvious racial animus that supported the law. In an act of extreme judicial restraint, the Court said: "This court is not a censor of the morals of other departments of the government; it is not invested with any authority to pass judgment upon the motives of their conduct."[49]

Seven years later, in apparent agreement with the substance of these exclusion acts, Justice John Marshall Harlan expressed blatant racism toward Chinese people in his famous dissent in *Plessy v. Ferguson*.[50] Harlan's dissent is often best remembered for this statement: "There is no caste here. Our constitution is color-blind, and neither knows nor tolerates classes among citizens. In respect of civil rights, all citizens are equal before the law. . . . In my opinion, the judgment this day rendered [upholding the segregationist Louisiana statute] will, in time, prove to be quite as pernicious as the decision made by this tribunal in the Dred Scott Case."[51] Yet his opinion also contained the following expression of deep prejudice against people of Chinese heritage:

> There is a race so different from our own that we do not permit those belonging to it to become citizens of the United States. Persons belonging to it are, with few exceptions, absolutely excluded from our country. I allude to the Chinese race. But, by the statute in question, a Chinaman can ride in the same passenger coach with white citizens of the United States, while citizens of the black race in Louisiana, many of whom, perhaps, risked their lives for the preservation of the Union, who are entitled, by law, to participate in the

political control of the state and nation, who are not excluded, by law or by reason of their race, from public stations of any kind, and who have all the legal rights that belong to white citizens, are yet declared to be criminals, liable to imprisonment, if they ride in a public coach occupied by citizens of the white race.[52]

Notice the logic of Harlan's reasoning. Because it is legally permissible and appropriate for Chinese citizens to be excluded from the United States, it cannot be constitutionally permissible to allow Chinese people but not Black people to sit beside white people in a railroad car. It is not that Black people are really equal to whites; it is just that Black people are better potential citizens than Chinese people. Of course, rather than being excluded from the United States, Black people were brought to the United States under conditions of slavery and, after the ratification of the Thirteenth and Fourteenth Amendments, were constitutionally eligible for citizenship. According to Harlan, the Louisiana legislation, which mandated separate railroad cars for white and Black people, should be understood as "sinister legislation" that placed a "condition of legal inferiority" on a "large body of American citizens."[53] But he was comfortable embracing the racial insults of his time with respect to Chinese people who sought to enter the United States legally.

The public vilification of Chinese immigrants focused on an unskilled, largely male, and unassimilated workforce, which pursuant to US law could not readily form a viable family unit. Negative public sentiment soon also targeted Japanese immigrants. Whereas Chinese immigrants were denigrated for not assimilating into US society, the Japanese were considered a threat because they *did* try to assimilate into US society. "Xenophobes used Japanese immigrants' propensity to assimilate as evidence of their competition in the labor market, thereby creating a greater threat than the 'unassimilable' Chinese."[54]

Drawing on the work of political scientist Benedict Anderson and sociologist Stanford Lyman, Keith Aoki argued that there was an "aggregate" conception of Asian, which constructed Asians as the racial "other."[55] A "word like 'slant,' for example, abbreviated from 'slant-eyed,' does not simply express an ordinary political enmity. It erases nation-ness by reducing the adversary to his biological physiognomy."[56] By merging together people from Vietnam, Korea, China, and the Philippines into one group, "nationalism thinks in term of historical destinies, while racism dreams of eternal contaminations, transmitted from the origins of time through an endless sequence of loathsome copulations: outside history."[57] Aoki argued that the negative public perceptions against Chinese immigrants ultimately also led to negative attitudes toward Japanese immigrants, even though their background and experiences in the United States were quite different.

Attempts to codify anti-Japanese animus took center stage in San Francisco. In 1900, San Francisco mayor James Duval Phelan openly declared:

> The Japanese are starting the same tide of immigration which we thought we had checked twenty years ago. . . . [T]he Chinese and Japanese are not bona fide citizens. They are not the stuff of which American citizens can be made. . . . [T]hey will not assimilate with us and their social life is so different from ours, let them keep at a respectful distance.[58]

With the mayor hurling such insults, it is no surprise that the city council supported laws that harmed the Asian community. San Francisco had historically segregated Chinese students in school, and it decided to extend that segregation to Japanese and Korean children in 1906. The campaign against Japanese people was led by several powerful factions, including politicians, the media, and civic organizations. The *San Francisco Chronicle* began an anti-Asiatic campaign with headlines declaring "Brown Men an Evil to the Public Schools" and "Brown Artisans Steal Brains of Whites."[59] White agriculturists formed the Asiatic Exclusion League in 1905, arguing that "[n]o large community of foreigners, so cocky, with such distinct racial, social and religious prejudices, can abide long in this country without serious friction."[60] The League sought to have the Chinese Exclusion Act cover Japanese and Koreans.[61] With this kind of open hostility to Japanese people, it is no surprise that laws were adopted to enshrine this bigotry. Public insults enabled direct mistreatment of Japanese people.

Japanese residents tried to fight back and enlist the support of the Japanese government. They took their complaints to the highest level, trying to win the support of President Theodore Roosevelt. Although Roosevelt tried to arrange a compromise, he was not able to stem the strong tide of anti-Japanese bias. California passed the Alien Land Law of 1913 by an overwhelming vote of 35–2 in the state Senate and 72–3 in the House. This law barred aliens who were ineligible to obtain citizenship (i.e., Chinese, Japanese, and Koreans) from acquiring land or entering into leases longer than three years. When that law did not sufficiently stem the flow of Japanese immigrants who owned land, California voters adopted a statewide ballot initiative that completely precluded any "alien" from owning or leasing land in California.[62] Japanese government protests against these adverse actions were seen "as proof of the Japanese immigrant population's disloyalty and racial undesirability."[63] Although these restrictive laws clearly violated basic constitutional principles of equal protection, the US Supreme Court upheld four of them in cases decided in the early 1920s.[64] One can understand the public insults as acting as a headwind against the application of traditional constitutional law principles under which all people are entitled to "equal protection of the law."

The Japanese internment that followed in the 1940s demonstrates how widespread racism can be validated and operationalized; the Supreme Court, the president, the military, and the media collaborated to manufacture the truly "fake news" that Japanese immigrants were committing sabotage and were a threat to the US population. Following the Japanese bombing of Pearl Harbor in 1941, President Franklin D. Roosevelt created the Roberts Commission to determine exactly what had led to the successful attack.[65] In a blatant violation of separation of powers, Roosevelt appointed Associate Supreme Court Justice Owen Roberts to head the commission. (Roberts would then fail to recuse himself in cases involving the internment of Japanese citizens during World War II, even though his report arguably was a factor in that internment.) The other members of the commission were military officials: Admiral William H. Standley, General Frank R. McCoy, General Joseph T. McNarney, and Admiral Joseph M. Reeves. While they cast blame on two members of the military, they also blamed the success of that attack on Japanese spies, characterized as "consular agents and other persons," without providing any specific names. That report arguably led to the US government asking the Supreme Court to take judicial notice of "the propensity of Japanese Americans to be disloyal."[66]

In the infamous *Korematsu* decision,[67] in which a majority of the Supreme Court upheld the internment of Japanese Americans, only one member of the Court, Justice Frank Murphy, attacked the prejudice and stereotypes that were the foundation of the internment order. He described the order as falling "into the ugly abyss of racism"[68] and then tore apart its justifications. He quoted at length from the general's final report on the evacuation from the Pacific Coast area to support this charge of racism. Here are some of the disturbing racial stereotypes he quoted from the report of the commanding general of the Pacific Coast area:

- "But we must worry about the Japanese all the time until he is wiped off the map. Sabotage and espionage will make problems as long as he is allowed in this area."
- Japanese individuals are described as "subversive" and belonging to an "enemy race."
- Japanese are condemned because they are said to be a "large, unassimilated, tightly knit racial group, bound to an enemy nation by strong ties of race, culture, custom and religion."
- Evidence of that disloyalty is that they like "emperor worshipping ceremonies" and like to send their children to Japanese-language schools.[69]

While the government's case rested on the supposed disloyalty of the Japanese people, Justice Murphy criticized the government for failing to offer any proof that Japanese people had committed sabotage. He concluded:

> The reasons [for the policy] appear, instead, to be largely an accumulation of much of the misinformation, half-truths and insinuations that for years have been directed against Japanese Americans by people with racial and economic prejudices—the same people who have been among the foremost advocates of the evacuation. A military judgment based upon such racial and sociological considerations is not entitled to the great weight ordinarily given the judgments based upon strictly military considerations. Especially is this so when every charge relative to race, religion, culture, geographical location, and legal and economic status has been substantially discredited by independent studies made by experts in these matters.[70]

In other words, the lengthy pattern of public insults acted as a headwind against the Supreme Court requiring factual evidence to support the allegations of Japanese disloyalty.

Justice Murphy was the *only* member of the Supreme Court to dissent despite the majority paying lip service to the notion that "all legal restrictions which curtail the civil rights of a single racial group are immediately suspect."[71] The majority insisted that "Korematsu was not excluded from the Military Area because of hostility to him or his race."[72] This blithe assertion ignores the profound racial animus underlying "the mass incarceration of 120,000 Americans of Japanese ancestry during World War II without charges, notice, trial or due process, and without any evidence of espionage and sabotage by persons of Japanese ancestry."[73]

The weakness of the government's justification became publicly evident in 1984 when Judge Marilyn Patel issued her decision in a modern-day *Korematsu v. United States*.[74] At the age of sixty-four, nearly forty years after his conviction was upheld by the Supreme Court, Korematsu filed a petition for a writ of *coram nobis* in Patel's court, seeking to have his conviction vacated. In granting the request, the court acknowledged that it was granting "extraordinary relief," which was required to "undo such profound and publicly acknowledged injustice."[75] The injustice did not rest merely in the fact that Korematsu had been afforded no due process when he was convicted on the basis of a statute that presumed he was disloyal to the United States due entirely to his Japanese ancestry; it also rested on the fact that the government *knew* it did not have strong evidence of Japanese disloyalty yet deliberately lied to the court throughout the original Korematsu trial to uphold the conviction.

I detail here the evidence in support of this horrific fraud upon the court to fully illustrate the potential power of insults to act as an enormous headwind against the application of principles of justice. First, Judge Patel recognized the findings of the Commission on Wartime Relocation and Internment of Civilians, which was established by Congress in 1980. The report concluded that "broad historical causes which shaped these decisions [exclusion and detention] were race prejudice, war hysteria and a failure of political leadership."[76]

Second, Judge Patel found that the "government knowingly withheld information from the courts when they were considering the critical question of military necessity in this case."[77] She noted that the government had changed a critical passage of what was called the "Final Report of General

DeWitt" to convey the idea that the government unanimously believed that evacuation and relocation were necessary rather than including the actual government finding that there were conflicting views on whether people of Japanese ancestry were illegally using radio transmitters and shore-to-ship signaling.[78] These lies were clearly pivotal in justifying the Supreme Court's decision, which had only weakly stated that it could not "reject as unfounded" the military's view even though the evidence was imprecise.

Judge Patel concluded with striking language concerning the power of insults:

> [The *Korematsu* case] stands as a caution that in times of international hostility and antagonisms our institutions, legislative, executive and judicial, must be prepared to exercise their authority to protect all citizens from the petty fears and prejudices that are so easily aroused.[79]

She powerfully acknowledged that "petty fears and prejudices" can be aroused and had helped lead to the mass incarceration of tens of thousands of people living lawfully in the United States who happened to be of Japanese ancestry. Such fears and prejudices can act as dead weights on the application of traditional legal principles.

The demonization of Asian people culminating in the Japanese internment during World War II is one of the strongest examples this book offers of the power of insults. Beginning in the late nineteenth century, public castigation of Chinese laborers was rampant in the United States. That animus led to a series of quite brutal laws that precluded them from citizenship or even having a family in the United States. While Japanese immigrants had different cultural traditions and represented a different socioeconomic class than Chinese immigrants, they fell victim to an expanding racial animus as all Asian people were lumped into the category "Orientals." Rampant xenophobia and racism engendered their exclusion from citizenship, exile from the United States, and internment. While Justice Hugo Black, writing for the *Korematsu* majority, bristled at the notion that these camps could be described as "concentration camps" and instead wanted to think of them as temporary security precautions, they would certainly have felt like concentration camps to those imprisoned behind their walls. While there was no government policy dictating that they be killed, they did live in substandard housing such as animal stables and stalls, which often did not even have roofs. Unsanitary conditions led to serious illnesses such as tuberculosis, and people who tried to escape were shot.[80] As one commentator has said:

> "Internment camp" doesn't do justice to the horrors experienced within them. Japanese Americans were uprooted from their homes and treated like criminals. They experienced enormous loss. They suffered great physical and emotional trauma. A racial minority was concentrated in specific areas for the security of the nation, imprisoned in deplorable conditions, and stripped of their dignity. They were living in concentration camps.[81]

It was not until 1988 that the US government offered a formal apology and compensated former inmates with a one-time payment, of only $20,000. That was forty-four years after Fred Korematsu lost his first case at the Supreme Court but four years after he prevailed before Judge Patel and had his conviction overturned.

Queried in 2015 about the Japanese internment, Donald Trump said: "I certainly hate the concept of it. But I would have had to have been there at the time to give you a proper answer."[82] Asked later several times if the internment violated American values, he did not respond. Trump's failure to acknowledge this human rights violation resonated with his administration's deep dive into racially tinged xenophobia. On the tactical level, the Trump administration echoed the *Korematsu* case by indulging in efforts to shore up white supremacy, lie to the courts, and encourage hostility toward immigrants.

These tactics are well illustrated by the administration's attempt to add to the 2020 Census a question that asked about respondents' citizenship status. As described by *Washington Post* columnist Dana Milbank, the Trump administration used a four-step strategy to preserve white hegemony by skewing Census results.[83]

First, they devised a governmental policy designed to reduce responses to the Census by Latinx, thereby undercounting their population for the purposes of congressional apportionment. That policy was the citizenship question.

Second, they had to come up with a lawful justification for this discriminatory policy. They invented the justification that the Justice Department had requested this question be added to the Census so that it could better enforce the Voting Rights Act. However, emails showed that the White House actually coerced the Justice Department into making the request for its own political gain. And later, after the Supreme Court had already engaged in oral argument on this case, it came to light that the true architect of this plan to aid white supremacy was Republican strategist Thomas Hofeller, who brazenly proposed such a plan knowing it would require a "radical redrawing" of legislative districts that would "be advantageous to Republicans and Non-Hispanic Whites."[84]

Third, the solicitor general tried to create confusion during oral argument by insisting that it could not quantify the effects of the citizenship question. In fact, the Census Bureau's own research had already quantified a 5.1 percent drop in participation from households with noncitizens if the question were added. In fact, it was that type of Bureau concern that had led to the removal of a citizenship question from the Census in 1960.

Fourth, the government cleverly blamed the victim by suggesting that if the Court disallowed the citizenship question, it would be "effectively empowering any group in the country to knock off any question on the census if they simply get together and boycott it."[85]

Curiously, this sounds a lot like the lying justifications offered for the Japanese internment during World War II. In *Korematsu*, the Justice Department came up with a pretextual explanation of national security to explain its incarceration of people of Japanese ancestry, foreshadowing the Trump administration's fabricated desire to better enforce the Voting Rights Act. Similarly, the government tried to create confusion in *Korematsu* by saying it could not quantify the amount of known Japanese domestic hostility when, in fact, it had no evidence of *any* hostility. Further, in *Korematsu*, the government tried to pretend that the internment policy was for the *benefit* of Japanese Americans, who might face adverse actions from their non-Japanese neighbors. Finally, as in *Korematsu*, some of the most damaging evidence regarding the Trump administration's policy emerged *after* the lower court cases, and even the Supreme Court oral argument, had already taken place.

In a rare legal maneuver, the ACLU filed a notice with the Supreme Court in the citizenship case (*Department of Commerce v. New York*) to make the Court aware of the new evidence, in the hope that the record could be expanded to include that evidence.[86] Legal observers had been predicting that the Court would permit the citizenship question to be added to the 2020 Census, and it would be highly unusual for the Court to reopen the record to consider evidence that the citizenship question was introduced for illegitimate reasons. In language harkening back to Judge Patel's conclusion about government pretext in the *Korematsu* case, the letter urged the Court to consider the new evidence because it appeared that the government had "falsely testified about the genesis of DOJ's request to Commerce in ways that obscured the pretextual character of the request."[87]

Unlike in *Korematsu*, however, in *Department of Commerce v. New York*, Chief Justice John Roberts, who had been appointed by Republican president George W. Bush, joined the Court's four liberals in concluding that the government had not satisfied its minimal burden under the Administrative Procedure Act of justifying the citizenship question because of the "unusual circumstances," in which "the evidence tells a story that does not match the explanation the Secretary gave for his decision."[88]

False testimony in pursuit of white supremacy is nothing new at the Supreme Court. But it was highly unusual for a conservative justice (Roberts) to join the liberal minority to call out the government for its lies. However, as discussed later, this was an unusual exercise in the application of so-called neutral judicial principles for the benefit of an immigrant community.

To understand why Chief Justice Roberts would diverge from his conservative colleagues to join the liberal majority in this case, it is important to understand the narrowness of the legal victory. This was not a grand constitutional case about the impropriety of insults being leveled against an immigrant community. This case was about a very narrow *legal* issue: whether the Census Bureau had offered any credible explanation of why it needed to add the citizenship question to the Census. The majority found that the secretary of commerce's rationale for adding this question to the Census was "arbitrary and capricious, based on a pretextual rationale." The majority did not conclude that the respondent had demonstrated an equal protection violation. When parties seek *constitutional relief*, as we will see, the power of insults acts as an insurmountable dead weight on the application of basic constitutional principles such as equal protection.

Operation Wetback

When the Mexican-American War ended in 1848, the United States annexed large portions of Mexico to form parts of Texas, California, New Mexico, Arizona, Colorado, Utah, Nevada, Oklahoma, Kansas, and Wyoming. Immigration policy has subsequently veered from wanting to facilitate cheap Mexican labor to excluding Mexicans, sometimes doing both simultaneously. "In a move that exemplified the United States' inconsistent immigration policy towards Mexico, the Department of Labor frequently issued *bracero* visas to immigrants deported to Mexico under Operation Wetback and immediately sent them back to the farms from which they had been arrested in the first place."[89]

Public officials rarely hesitated in voicing their open hostility toward Mexican immigrants even as the country benefited enormously from their low-paid agricultural labor. For example, Representative James L. Slayden published an article in 1921 in which he said:

- Mexican workers suffered from "hopeless inefficiency."
- They did not know the difference "between a saw and a hammer."
- They were "ragged, filthy paupers."
- Their US migration was an "invasion."[90]

In the 1930s, a program inaccurately described as "repatriation" forced an estimated one million persons of Mexican ancestry to relocate to Mexico. Under this program of forcible exclusion, "[a]pproximately 60 percent of the persons of Mexican ancestry removed to Mexico in the 1930s were U.S. citizens, many of them children who were effectively deported to Mexico when their immigrant parents were sent there."[91] These practices violated a bedrock immigration and human rights principle: "that U.S. citizens cannot be deported, removed, or banished from this country."[92]

But the 1930s was not the only period of open, mass deportation of people of Mexican ancestry. In 1954, the federal government instituted Operation Wetback, openly endorsing a program that resulted in "hundreds of thousands of Mexican immigrants and U.S. citizens of Mexican descent [being] rounded up and deported."[93] The public slur ("Operation Wetback") was openly combined with the public deportation policy.

Hostility to Mexican immigrants has resulted in many governmental policies that impose harsh sanctions on undocumented Mexican immigrants who are residing in the United States. Some of the legal doctrines that allowed the federal government to intern Japanese people during World War II also gave Congress supremacy in dictating immigration policy. In a few instances, the Supreme Court has narrowly stopped states from directly sanctioning Mexican immigrants, but the constitutional policy of equal protection has rarely been applied to Mexican immigrants when the federal government takes adverse action against them.

In 1982, the Supreme Court in *Plyler v. Doe*[94] overturned a Texas statute and school district policy that allowed the school district to bar the children of undocumented immigrants from receiving a public education. Rather than acknowledge that it wanted to punish Mexican immigrants, the state argued that the law was a "financial measure designed to avoid a drain on the State's fisc."[95]

The Supreme Court majority rejected the rationality of the state's argument. First, the Court noted federal policy had helped create a "shadow population" of "illegal migrants" who are "encouraged by some to remain here as a source of cheap labor, but nevertheless denied the benefits that our society makes available to citizens and lawful residents."[96] Second, the Court sympathetically noted that the child plaintiffs were facing a "discriminatory burden on the basis of a legal characteristic over which children can have little control."[97] It also rejected the state's underlying financial logic, stating that "the available evidence suggests that illegal aliens underutilize public services, while contributing their labor to the local economy and tax money to the state fisc."[98] Concluding that the state statute could not even withstand low-level rationality review, the Court said: "It is difficult to understand precisely what the State hopes to achieve by promoting the creation and perpetuation of a subclass of illiterates within our boundaries, surely adding to the problems and costs of unemployment, welfare, and crime."[99] But of course the Texas legislature may well have intended to reinforce the status of Mexican immigrants as a pliable and exploited workforce ineligible for public benefits.

Four members of the Supreme Court dissented in *Plyler*: Justices Warren Burger, Byron White, William Rehnquist, and Sandra Day O'Connor. Chief Justice Burger authored the dissent, which began by paying lip service to the notion that he disagreed with the state's policy choice, sympathizing with the plight of the children. "Were it our business to set the Nation's social policy, I would agree without hesitation that it is senseless for an enlightened society to deprive any children—including illegal aliens—of an elementary education."[100] But then the dissent went on to say that it was inappropriate for the courts to intervene to upset the state's policy choice because, in fact, it did have a reasonable and legitimate explanation for its choice. "By definition, illegal aliens have no right whatever to be here, and the state may reasonably, and constitutionally, elect not to provide them with governmental services at the expense of those who are lawfully in the state."[101] The dissenters felt no need to respond to the majority's factual observation that immigrants pay taxes yet underutilize their share of state-provided services. The dissent described the majority as "disingenuous when it suggests that the State has merely picked a 'disfavored group' and arbitrarily defined its members as nonresidents."[102] The majority opinion's narrow focus on the plaintiffs' status as children and the importance of education created a weak constitutional precedent for other immigrants when facing adverse state action.

The *Plyler* decision also had no bearing on the *federal* government's right to deliberately harm undocumented immigrants. As the *Plyler* dissent acknowledged, the federal government already directly barred undocumented immigrants from receiving a host of federal services: the food stamp program, the old-age assistance program, aid to families with dependent children, aid to blind people, aid to people with permanent and total disabilities, supplementary security income programs, Medicare hospital insurance benefits, and Medicaid hospital insurance benefits for the aged and disabled.[103]

Following *Plyler*, the federal government stepped up its attempts to deter Mexican immigration and deny benefits to Mexican immigrants. In 1986 and 1990, Congress passed increasingly stringent laws designed to limit Mexican immigration while increasing "the number of visas going to well-educated job seekers—primarily from developed European countries—thus revealing Congress's preference for European immigrants over those from other regions."[104]

States rushed to pass anti-immigrant measures, often targeting Mexican immigrants. In states in which liberals controlled the state legislature, the voters sometimes passed anti-immigrant measures through statewide initiatives. One example was the passage of Proposition 187 in California on November 8, 1994. In addition to requiring the state government to cooperate with the federal government with respect to notifying it of "illegal aliens" in the state, the proposition also required that those individuals be denied social services, health care, and education.[105] Although this rule was created through the initiative process, rather than the legislative process, the state of California vigorously defended it in the courts (until Democrats took over the governorship).

The campaign for Proposition 187 was openly hostile to Mexican immigrants. California governor Pete Wilson "ran television advertisements supporting the measure that showed dark, shadowy figures storming the U.S./Mexico border, with the narrator eerily stating 'They keep coming.' An initiative supporter explained to voters: 'You are the posse and [the Save Our State initiative] is the rope.'"[106] The open vilification of Mexican immigrants was successful; 59 percent of voters supported the measure, and Pete Wilson was reelected, in part because of his support of Proposition 187.

While the federal courts were considering the constitutionality of Proposition 187, President Bill Clinton signed the Personal Responsibility and Work Opportunity Act (PRA) on August 22, 1996, which he heralded as ending "welfare as we know it." In addition to sharply cutting the welfare rolls by placing time limits on the receipt of benefits, it ended nearly all public benefits to both documented and undocumented immigrants. In one of the strongest public criticisms of this new law, Marian Wright Edelman, who founded the Children's Defense Fund and had given Hillary Rodham Clinton her first job, called the law "sad and painful."[107] Her husband, Peter Edelman, quit his job with the Clinton administration in protest against the draconian measures. Many of the California restrictions on public benefits for immigrants were already contained in the PRA; supremacy law principles dictated that states needed to implement the federal policies. Thus, California was not permitted to enforce its own restrictions on immigrants under Proposition 187, separate from the draconian measures already approved by the US Congress.

During the 1990s, hostility against both documented and nondocumented immigrants was widespread. Newt Gingrich's "Contract with

America" supported an overhaul of the welfare system with severe limits on the rights of immigrants to receive any benefits. "The welfare law conditioned eligibility on citizenship status rather than legal status, extending to most legal immigrants the eligibility restrictions that had traditionally applied only to undocumented immigrants."[108] Those rules were highly popular. A Gannett News Service poll in 1996 reported that 71 percent of respondents believed "immigrants got too many public benefits such as welfare, medical care, and food stamps."[109] Not surprisingly, Gingrich supported Clinton's anti-immigrant efforts, including the Illegal Immigration Reform and Immigrant Responsibility Act of 1996 (IIRIRA), which passed by a vote of 380–37 in the House and was signed into law by President Clinton. IIRIRA took away judicial discretion over deporting immigrants who had committed crimes, including seemingly minor crimes like shoplifting or public urination.[110]

These measures suggest the substantial success achieved by the onslaught of anti-immigrant public insults. The federal government passed draconian measures that greatly hindered the well-being of immigrants to the United States. The *Plyler* decision acted as a partial limitation on these measures, but in the immediate aftermath of *Plyler*, state and federal governments competed to outdo each other in passing the most draconian anti-immigrant measures. The *Plyler* decision demonstrated how courts could apply equal protection principles for the benefit of castigated immigrant communities. But more typically, courts and legislatures caved to the public insults of the time. These insults acted as dead weights on the courts to stop them from applying settled equality principles and as headwinds to the legislatures to prevent progressive legislation from gaining traction.

THE TRUMP ERA

The previous section documented that open hostility to many immigrant communities has been a long-standing aspect of US policy. This section delves into a simple legal principle that should be useful in the modern era to prevent the government from pursuing such policies merely out of animus against a group. I show how the Supreme Court under the leadership of Chief Justice Roberts has been willing to use the anti-animus legal principle to protect a Christian baker from purported religious animus but has not been willing to use that same principle to protect various racial and religious minorities from discrimination.

In constitutional law, there is a long-standing principle that state actors cannot act with invidious intent against various protected categories like racial or religious minorities. When actions have a disparate impact on a religious or racial minority group, and public statements make clear that that impact was intentional, such actions are considered to be presumptively unconstitutional absent a compelling justification for the conduct. The Supreme Court explained this bedrock legal principle in 1979 in its decision in *Personnel Administrator of Massachusetts v. Feeney*:[111]

> Certain classifications . . . supply a reason to infer antipathy. Race is the paradigm. A racial classification, regardless of purported motivation, is presumptively invalid and can be upheld only upon an extraordinary justification. This rule applies as well to a classification that is ostensibly neutral but is an obvious pretext for racial discrimination. But, as was made clear in *Washington v. Davis* and *Arlington Heights v. Metropolitan Housing Development Corporation,* even if a neutral law has a disproportionately adverse effect upon a racial minority, it is unconstitutional under the Equal Protection Clause only if that impact can be traced to a discriminatory purpose.[112]

Thus, actions that are facially discriminatory are presumptively unconstitutional, and actions that on their face are race or religion neutral, but are actually for the purpose of discrimination, are also presumptively unconstitutional. In both instances, the action is invalidated unless it has an extraordinary justification.

Nonetheless, Trump ran a campaign for president premised on his desire to deport Mexicans and bar Muslims from entering the country. He was not subtle about it. In August 2016, *Time Magazine* ran an article with the headline, "Here Are All the Times Donald Trump Insulted Mexico,"[113] which included some of these statements:

> When Mexico sends its people, they're not sending their best. They're not sending you. They're not sending you. They're sending people that have lots of problems, and they're bringing those problems with us. They're bringing

drugs. They're bringing crime. They're rapists. And some, I assume, are good people.

Sadly, the overwhelming amount of violent crime in our major cities is committed by blacks and Hispanics—a tough subject—must be discussed.

When will the U.S. stop sending $'s to our enemies, i.e., Mexico and others.

The Mexican legal system is corrupt, as is much of Mexico. Pay me the money that is owed now—and stop sending criminals over our border.

Mexico's court system corrupt. I want nothing to do with Mexico other than to build an impenetrable WALL and stop them from ripping off U.S.

The border is wide open for cartels & terrorists. Secure our border now. Build a massive wall & deduct the costs from Mexican foreign aid!

I've been treated very unfairly by this judge [U.S. District Court judge Gonzalo Curiel]. Now, this judge is of Mexican heritage. . . . This judge is giving us unfair rulings. Now I say why. Well, I want to—I'm building a wall, OK? And it's a wall between Mexico, not another country.[114]

Hence, Donald Trump's actions as president, as he sought to keep those promises with respect to immigration policy, could not more perfectly meet the rigorous constitutional law test for actions premised on invidious statements. And as his attempts to limit immigration were put into effect, many lower courts reached that conclusion. A brief review of the underlying facts and a glance at some of these lower court decisions reflects the strength of the argument that Trump's immigration policies often violated clear rules of law with regard to acting with invidious intent.

On January 27, 2017, seven days after taking the oath of office, Trump signed Executive Order 13,769,[115] which immediately suspended for ninety days the immigrant and nonimmigrant entry of foreign aliens from seven predominantly Muslim countries. It also reduced the number of refugees to be admitted and indefinitely barred the admission of Syrian refugees. Finally, it directed the secretary of state to prioritize refugee claims on the basis of religious-based persecution in which the individual is a member of a minority religion in the individual's country of nationality.

Numerous legal actions were filed within days of the issuance of this executive order. For example, on January 30, 2017, the state of Washington sought a nationwide injunction against enforcement of the order. On February 3, 2017, the district court granted that request.[116] Four days later, the Ninth Circuit denied the government's motion to stay the injunction pending appeal.[117] The court did not have to reach the religious animus issue because the executive order's violation of basic procedural due process rights for both lawful permanent residents and others was so blatant. "The Government has not shown that the Executive Order provides what due process requires, such as notice and a hearing prior to restricting an individual's ability to travel."[118] Although the court could have rested its decision entirely on the due process problems with the executive order, it noted the serious First Amendment and equal protection issues raised by the executive order due to the president's stated intention to disfavor Muslims. "In support of this argument, the States have offered evidence of numerous statements by the President about his intent to implement a 'Muslim ban' as well as evidence they claim suggests that the Executive Order was intended to be that ban."[119] Further, the court noted that it was appropriate under settled constitutional jurisprudence to consider circumstantial evidence of invidious intent, analogous to the statements made by President Trump.

In the face of the plaintiffs' strong cases, the administration quickly backtracked. Rather than vigorously defending this executive order before the US Supreme Court, the government revoked the first travel ban executive order and issued a new one, Executive Order 13,780, on March 6, 2017, with the same name: "Protecting the Nation from Foreign Terrorist Entry into the United States." The primary difference between the first and second travel bans was that Iraq was excluded from the ninety-day visa ban because the Iraqi government had supposedly made "firm commitments" to the United States regarding information sharing.[120] The new executive order continued to suspend US participation in the refugee assistance program for 120 days but no longer referred to an individual's status as a "religious minority" as a reason favoring refugee status. It also no longer included a Syria-specific ban on refugees. The effective date of the March 6 executive order was March 16, 2017. The entry suspension would therefore lapse on June 14, 2017.

On March 15, 2017, a Hawaii district court issued a temporary restraining order and then, on March 29, 2017, issued a nationwide preliminary injunction to prevent the implementation of the executive order.[121] On May 15, 2019, the Ninth Circuit Court of Appeals affirmed that injunction, although on statutory rather than constitutional law grounds.[122]

The March 15 decision provides a strong constitutional argument for why Trump's conduct in issuing these two executive orders violated the establishment clause, which prohibits the government from officially preferring one religious denomination over another. A government action that does not have a "secular purpose" violates this rule. The district court found that the historical background of the executive order was "unique." "It includes significant and unrebutted evidence of religious animus driving the promulgation of the Executive Order and its related predecessor."[123] The court relied on these kinds of statements from Trump to reach this conclusion:

- "I think Islam hates us."
- "But there's a tremendous hatred. And we have to be very vigilant. We have to be very careful. And we can't allow people coming into this country who have this hatred of the United States . . . [a]nd of people that are not Muslim."
- "People were so upset when I used the word Muslim. Oh, you can't use the word Muslim. Remember this. And I'm okay with that, because I'm talking territory instead of Muslim."
- "The Muslim ban still stands. . . . It's called extreme vetting."
- "Donald J. Trump is calling for a total and complete shutdown of Muslims entering the United States."[124]

While recognizing that the case law precluded judges from undertaking a "judicial psychoanalysis of a drafter's heart of hearts," the court concluded this case posed no such risk.

> The remarkable facts at issue here require no such impermissible inquiry. For instance, there is nothing "*veiled*" about this press release. . . . Nor is there anything "*secret*" about the Executive's motive specific to the issuance of the Executive Order. . . . These plainly-worded statements, made in the months leading up to and contemporaneous with the signing of the Executive Order, and, in many cases, made by the Executive himself, betray the Executive Order's stated secular purpose.[125]

Similarly, a federal district court in Maryland concluded that the provision suspending entry from six countries likely violated the establishment clause, and it entered a nationwide preliminary injunction.[126] The

Supreme Court reviewed those injunctions on an expedited basis and concluded in a per curiam opinion (i.e., not signed by any member of the Court) that the suspension of visas could "not be enforced against foreign nationals who have a credible claim of a bona fide relationship with a person or entity in the United States. All other foreign nationals are subject to the provisions of EO-2."[127] Similarly, with respect to the suspension of refugees, the ban could not be enforced when an American individual or entity "has a bona fide relationship with a particular person seeking to enter the country as a refugee [and] can legitimately claim concrete hardship if that person is excluded."[128] The per curiam decision offered no explanation of why the Court thought that the plaintiffs were likely to prevail on the merits so that these partial injunctions should be issued. Justices Clarence Thomas, Samuel Alito, and Neil Gorsuch dissented, finding no credible claim by the plaintiffs to authorize any injunction at all.

Trump then issued a presidential proclamation on September 24, 2017, which added North Korea and Venezuela to the list of affected countries.[129] The state of Hawaii challenged the proclamation, arguing that the president continued to violate the establishment clause, and that the proclamation also violated various statutory rules with respect to the president's authority in the immigration field. Specifically, the state argued that the president's conduct violated the rule against nationality-based discrimination in the issuance of immigrant visas. Because the lower courts ruled on the basis of the statutory problems with the executive order, they did not need to reach the establishment clause issue. The Supreme Court, however, found that the president did not violate the statutory rules regarding his immigration authority and therefore had to reach the establishment clause issue, which as I discussed earlier had been previously considered by the Hawaii district court with regard to the second executive order.

The Supreme Court majority was quickly dismissive of the establishment clause argument recounting only a few of Trump's statements that evinced clear hostility to Muslims. As Justice Sonia Sotomayor said in her dissent, "The full record paints a far more harrowing picture, from which a reasonable observer would readily conclude that the Proclamation was motivated by hostility and animus toward the Muslim faith."[130]

For the purposes of this book, the obvious question is: Whose insults count? The majority opinion in *Trump v. Hawaii* went out of its way to ignore the president's insulting rhetoric, which clearly demonstrated an anti-Muslim bias. A similar pattern occurred in the Supreme Court's decision overturning Trump's attempt to rescind the Deferred Action for Childhood Arrivals (DACA). Although Chief Justice Roberts, once again, joined the four liberal justices to conclude that the Trump administration had violated the Administrative Procedure Act by engaging in "arbitrary and capricious behavior," a majority was unwilling to conclude that the Trump administration had violated the constitutional principle of equal protection despite Trump's long-standing vilification of Latinos. The majority opinion, authored by Chief Justice Roberts, found Trump's critical statements about Latinos too "remote in time and made in unrelated contexts" to qualify as unconstitutional animus against a group in society.[131]

To really answer the question of whose insults count, one needs to contrast the Court's consideration of anti-Muslim animus in *Trump v. Hawaii* with its consideration of the statements of one low-level actor in a very different case: the one brought against Masterpiece Cakeshop when it refused to follow Colorado's sexual orientation nondiscrimination law in providing service to the public. Although the lawsuit against Masterpiece Cakeshop, which was decided two weeks before *Trump v. Hawaii*, seems very different than the one against the Trump administration, antireligious animus played a role in both cases. In fact, the Supreme Court's decision in *Trump v. Hawaii*,[132] in contrast with its decision in *Masterpiece Cakeshop v. Colorado Civil Rights Commission*,[133] is a perfect illustration of the selective deployment of and protection of insults by and on behalf of the powerful in society.[134]

The reader likely remembers the gay rights story contained in the *Masterpiece Cakeshop* decision. Although the state of Colorado had a nondiscrimination law that precluded a store owner from denying service to someone due to sexual orientation, the bakery owner, Jack Phillips, refused to make a cake for Charlie Craig when he learned that Craig wanted to celebrate his union with another man. But for Craig's sexual orientation, Phillips would have baked him a cake. It should have been an easy case of enforcing a state nondiscrimination statute. But it was not.

Initially, it was Charlie Craig and Dave Mullins who were insulted when Jack Phillips refused to bake them a cake, saying, "I just don't make cakes for same sex weddings."[135] This action was a straightforward violation of the state's nondiscrimination law, which prohibited places of public accommodation from discriminating on the basis of sexual orientation.[136] The case proceeded through a multistep investigative process. A state administrative law judge found that Phillips had violated state law,[137] then a seven-member Colorado Civil Rights Commission affirmed that decision,[138] and finally, a three-member Colorado Court of Appeals affirmed.[139] In total, eleven adjudicators heard the case and concluded that Masterpiece Cakeshop had violated the Colorado statute, and that relief was appropriate against the bakery.

Even though the Colorado Supreme Court declined to hear the case, the bakery owner persisted in seeking certiorari in the US Supreme Court. The Supreme Court agreed to hear the case and ultimately ruled that Phillips was the victim in this instance: he was a victim of intentional discrimination because of his Christian beliefs. This is the lone statement made by one member of the Civil Rights Commission that the Court used to support that conclusion:

> I would also like to reiterate what we said in the hearing or the last meeting. Freedom of religion and religion has been used to justify all kinds of discrimination throughout history, whether it be slavery, whether it be the holocaust, whether it be—I mean, we—we can list hundreds of situations where freedom of religion has been used to justify discrimination. And to me it is one of the most despicable pieces of rhetoric that people can use to—to use their religion to hurt others.[140]

This statement was found to violate the requirement of a fair and neutral enforcement of Colorado's antidiscrimination law because of its use of the word "despicable" and alleged comparison of Phillips's actions to those of slavery and the Holocaust,[141] even though those views were not embraced in any written opinion justifying enforcement of the Colorado statute. The commissioner did not actually make a comparison; he merely stated a historical fact about the justifications for slavery and the Holocaust. He also said he spoke for himself, not for the seven-member commission. Further, those views were not essential to the enforcement of the Colorado statute. Phillips never contested that he refused to sell the cake to Craig and Mullins due to his disapproval of their sexual orientation.

Although the result of the Supreme Court's decision was to cause no sanctions to be levied against Phillips (and no relief to be provided to Craig and Mullins), one might praise the decision for giving teeth to the rule that government officials are not supposed to engage in overt expressions of religious hostility as part of their justifications for their actions. Because government actors are more likely to express hostility toward minority religions than majority religions, one might hope that this ruling could protect religious minorities from government insults.

Unfortunately, the Supreme Court's decision in *Trump v. Hawaii*[142] makes it clear that the courts will only protect against insults directed against the Christian majority rather than the Muslim minority. In *Masterpiece Cakeshop*, the Court was faced with *one* arguably anti-Christian comment from one member of a seven-person tribunal in a context where non-religiously biased explanations could justify the tribunal's decision to enforce the state's nondiscrimination policy. (Craig did not deny that he had refused to bake the cake because of the sexual orientation of the customers.) By contrast, in *Trump v. Hawaii*, the Court was faced with overwhelming evidence that one person—the president of the United States—had engaged in overt religious bias when he announced and implemented his immigration executive orders. Justice Sotomayor detailed some of that evidence in her dissent:

- On December 7, 2015, candidate Trump called "for a total and complete shutdown of Muslims entering the United States" and kept that statement on "his campaign website until May 2017 (several months into his Presidency)."

- In January 2016, he said that he did not want to "rethink" his position on "banning Muslims from entering the country."

- In March 2016, he asserted that "[w]e're having problems with the Muslims, and we're having problems with Muslims coming into the country" and "called for surveillance of mosques in the United States, blaming terrorist attacks on Muslims' lack of 'assimilation' and their commitment to 'sharia law.'"

- In March 2016, "he opined that Muslims 'do not respect us at all' and don't respect a lot of the things that are happening throughout not only our country, but they don't respect other things.'"

- When his campaign started talking about "radical Islamic terrorism" rather than a "Muslim ban," he explained, "I actually don't think it's a rollback. In fact, you could say it's an expansion." He used different terminology because "[p]eople were so upset when [he] used the word Muslim."

- On January 27, 2017, when Trump moved to apparently religiously neutral terminology in his first immigration executive order, he "read the title, looked up, and said 'We all know what that means.'" He also explicitly said that the executive order was "designed 'to help' the Christians in Syria."

- While litigation was ongoing about his second anti-immigration executive order, Trump told his supporters at a campaign rally that "it was 'very hard' for Muslims to assimilate into Western culture."

- As candidate, Trump also told an apocryphal story about US general John J. Pershing killing a large group of Muslim insurgents in the Philippines with bullets dipped in pigs' blood in the early 1900s. As president, he repeated that story and then said: "Study what General Pershing . . . did to terrorists when caught. There was no more Radical Islamic Terror for 35 years!"

- "On November 29, 2017, President Trump 'retweeted' three anti-Muslim videos, entitled 'Muslim Destroys a Statue of Virgin Mary!', 'Islamist mob pushes teenage boy off roof and beats him to death!', and 'Muslim migrant beats up Dutch boy on crutches!' Those videos were initially tweeted by a British political party whose mission is to oppose 'all alien and destructive polit[ical] or religious doctrines, including . . . Islam.'"[143]

Despite this overwhelming evidence of anti-Muslim bias by the president of the United States in his immigration policies, the Supreme Court majority concluded that there was insufficient evidence that "the primary purpose of the Proclamation is to disfavor Islam and its adherents by excluding them from the country."[144] As Professor Daniel Tokaji has said: "The Court's disregard for the overwhelming evidence of President Trump's animus toward Muslims is painful enough. But placing this decision alongside the others from the Term makes it look even worse. . . . The Kennedy Court had its favored children and left no doubt of who they were."[145] Christians were clearly favored over Muslims and gay men.

The contrast between *Masterpiece Cakeshop* and *Trump v. Hawaii* is a very powerful example of the non-neutrality of the power of insults. President Trump could wield insults with impunity even when they flatly contradicted basic First Amendment norms of religious neutrality. As someone holding the highest pinnacle of power in the United States, he had a Teflon coating; the Supreme Court used the lowest possible scrutiny to assess the constitutionality of his actions against a religious minority.[146] Context matters. Not all insults are treated equally under the law. Insults are most powerful in the hands of the powerful. They can serve as a dead weight against application of basic constitutional principles and a headwind against progressive reform.

5 Pedophiles or Welcome Entrants to the Institution of Marriage

Although considerable progress has occurred in the public acceptance of members of the LGBTQ+ community, hateful messages still permeate the internet. In June 2019, Carlos Maza, a video producer for the news site Vox, created a video compilation of the public insults he had faced on You-Tube from conservative pundit Steven Crowder:

- Lispy sprite
- Little queer
- Mr. Gay Vox
- Mr. Lispy queer from Vox
- An angry little queer
- Gay Mexican
- Gay Latino from Vox
- A caricatured gay voice appearing to pantomime oral sex with his microphone while saying "Socialism is for fags."[1]

Crowder also sold shirts with messages like "Socialism is for Fags" at his online store. To understand the power of Crowder's homophobic messages, it is important to connect them to his antisocialism political position. He sought to discredit socialism by connecting it to an openly gay video producer who had a platform on Vox for disseminating his own political views. The power of insults in this example is not merely that Maza felt harassed, but that Crowder calculated that these kinds of homophobic messages were likely to resound with his conservative base and advance his own political agenda.

This chapter explores how power bullies have hurled insults against LGBTQ+ people to diminish their humanity. In contrast to the discussion of the struggle for immigrant rights in chapter 4, this chapter offers an example of progress despite debilitating insults. In part, LGBTQ+ advocates initially succeeded because their goals were relatively conservative: the right to have private sexual relations in one's bedroom or join the institution of marriage. But victory was also possible because of a successful campaign to combat the insults with human faces as well as facts and figures. As the Crowder example reflects, however, it would be wrong to conclude that public insults against the LGBTQ+ community have disappeared. In fact, in September 2019 the American Medical Association noted an increase in hate crimes against transgender people, especially transgender women of color, and characterized these crimes as an "epidemic."[2] Some Black Lives Matter activists have sought to highlight the murders of trans and gender nonconforming people.[3] While some modest advances have been made, there is much work yet to be done.

Historically, the legal-political strategy of the lesbian and gay movement reflected some understanding of the conservative aim of what came to be called "marriage equality" rather than "same-sex marriage." (It would not be accurate to describe this movement in its early days as an LGBTQ+ movement; it was mostly led by gay men and some lesbians.) The move from the terminology "same-sex marriage" to "marriage equality" was a powerful effort to reclaim the ability to name. By endorsing the concept of "marriage equality," one did not even have to acknowledge who ("homosexuals"!) would now be entering into that institution. Instead, one only had to embrace the concept of equality. Nonetheless, some lesbian feminists argued that marriage equality should not be a key priority of the gay rights movement due to the institution's patriarchal underpinnings.[4] They argued that granting gay men and lesbians access to marriage would not transform marriage but instead might strengthen the patriarchal norms within marriage. These lesbians joined other feminists in criticizing the whole concept of state-sanctioned marriage, which privileges those who live in middle-class households with a traditional breadwinner and a dependent spouse through tax breaks and access to health care. They argued that marriage has never been an institution premised on "equality" and would not become one due to the entry of gay men and lesbians into that institution.

Everyone knows the happy ending to the marriage story. The Supreme Court ultimately concluded that banning gay men and lesbians from the institution of marriage violated the US Constitution. One must ask why the Court dismissed public insults against gay men and lesbians in the marriage context but was less dismissive of public insults hurled at Muslim or Mexican immigrants. Of course, the transgender community was not able to successfully fight such public insults in the Trump era, as reflected in the Supreme Court's willingness to uphold a ban on transgender individuals' service in the military.[5] By contrast, it was able to obtain a victory in an important Title VII case, in which the Court held that transgender people are protected from sex discrimination.

Why have marriage and immigration been treated so differently? First, the defendants differ. The gay rights cases were principally brought against states. The Court may have been more protective of a Republican president than conservative states. Although epithets against the LGBT community are a historical problem, none of the successful gay rights cases involved the president hurling those epithets. When confronted with public insults by the president of the United States, the Supreme Court, led by Chief Justice John Roberts, may have been reluctant to apply its long-standing precedent. Second, the end goal of the marriage cases is also more conservative than the end goal of the immigration rights community. The right to marry is a conservative legal principle. It arguably helps preserve the patriarchy by favoring traditional families headed by a breadwinner and a dependent spouse. After all, one of the champions of the marriage movement was Ted Olson, whom the *New York Times* called "a towering figure in the conservative legal movement."[6] The immigration rights community, by contrast, wants to extend principles of religious freedom and racial nondiscrimination to noncitizens who often identify as Muslim.

Unfortunately, the transgender community's experience in the Trump era may offer the most fitting example for exploring the power of public insults to deter significant structural advances. While it may be the case that even the conservative Trump judiciary will not seek to turn back LGBT marriage gains, it has been willing to be a partner in overturning some transgender advances, such as serving openly in the military, which are much more radical in nature. Thus, resistance to public insults may be possible, and even successful, on behalf of some disadvantaged groups, but we should be careful not to overstate the extent of progress. Only the most conservative of rights are likely to be sustained, despite supposed principles of stare decisis (i.e., preserving precedent), when the political climate moves in a dramatically conservative direction. The courts are not a backstop against the power of all public insults although, as we have seen, a president can issue a temporary reprieve through executive orders, such as Obama's immigration executive orders, discussed in chapter 4, and President Biden's executive order overturning the ban on military service by members of the transgender community.

THE PUBLIC INSULT PLAYBOOK

Long-standing judicial approval of the second-class status of lesbians and gay men is strikingly illustrated by the Supreme Court's decision in 1986 in *Bowers v. Hardwick*. This case involved the constitutionality of the Georgia sodomy statute, which provided that a person "commits the offense of sodomy when he or she performs or submits to any sexual act involving the sex organs of one person and the mouth or anus of another."[7] The punishment for violating the statute was between one and twenty years in prison. Although the statute, today, is considered to be unconstitutional, it has never been repealed by the Georgia legislature.

The language of the Georgia statute would apply to heterosexual couples who engage in anal or oral sex. Thus, the original case challenging the Georgia statute in *Bowers* was filed by Michael Hardwick, who had been arrested for having sex with another man, and a married, heterosexual couple, John and Mary Doe, who claimed that they sought to engage in the sexual activities prohibited by the statute. The lower courts, however, concluded that the Does did not have standing because the state conceded that it would not use the statute to prosecute a heterosexual couple.

The state defended its sodomy statute through a campaign of insults. A lengthy footnote from the state's brief reminds us of the harsh public justifications offered as recently as 1986 in support of imposing a twenty-year prison sentence on "practicing homosexuals":

> Sodomy was proscribed in the laws of the Old Testament (Leviticus 18:22) and in the writings of St. Paul (Romans 1:26, 27; 1 Corinthians 6:9, 10). Sodomy was a capital crime in ancient Rome under the Theodosian law of 390 A.D. and under Justinian. Sodomy was proscribed by the teachings of St. Thomas Aquinas. Sodomy was prosecuted as heretical in the ecclesiastical courts throughout the Middle Ages. During the English Reformation when powers of the ecclesiastical courts were transferred to the King's courts, the first English statute criminalizing sodomy was passed.
>
> In the first half of the 17th Century, Lord Coke expounded upon the crimes of buggery and sodomy, noting that the "ancient authors doe conclude, that it deserveth death, *ultimum supplicium,* though they differ in the manner of punishment." Blackstone considered "the infamous crime against nature" as an offense of "deeper malignity" than rape, and an act so heinous, "the very mention of which is a disgrace to human nature," "a crime not fit to be named."
>
> Coke's *Institutes* and the *Commentaries* were studied by colonial lawyers in America. The popularity of Coke in the colonies and the significance of that popularity was recognized by this Court in *Payton v. New York,* 445 U.S. 573, 594 n. 36 (1980). Two thousand five hundred copies of the *Commentaries* were sold in America before the Revolution, and a subscription reprint was published in Philadelphia between 1771 and 1772. "John Adams, Esq., Barrister at Law, Boston, Massachusetts Bay," was among the subscribers.
>
> In Georgia, the common law of England in force prior to May 14, 1776, was adopted as the law of the state by an act of the General Assembly approved February 25, 1784 (Prince's 1837 Digest 570; *see also* Cobb's 1851 Digest 720).
>
> In 1816, the crimes of sodomy and bestiality were made punishable in Georgia by life imprisonment at hard labor (Lamar's Laws of Georgia, 1810-1819, at 571, § 35) and have continuously been statutory crimes ever since.[8]

In addition to the supposition that religious hostility to a behavior by itself constitutes justified moral condemnation, the state's brief hurled remarkably harsh insults against the gay and lesbian community. The state supported the notion that consensual sodomy could even be prosecuted as a capital crime, and certainly by imprisonment for life at hard labor. It was considered more heinous than rape.

Later in its defense of the sodomy statute, the state responded to the plaintiff's argument that he had a constitutional right of association to engage in an intimate relationship with someone he loved. Again, parroting the public insults usually hurled against gay couples, the state argued:

- Perhaps the most profound legislative finding that can be made is that homosexual sodomy is the anathema of the basic units of our society— marriage and the family. To decriminalize or artificially withdraw the public's expression of its disdain for this conduct does not uplift sodomy, but rather demotes these sacred institutions to merely other alternative lifestyles.

- If the legal distinction between the intimacies of marriage and homosexual sodomy are lost, it is certainly possible to make the assumption, perhaps unprovable at this time, that the order of society, our way of life, could be changed in a harmful way.

- Because of the harmful results that would inevitably occur if sodomy were legalized, the state claimed it had a "compelling interest in the organization of society."[9]

Those arguments were not anachronistic. The state felt entirely comfortable describing "a practicing homosexual" as having that potential impact on society if the law did not ban sodomy through a harsh twenty-year sentence. The state understood that overturning sodomy bans would likely result in the ultimate acceptance of "homosexual marriage" or what the state of Georgia cast as the destruction of organized society.

Public insults against homosexual marriage were emphatically made in public forums to persuade the courts to uphold the state's sodomy ban. For example, James Dobson of Focus on the Family argued:

The legalization of homosexual marriage will quickly destroy the traditional family. . . . When the State sanctions homosexual relationships and gives them its blessing, the younger generation becomes confused about sexual identity and quickly loses its understanding of lifelong commitments, emotional bonding, sexual purity, the role of children in a family, and from a spiritual perspective, the "sanctity" of marriage.[10]

In 1986, the power of insults prevailed. In a 5–4 decision, the Supreme Court concluded that the statute was not rendered unconstitutional because it was supported by "the presumed belief of a majority of the electorate in Georgia that homosexual sodomy is immoral and unacceptable." The Court approved of that kind of rationale, concluding that "if all laws representing essentially moral choices are to be invalidated under the Due Process Clause, the courts will be very busy indeed."[11] But that response reduces the plaintiff's argument to a straw man. The plaintiffs were not arguing that morality has no role in law; the plaintiffs were arguing that a morality based merely on hostility to a particular group cannot be the basis of valid laws.

From reading the opinion in *Bowers*, it is clear that the justices did not conceive of the plaintiff, Michael Hardwick, as a whole person. He was just a sexual act. As the Court said, in explaining why the state statute was constitutional: "It is obvious to us that neither of these formulations would extend a fundamental right to homosexuals to engage in acts of consensual sodomy."[12] Michael Hardwick had been reduced to a sodomy-creating machine. He had no joy, no frustrations, no life aside from his apparently uncontrolled propensity to engage in sex, despite the illegality of his conduct. Public insults had defined him.

Not surprisingly, the public insults did not end when the Supreme Court announced its decision in 1986. If anything, the political right felt emboldened to use its public insults to influence public policy. It next turned its attention to the state of Colorado, where it persuaded voters on November 3, 1992, to ban local nondiscrimination ordinances. In preparation for the vote on this statewide initiative (Amendment 2), the airwaves were filled with messages that gay and lesbian people were pedophiles and perverts who should not be granted "special protection." In their LGBT rights casebook, William Eskridge and Nan Hunter provide an appendix with eleven pages of these pamphlets. Here are some of the claims made in these pamphlets:

TARGET: CHILDREN
   Lately, America's been hearing a lot about the subject of childhood sexual abuse. This terrible epidemic has scarred countless young lives and destroyed thousands of families. But what militant homosexuals don't want you to know is the large role they play in this epidemic. In fact, pedophilia (the

sexual molestation of children) is actually an accepted part of the homosexual community!

√ David Thorstad, founding member of the gay organization called the North American Man-Boy Love Association, a group whose motto is "Sex by eight, or it's too late" and a former president of Gay Activist Alliance of New York, writes:

"The issue of man-boy love has intersected the gay movement since the late nineteenth century." Thorstad complains that pedophilia is being swept under the rug by the gay-rights movement, which ". . . *seeks to sanitize the image of homosexuality to facilitate its entrance into the social mainstream."*

***

Homosexual indoctrination in the schools?
IT'S HAPPENING IN COLORADO!

***

In Laguna Beach, California, a city with one of the country's largest gay communities and strongest "gay-rights" ordinances, a three-year old boy entered a public park restroom. What he saw there traumatized him severely. Three grown gay men were engaging in group sex, right there in the bathroom! When he ran out to his mother, crying and upset, she attempted to file a complaint with the Laguna Beach Police Department. Their reply: with a "gay-rights" ordinance in place, there was nothing they could do. You can stop this from happening in Colorado with your "YES" vote on Amendment 2.[13]

That is only a small sampling of the eleven pages of pamphlets, but the message is consistent throughout. Gay men and lesbians (mostly gay men) are accused of being pedophiles; living unhealthy, AIDS-ridden lifestyles; trying to destroy the church and family; and seeking work opportunities like schools or day-care centers where they can prey on young people. While the state used more modulated arguments in defense of the initiative, the important point is that the campaign of public insults was quite persuasive with the voters, who overwhelmingly approved Amendment 2.

Somewhat surprisingly, however, in 1996, the US Supreme Court invalidated the Colorado initiative in the landmark case *Romer v. Evans*.[14] In writing for the Court, Justice Kennedy concluded for a six-member majority that "a bare desire to harm a politically unpopular group cannot constitute a legitimate governmental interest."[15]

The decision in *Romer* did not, however, stop the campaign of public insults and hate. As recently as 2008, in so-called liberal California, the voters approved a statewide initiative, Proposition 8, on November 4. This initiative provided that "only marriage between a man and a woman is valid or recognized in California." It was supported by religious organizations such as the Roman Catholic Church and the Church of Jesus Christ of Latter-Day Saints. In the public material prepared to describe the arguments in support of this initiative, the proponents claimed:

> It protects our children from being taught in public schools that "same-sex marriage" is the same as traditional marriage.
>
> Proposition 8 protects marriage as an essential institution of society. While death, divorce, or other circumstances may prevent the ideal, the best situation for a child is to be raised by a married mother and father.
>
> If the gay marriage ruling is not overturned, TEACHERS COULD BE REQUIRED to teach young children there is *no difference* between gay marriage and traditional marriage.[16]

Those quotations are from materials publicly disseminated by the state of California. In their public relations campaign, handled at their own expense, the Proposition 8 proponents were even more clear in seeking to "play[] on the fear that exposure to homosexuality would turn children into homosexuals and that parents should dread having children who are not heterosexual."[17] In one not-so-subtle attempt to play off those fears and stereotypes, Proposition 8 proponents aired a video entitled *Have You Thought About It?* in which a young girl is asked "whether the viewer has considered the consequences to her of Proposition 8 but not explaining what those consequences might be."[18] Because of the pervasiveness of antigay stereotypes, the video could rely on viewers filling in that answer in a way that would cause them to support Proposition 8. But the Proposition 8 proponents did not always rely on the viewer to connect the dots. In another video, entitled *It's Already Happened*, a mother expresses horror "upon realizing her daughter now knows she can marry a princess."[19]

Proposition 8 was approved by 52 percent of the voters. The campaign of hate worked. However, both the district court and the court of appeals concluded that Proposition 8 could not survive constitutional challenge because its passage was based on "disapproval of gays and lesbians as a class."[20] As the court of appeals observed, "These messages were not crafted accidentally." These tactics were not new: "[F]or decades, ballot measures regarding homosexuality have been presented to voters in terms designed to appeal to stereotypes of gays and lesbians as predators, threats to children, and practitioners of a deviant 'lifestyle.'"[21]

Given this campaign of hate against the LGBTQ+ community, the legal community had difficult decisions to make. Should they seek to enact non-discrimination measures in employment and housing to help LGBTQ+ people have access to basic rights to housing and employment? Rather than seek structural remedies, such as legislation, should they open up legal aid offices to help people with basic issues like landlord abuse that might be keeping them from living even at a basic level of human dignity? Or should they push for legalizing same-sex marriage through legislation and litigation because marriage is a cornerstone for respectability in society? The next section discusses how the marriage equality issue became the top LGBTQ+ priority in the late twentieth century.

MARRIAGE AS A GOAL

Marriage equality was not always at the top of the gay rights agenda; in fact, the gay rights legal community initially argued against what was then termed "same-sex marriage." A little LGBTQ+ history can track the development of marriage equality as a goal.

The public birth of the gay rights movement is often considered to be the Stonewall protests of 1969. The Stonewall protesters "wanted freedom of sexual expression and autonomy and basic legal protections from discrimination in many aspects of their lives. Marriage was not only the furthest thing from their minds, it was an object of derision, [with protesters] calling it 'one of the most insidious and basic sustainers of the system.'"[22] While it is true that Michael McConnell and Jack Baker unsuccessfully applied for a marriage license in Minnesota in the early 1970s and took their case to the US Supreme Court, the Stonewall activists described their case as "reactionary."[23] The priority of the gay rights movement was "abolishing anti-sodomy laws, passing hate-crimes legislation, and expanding employment protections for gay workers."[24]

In 1989, the marriage debate within the gay and lesbian movement gained a public stage. Tom Stoddard and Paula Ettelbrick published dueling essays in the LGBT magazine *Out/Look* on whether same-sex marriage should be a priority of the gay rights movement.[25] In recounting the story behind those dueling essays, Carlos Ball asserts that Stoddard held the minority position within the LGBT community. "Tom Stoddard was one of only a handful of movement leaders who was urging the LGBT community to take the pursuit of same-sex marriage seriously."[26] Yet Stoddard was hired by Lambda Legal Defense Fund in 1986 as its executive director. Stoddard hired Ettelbrick as the organization's first staff attorney.

The debate between Stoddard and Ettelbrick is an important development in the LGBT rights legal struggle. When the *New York Times* published Ettelbrick's obituary in 2011, it quoted from her 1989 *Out/Look* essay.[27] In that essay, she argued that she did not "want to be known as 'Mrs. Attached-to-Somebody-Else,'"; nor did she "want to give the state the power to regulate [her] primary relationship."[28] She argued: "Marriage, as it exists today, is antithetical to my liberation as a lesbian and as a woman because it mainstreams my life and voice."[29]

While Ettelbrick pushed a feminist perspective to argue that same-sex marriage should not be a priority of the lesbian and gay rights movement, others embraced her views from a more practical perspective. "What lesbian employee, for example, would publicly exchange vows with her partner on Saturday if her boss could legally fire her the following Monday?"[30] Strategically, as documented by William Eskridge and Darren Spedale, states were likely to move in an LGBT rights direction by first repealing their sodomy laws, then adding sexual orientation to hate crimes protection, and eventually prohibiting employment discrimination.[31] Only after those legal protections were in place did states begin to offer some kind of legal recognition of same-sex relationships, often in the form of domestic partnership legislation.[32]

It is also likely that financial considerations were a factor in the choice of marriage as a legal priority. As documented by Leonore Carpenter, LGBT-rights groups have become extremely well funded in the last decade.[33] That money poured in as marriage equality advances began to materialize in the courts. As an insider to the priority-setting decisions of the LGBT community, Carpenter documents how an assimilationist, well-funded perspective prevailed during strategy discussions:[34]

- A group of wealthy Californians hired former solicitor general Ted Olsen and his former opposing counsel, David Boies (from *Bush v. Gore*), to argue that California's Proposition 8 was unconstitutional.

- Edith Windsor hired private lawyer Roberta Kaplan of Paul, Weiss, Rifkind, Wharton & Garrison to bring the case *Windsor v. United States*. Edith Windsor was seeking a significant tax benefit when the federal government recognized her marriage.

In both of those cases (and others documented by Carpenter), the national LGBT organizations supported marriage equality efforts *after* well-financed groups decided to back these conservative, assimilationist goals. The conservative, assimilationist aspect of these choices did not go unnoticed. Dean Spade and Craig Willse, for example, observed:

> In our view, the individual rights perspective has been chosen as the LGBT agenda, and redistributionist liberation struggles have been undermined or cast aside. . . . It is the choice to bring individual lawsuits for rich queers denied the rights to pass on apartments to their partners, but to take no stand in the struggle for affordable housing. . . . It is the choice to virtually ignore the most vulnerable members of our "community."[35]

Not surprisingly, as documented by Carpenter, the LGBT legal community was also making decisions based on what legal theories they thought might prevail. The right to enter the conservative institution of marriage was arguably an easier argument than the right to live in affordable housing, especially when the courts have never given much weight to arguments made on behalf of poor people. Further, as discussed later, it was unthinkable in terms of legal strategy to question whether the state should even be permitted to tie benefits to the institution of marriage. To the extent that the LGBT community could make an argument that they were "just like" heterosexuals, but for their sexual orientation, and even revered marriage, they stood a stronger chance of prevailing.

If acquiring the right to be married is a conservative legal principle, then it makes sense that people in society with ample resources to contribute to a political-legal cause would jump on the marriage bandwagon. In fact, organizations such as The American Foundation for Equal Rights were started specifically for the purpose of advancing marriage for the

LGBT community after that goal appeared possible.[36] One can think of it as a cycle: the marriage movement makes legal gains, money flows in to support such efforts, and those efforts then accelerate. The result, as many scholars have noted, is that access to marriage got ahead of the movement toward a national nondiscrimination statute. As of 2020, the Supreme Court decision in 2015 in *Obergefell v. Hodges* was settled constitutional precedent, but a national nondiscrimination statute was stalled in Congress.

The fact that a marriage victory has some conservative roots does not make the recognition of same-sex marriage a failure, but it does make that result a conservative victory.

THE CONSERVATIVE CLOTHING OF THE MARRIAGE VICTORY

Close consideration of the *Obergefell* decision reveals its conservative nature. The *Obergefell* Court described the victory as one for "same-sex marriage," the "freedom to marry," and the "right to marry,"[37] while the LGBT community applauded the decision as one for "marriage equality" or the "freedom to marry."[38] Although the *Obergefell* decision did require states to allow all persons to enter the institution of marriage irrespective of the gender or sexual orientation of their partner, saying that *Obergefell* genuinely created marriage "equality" is misleading. True marriage equality would give people the *choice* whether to enter the institution of marriage. Bluntly, the *Obergefell* decision coerced more people to marry in order to obtain privileges or benefits that would otherwise be unavailable to them. It made marriage available to same-sex couples but did not sufficiently protect their *choice* of whether to get married or not. In other words, it may have allowed the LGBT community to enter marriage while promoting discrimination against nonmarital couples (or other kinds of unions).

The limitations of the rights gained in *Windsor* and *Obergefell* are evident in the stories of the lead plaintiffs. The Court's decision meant that in order to improve their status in society, they *had* to seek to marry their partners. The government was permitted to continue to withhold certain rights unless couples in their position chose to marry.

The first story is that of Edith Windsor. Edith Windsor and Thea Spyer held a commitment ceremony and exchanged circular diamond brooches in 1967, but they could not become legally "married" due to widespread restrictions on same-sex marriage at the time.[39] Later in their lives, in 2007, they traveled to Canada to get married, at a time when their home state of New York was not yet allowing same-sex marriages. When Spyer died in 2009, she left her estate to Windsor, but the federal government would not allow Windsor to take advantage of the favorable tax treatment provided to married couples. Thus, Windsor had a tax bill of $363,053 to pay. Under US tax law, Windsor had to pay the $363,053 and then file a legal claim for a tax refund. When she prevailed in 2013, she became eligible for that refund. But notice that she only became eligible for that refund because she had gone to Canada with Spyer in 2007 and gotten married. But for her marriage, she would not have been eligible for that refund. In other words, wealthy couples who want to pass their estate to each other tax-free *need* to get married. The state strongly encourages or coerces them to get married to receive that significant financial benefit.

Windsor and Spyer were not unusual, in the sense that they would have benefited from being able to be legally married. The tax benefits of marriage are especially strong for those couples who reflect a traditional marriage by having one high-income and one low-income partner. Those benefits include a lower tax rate and various Social Security benefits.[40] Tara Siegel Bernard and Rob Lieber estimated in 2009 that the annual costs of being unmarried in the United States range from $28,595 to $211,993 in health insurance costs, $32,253 in pension costs, and $112,192 in spousal IRAs. Poor people, however, face a financial disincentive to marry. "Getting married might, say, reduce eligibility for Medicaid benefits, the earned-income tax credit or the tax credit that can help pay for health insurance under the Affordable Care Act."[41] In other words, the legal system is not marriage neutral. It provides financial incentives for traditional, middle-class families with one high-wage earner to marry but provides financial disincentives for poor people to marry. The *Windsor* decision merely extended those coercions to same-sex couples.

The second story is that of April DeBoer and Jayne Rowse, plaintiffs in one of the cases that became the *Obergefell* litigation.[42] They were an unmarried same-sex couple residing in Michigan. As single people,

DeBoer had adopted one child and Rowse had adopted two. Under Michigan law, they could not jointly adopt those children unless they were married. Similarly situated, unmarried opposite-sex adults would have faced the same problem: they would not have been allowed to jointly adopt the three children.

In their original complaint, DeBoer and Rowse alleged that the state adoption law impermissibly discriminated against unmarried couples. They sought a victory for all unmarried couples: the ability to jointly adopt children without getting married. But they amended their complaint after the trial court judge made it clear that he thought the legal impediment they faced was an inability to *get married* rather than an inability to adopt as an unmarried couple. Upon his invitation, they amended their complaint, and he ruled that the state marriage law was unconstitutional. After the US Supreme Court ruled in their favor, they reportedly said: "Now apparently we have to plan a marriage."[43] They did *not* say: "Now apparently we have to file for an adoption," because their right to adopt was still contingent on their willingness to marry, and Michigan law still only allows a second-parent adoption if a couple is married. A couple that wants to adopt children jointly does *not* have the choice of remaining unmarried. Like Windsor and Spyer, they must marry in order to obtain the government benefit. One can only hope they really cherished the ability to marry when they finally exchanged their marriage vows on August 23, 2015,[44] and adopted their children on November 5, 2015.[45]

The compulsory marriage aspects of *Obergefell* were not accidental. As Melissa Murray has said, "From start to finish, the majority opinion in *Obergefell* reads like a love letter to marriage."[46] "In short, the majority's rhetoric suggests that the prospect of willingly being unmarried is utterly unimaginable."[47]

But even more important is that the Court's decisions in *Windsor* and *Obergefell* do not pay homage to the developing case law on the right *not* to be married. As discussed by Murray,[48] the nonmarital rights case law includes

- the rights of children born outside of marriage to receive wrongful death benefits, welfare benefits, inheritance benefits, workers' compensation benefits, and a relationship with their father;

- the rights of nonmarried people to have access to contraception and abortion;
- access to Food Stamps and single-family housing for nonmarital households; and
- the right to have a sexual relationship.

The extension of that case law could have yielded somewhat different rulings in *Windsor* and *Obergefell*. Instead of conditioning Windsor's tax benefit on proof that she had married Spyer in Canada, the Court could have said that it was unconstitutional to condition an important tax benefit on a marital relationship. Similarly, the Court could have ruled that it was unconstitutional to limit adoption rights, death benefits, and military benefits based on the marital status of one's partner in the various cases underlying the *Obergefell* decision.

Instead, the victory in *Obergefell* and *Windsor* is not merely a loss for the members of the LGBT community who do not want to get married. It is a loss for *all* couples who would prefer to be in a relationship but not be "married." As Murray aptly notes, the Court's placement of marriage on a pedestal "is at odds with the experiences of those who are divorced, in marriage counseling, or in abusive marriages or families."[49] Or, as Dana Harrington Conner has more starkly observed: "Marriage is the batterer's gateway to establishing power over the family finances and property."[50] The *choice* to not marry is essential if some people are to live fulfilling lives.

We will truly have the freedom to marry when people choose marriage out of love rather than as a way to obtain state-sanctioned material gain. Evidence from other countries suggests that this path is possible. In New Zealand, for example, marriage has lost most of its legal value. Financial benefits are not contingent upon entering the relationship of marriage. Couples who do choose marriage report that they feel that they can choose a ceremony that reflects their "personal values and lifestyles."[51] And some couples report that they choose not to get married to avoid the "religious connotations or gendered traditions" of marriage.

Of course, if the LGBT community would prioritize genuine marriage equality—the choice *not* to get married—it would play right into the hands of the LGBT bigots who have always claimed that the LGBT community wants to destroy marriage as we know it. Note this passage from Kennedy's majority opinion in *Obergefell* in describing the position of the plaintiff-petitioners:

> Were their intent to demean the revered idea and reality of marriage, the petitioners' claims would be of a different order. But that is neither their purpose nor their submission. To the contrary, it is the enduring importance of marriage that underlies the petitioners' contentions. This, they say, is their whole point. Far from seeking to devalue marriage, the petitioners seek it for themselves because [of] their respect—and need—for its privileges and responsibilities. And their immutable nature dictates that same-sex marriage is their only real path to this profound commitment.[52]

Look at what Kennedy is saying. He is saying that marriage's "immutable nature" is such that it is the only proper way to make a commitment to someone one loves. The heart of the plaintiffs' claim is that they accept that one can only live a fulfilled life by getting married. They *seek* the privileges of marriage and support those privileges being limited to those who are married due to the "immutable nature" of marriage. There is no doubt how Kennedy would have ruled if the plaintiffs had requested that the state stop allocating privileges on the basis of marriage. He would have correctly understood that argument as seeking to undermine the importance of the institution of marriage.

So, in hindsight, one can say that the LGBT community made the correct political calculation in understanding that they could only win the right to marry if they did not contest marriage's exalted place on the pedestal. Trenchant critique of the institution of marriage was not a viable path to legal victory.

THE DIFFICULT PATH TO SAME-SEX MARRIAGE

Despite the fact that same-sex marriage was a conservative victory, it is important to recognize how difficult it was to get to that step. Overcoming the power of insults was important and challenging. To better understand the power of insults, it is helpful to recount the successful LGBT legal and political strategy used to confront endemic anti-LGBT stereotypes.

As Ball carefully documented, the LGBT legal community was initially unwilling even to bring cases challenging the exclusion of same-sex couples from marriage because they thought the cases were impossible to win.[53] In the earliest same-sex marriage cases, the courts merely said that marriage, by definition, was a union of a man and a woman and did not take seriously arguments for same-sex marriage.[54] It wasn't merely that the courts thought that gay men and lesbians were immoral pedophiles who could not sustain long-term relationships; they simply thought it was not credible that gay men and lesbians would even consider entering the institution of marriage. Early litigation resulted in brief sentences or paragraphs denying relief because the judges denied that the cases raised any serious constitutional issue.

Critical gains in public support for same-sex marriage came about because of sustained efforts by the LGBT community and their allies to counter vitriolic insults. Before turning to a discussion of the California Proposition 8 litigation in *Hollingsworth v. Perry*, 558 U.S. 183 (2010), it is helpful to remember some of those arguments and the resources that the LGBT community deployed to counter them.

The Southern Poverty Law Center published a blog entry entitled *10 Anti-Gay Myths Debunked* in which it recounted many of these insults and the LGBT response.[55] I discuss here four of these myths below and how the LGBT community has responded to them outside the courtroom. I then discuss that response in the context of the *Perry* litigation.

1. Gay men molest children at far higher rates than heterosexuals.

Antigay activists have popularized this claim by drawing on right-wing organizations such as the American College of Pediatricians (ACPeds) and the Family Research Council, which were formed for the purpose of promoting antigay propaganda, making fake claims that "the research is overwhelming that homosexuality poses a [molestation] danger to children." The creation of ACPeds was a clever move by antigay rights forces, because its name sounds similar to the mainstream American Academy of Pediatrics.[56]

In response, well-respected researchers have reviewed reputable studies and concluded there is no evidence to support this view. Further, mainstream organizations like the Child Molestation Research & Prevention

Institution, the American Psychological Association, and the American Academy of Pediatrics have publicly argued that the views of ACPeds have no scientific basis.[57]

2. Same-sex parents harm children.

Anti-LGBT think tanks spent $1 million to fund a study by Mark Regnerus claiming to prove that lesbians and gay men are bad parents.[58]

In response, mainstream organizations such as the American Academy of Child & Adolescent Psychiatry, the American Academy of Pediatrics, the Child Welfare League, and the American Psychological Association stated their disagreement with his study. They pointed out that "beliefs that lesbian and gay adults are not fit parents have no empirical foundation."

In a highly unusual move, the Regnerus study was discredited by his own department chair at the University of Texas. She issued a statement in which she said that the American Sociological Association "takes the position that the conclusions he draws from his study of gay parenting are fundamentally flawed on conceptual and methodological grounds."[59]

3. People become homosexuals because they were sexually abused as children or there was a deficiency in sex-role modeling by their parents.

Antigay advocates have made assertions that "if you traumatize a child in a particular way, you will create a homosexual condition" and have published a study, based on aggregated anecdotal data from a biased sample, claiming that gay couples model "gay behavior" to raise gay or lesbian children.[60]

Organizations such as the National Organization on Male Sexual Victimization and Advocates for Youth have debunked such claims. The antigay claims have even been criticized by Dr. Warren Throckmorton, who holds a faculty position at Christian Grove City College. Throckmorton became particularly incensed when Scott Lively (a Christian minister) pushed the false claim that "the Nazi Party was entirely controlled by militaristic male homosexuals." Throckmorton warned other Christians: "When Christians make spurious comparisons to the Nazis, they should not be surprised when the targets of these comparisons lash back and consider them hateful. There should be little wonder why they don't feel the Love."[61] Obtaining support from faculty at traditionally conservative, religious entities was a useful strategy and reflects how antigay animus was moving out of mainstream circles.

4. LGBT people don't live nearly as long as heterosexuals.

The Family Research Institute published a study in 1994 based on obituaries from newspapers serving the gay community and concluded that, on average, gay men died at age forty-three, compared to the overall life expectancy of seventy-three for all men in the United States. These statistics were cited as recently as 1997 by William Bennett, who formerly served as the secretary of education for President Ronald Reagan.[62] Further, antigay advocates claimed that a Canadian study also supported that conclusion.

With respect to the Canadian study, the authors issued a response saying that their work was being misrepresented.[63] Furthermore, the LGBT community was even able to gain the support of the conservative American Enterprise Institute, which called the results from the Family Research Institute "just ridiculous."[64]

.   .   .   .   .

In each of these instances, the LGBT community worked with mainstream organizations, including ones that might have conservative or religious affiliations, to respond to the antigay claims through new research or criticism of the existing research. They also got civil rights organizations such as the Southern Poverty Law Center to list the antigay groups as "hate groups" and use their extensive resources to respond to these antigay claims. They also used their own publicity arms to circulate those responses. In general, LGBT advocates tried to stand with science and respected empirical research to further their point of view. We will see that legal advocates in the *Perry* case used a similar strategy inside the courtroom.

The LGBT community and its allies also tried to move beyond academic circles to criticize antigay stereotypes in the media. One mechanism for countering those stereotypes was the formation of GLAAD.[65] When it was founded in 1985, it was called the Gay & Lesbian Alliance Against Defamation, but changed its name to "GLAAD" in 2013 to become more inclusive of bisexual and transgender issues. Initially, GLAAD worked to persuade media organizations to use terms like "gay" instead of "homosexual" or "homophile." The group also held rallies in the 1980s to protest the biased nature of HIV and AIDS coverage in the media. In 1988, it challenged the stereotypical portrayal of a bisexual character in a show, *Midnight Caller*, featured on NBC. Also in 1988, it persuaded the phone book publisher to list "Gay and Lesbian Services" as one of its yellow pages' headers. While phone books may be scarce today, they were an important source of visibility in the late twentieth century. In a creative move to increase visibility, GLAAD persuaded the US Postal Service to issue a Stonewall anniversary stamp in 1989, celebrating Stonewall's twentieth anniversary. In 1990, GLAAD created Project 21, which sought to ensure that fair, accurate, and unbiased information regarding sexual orientation was presented in the nation's public schools.

GLAAD was not the only group trying to change public perceptions of the LGBT community. ACT UP was founded in 1987, in response to the AIDS crisis, and used a direct-action approach, including civil disobedience, to advocate on behalf of the LGBT community.[66]

Researchers believe that the media has helped change the public's views about the LGBT community. Phillip Ayoub and Jeremiah Garretson have concluded that the combination of personal contacts and positive portrayals of the LGBT community in the media "can shape opinions and values, even across national borders."[67] Thus, it is likely that the kind of media work that GLAAD has done has had some influence on public perceptions of the LGBT community, thereby making it easier to counter negative stereotypes in the courtroom. In other words, the LGBT community formulated a strong playbook of its own, starting in the mid-1980s, to counter the political right's homophobic playbook.

When same-sex marriage litigation began, the political right used its political insult playbook to support its homophobic measures. In the *Perry* Proposition 8 litigation, which challenged the California proposition which banned same-sex marriage, the proponents of Proposition 8 made the following disparaging arguments:

1. Denial of marriage to same-sex couples preserves marriage.
2. Denial of marriage to same-sex couples allows gays and lesbians to live privately without requiring others, including (perhaps especially)

children, to recognize or acknowledge the existence of same-sex couples.

3. Denial of marriage to same-sex couples protects children.

4. The ideal child-rearing environment requires one male and one female parent.

5. Marriage is different in nature depending on the sex of the spouses, and an opposite-sex couple's marriage is superior to a same-sex couple's marriage.

6. Same-sex couples' marriages redefine opposite-sex couples' marriages.[68]

Notice how these arguments often rested on the stereotypes mentioned earlier in this chapter. Moreover, the Proposition 8 proponents were comfortable arguing directly that opposite-sex couples are "superior" to same-sex couples. These were not hidden or subtle public slurs and appeared in legal briefs as recently as 2010.

The plaintiffs in the *Perry* litigation had to do a lot of work to counter this parade of insults. They presented nine expert witnesses to counter the proponents' arguments in support of Proposition 8. The expert witnesses presented the following testimony:

- Harvard University historian Nancy Cott testified about the "public institution of marriage and the state's interest in recognizing and regulating marriages."[69]

- UCLA psychologist Letitia Anne Peplau "testified that couples benefit both physically and economically when they are married."[70]

- University of Massachusetts economist Lee Badgett provided evidence that same-sex couples would benefit economically if they were able to marry, and there would be no adverse effect on marriage or opposite-sex couples.

- U.C. Davis psychologist Gregory Herek testified that "homosexuality is a normal expression of human sexuality" and that therapeutic attempts to change one's sexual orientation have been found to "pose a risk of harm to the individual."[71]

- Columbia University social epidemiologist Ilan Meyer testified about the likelihood of mental and physical harms occurring to gays and lesbians as a result of the implementation of Proposition 8.

- University of Cambridge psychologist Michael Lamb testified that children raised by gay or lesbian parents are as likely to be well adjusted as children raised by heterosexual parents.
- Yale historian George Chauncey testified that the advertisements to support Proposition 8 relied on stereotypical images of gays and lesbians. He testified that "stereotypes of gays and lesbians as predators or child molesters were reinforced in the mid-twentieth century and remain part of current public discourse."[72]
- Stanford political scientist Gary Segura "testified that negative stereotypes about gays and lesbians inhibit political compromise with other groups."[73]
- City of San Francisco economist Edmund Egan testified that "San Francisco faces direct and indirect economic harm as a consequence of Proposition 8."[74]

The plaintiffs also tried to humanize the case by offering testimony from four of the plaintiffs and various lay witnesses. One lay witness, Ryan Kendall, for example, testified about his mental anguish when his parents forced him to undergo therapy to change his sexual orientation:

- "I remember my mother looking at me and telling me that I was going to burn in hell."[75]
- "My mother would tell me that she hated me, or that I was disgusting, or that I was repulsive. Once she told me that she wished she had had an abortion instead of a gay son."[76]

Although the proponents of Proposition 8 presented the court with a long witness list, they only called two of those witnesses to testify in court, whom they asked the court to qualify as experts. The first witness was David Blankenhorn, who was called as an expert on marriage, fatherhood, and family structure. While the court permitted Blankenhorn to testify, it reserved judgment on whether he qualified as an expert or was just offering "opinion" testimony. Blankenhorn had received a BA in social studies from Harvard and an MA in comparative social history from the University of Warwick in England. The court was troubled by Blankenhorn's lack of formal training in sociology, psychology, or anthropology despite the importance of those fields to his conclusions, as well as his lack of intellectual rigor in reaching his conclusions. "The court concludes that

Blankenhorn's proposed definition of marriage is 'connected to existing data only the by *ipse dixit*' of Blankenhorn and accordingly rejects it."[77] In sum, the court concluded that "Blankenhorn's opinions are not supported by reliable evidence or methodology and Blankenhorn failed to consider evidence contrary to his view in presenting his testimony."[78]

The proponents' second witness had stronger qualifications. He was Kenneth P. Miller, professor of government at Claremont McKenna College, who had a PhD from the University of California (Berkeley). He testified on gay and lesbian political power, but the court refused to certify him as an expert on that subject because "the opinions he offered at trial were inconsistent with the opinions he expressed before he was retained as an expert."[79]

The court therefore was presented with nine credible expert witnesses by the LGBT community and two weak witnesses by the proponents of Proposition 8. After spending nearly eighty pages summarizing the testimony in the case, the court rejected each of the proponents' justifications for Proposition 8:

1. "The evidence shows that the state advances nothing when it adheres to the tradition of excluding same-sex couples from marriage. Proponents' asserted stated interests in tradition are nothing more than tautologies and do not amount to rational bases for Proposition 8."[80]

2. "[A]llowing same-sex couples to marry has at least a neutral, if not a positive, effect on the institution of marriage."[81]

3. "To the extent proponents seek to encourage a norm that sexual activity occur within marriage to ensure that reproduction occur within marriage to ensure that reproduction occurs within stable households, Proposition 8 discourages that norm because it requires some sexual activity and child-bearing and child-rearing to occur outside marriage."[82]

4. Rather than protect the rights of those morally opposed to same-sex marriage, "Proposition 8 does nothing other than eliminate the right of same-sex couples to marry in California."[83]

5. There is no secular basis for opposing same-sex marriage. "The evidence shows conclusively that moral and religious views form the only basis for a belief that same-sex couples are different from opposite-sex couples."[84]

6. "The evidence shows that, by every available metric, opposite-sex couples are not better than their same-sex counterparts; instead, as partners, parents and citizens, opposite-sex couples and same-sex couples are equal."[85]

Notice all the heavy lifting that was required for the court to conclude that same-sex couples are not inferior people but can form loving unions and even raise children in those unions who will not be harmed by their parents' sexual orientation.

And that opinion is not ancient history. It was issued by a federal district court judge in 2010 at a time when it was not clear whether his decision would be sustained on appeal. *Obergefell* had not yet been decided.

Thus, although *Obergefell*, in my opinion, was a conservative decision upholding the traditional institution of marriage, it still took a lot of heavy lifting (and a well-resourced legal community) to lay the foundation to disprove the stereotypes underlying the exclusion of the LGBT community from marriage. Even conservative gains are difficult if those gains require countering the political right's public insult playbook.

The marriage equality journey is an excellent example of how progressive advocates can try to win despite the public insult playbook. The LGBT community smartly recognized the importance of changing their portrayal in the media and devoted substantial resources to overcoming those media stereotypes. Further, the LGBT community encouraged mainstream scholars to generate scholarship that could counter unfounded myths. But none of that might have been enough if some wealthy benefactors had not supported the expensive litigation efforts that were mounted. The description of the *Perry* litigation alone gives the reader the sense of the enormous resources necessary to mount a successful legal campaign. One has to be a virtual member of the power elite to provide the resources necessary to beat the power elite at its own game.

And while I have described the marriage victory as conservative, it remains imperiled. The political right has continued to challenge the availability of marriage to same-sex couples by withholding marriage licenses on religious grounds. Same-sex couples cannot assume that their local florist or bakery will help them celebrate their weddings. Nothing is beyond the scope of our imagination. It is a fragile victory.

A TRANSGENDER CODA

I have been reluctant to use the initialism "LGBT" throughout this chapter because the cases discussed have rarely advanced the interests of transgender people and only indirectly have sometimes advanced the interests of bisexuals. My book *Hybrid: Bisexuals, Multiracials and Other Misfits under American Law*, discusses this issue at length. Briefly, when bisexuals enter any union—be it marriage or any other—the outside community is likely to conclude that they are gay or straight. The mere existence of bisexuals is generally invisible, which leads to its own kind of stereotypes.

But the status of transgender people requires further amplification. While they were able to achieve some successes at the end of the Obama presidency, many of those advances were reversed by President Trump. While the Supreme Court did affirm their coverage under Title VII, it left open the possibility that religious freedom claims or obsession with single-gender bathrooms could take away some of those gains.

It is helpful to remember that the embrace of "T" issues within the LGB community is relatively new. Until recently, one could argue that the public insult playbook was so effective that it even influenced the gay and lesbian communities.

For transgender people, the insults often do not end with words. They sometimes end with violence or even murder. November 20 is the annual International Transgender Day of Remembrance. While it is hard to gather statistics about violence against the transgender community, it is well recognized that a disproportionate percentage of LGBT people who report violence are transgender, and many of them are people of color.[86]

In addition to the violence, transgender people are castigated and demonized as

- oversexualized, uncontrollable freaks;
- drugged out prostitutes;
- flamboyant drag queens;
- living crazy lives characterized by drag performances, hypermasculine or hyperfeminine behavior, drugs, or prostitution;
- confused about their sex and gender;
- mentally disturbed;

- performers at drag shows;
- not "real" men or women; and
- rapists who want to prey on women in bathrooms.[87]

For many years, the gay rights community did not consider transgender issues to be a legislative or legal priority. A brief legislative history of the Equality Act (which has not yet passed Congress) can help the reader see the evolution, which has led to increased support for transgender people.[88]

In 1974, Representative Bella Abzug introduced the Equality Act. It was intended to prohibit discrimination on the basis of sexual orientation or marital status in places of public accommodation and in federally assisted programs. Then the LGB community began to favor amending Title VII of the Civil Rights Act of 1964 to ban discrimination based on sexual orientation.

In 1995, the strategy shifted to drafting a freestanding law that would ban sexual orientation discrimination. It was called the Employment Non-Discrimination Act (ENDA). It was introduced by Gerry Studds, who was the first openly gay member of Congress.

Reflecting the weak political position of the LGB community, this bill was quite narrow in scope. It did not cover employee benefits such as health insurance. It also stated that plaintiffs could not pursue "disparate impact" legal theories. Those kinds of legal theories, which attack practices that are neutral on their face, are crucial to achieving structural reform. But ENDA foreclosed such legal theories. The bill also precluded affirmative action and exempted many religious entities and the armed forces from coverage. And relevant to this discussion, ENDA did not seek to cover discrimination on the basis of gender identity.

The issue of whether ENDA should ban gender identity discrimination divided the LGB community. On April 24, 2007, Representative Barney Frank introduced a version of ENDA in the House that prohibited discrimination on the basis of gender identity while continuing to exempt religious entities and the armed forces from coverage. Further, the bill had specific language regarding bathrooms and grooming rules that would have foreclosed complaints against many common examples of discrimination against transgender people. Later that year, on September 27, 2007, Representative Frank introduced another version of ENDA that did *not* cover gender identity issues. That bill passed the House on November 7, 2007, but never passed the Senate. And then, on November 7, 2013, a version of ENDA passed the Senate that included some protection for transgender people, but it never passed the House. It also exempted religious entities and the armed forces.

In 2015, LGBT advocates decided to pursue a much more aggressive approach to nondiscrimination protection. Representative David Cicilline introduced a bill called the Equality Act in 2015. It provided for comprehensive nondiscrimination on the basis of sex; sexual orientation; gender identity; pregnancy, childbirth, or a related medical condition of an individual; and sex-based stereotypes. It covered public accommodation, public facilities, public education, federally funded programs, employment, housing, credit, and juries. Rather than broadly exempting religious entities, it provided that the Religious Freedom Restoration Act of 1993 would *not* provide a defense to discrimination. The Equality Act continues to gain increasing support in Congress but has not yet been enacted into law.

Thus, we can see a substantial evolution in attitudes within the legal community, paralleling the legal advances we have seen with respect to marriage equality. After the LGBT community obtained the right to marry, it also became more aggressive in pushing for more protective legislation. Of course, the Equality Act has not become law.

Ironically, the transgender community did not even need new legislation to obtain legal protection. Title VII of the Civil Rights Act of 1964 already banned discrimination on the basis of "sex." Likewise, Title IX of the Education Amendments of 1972 already banned discrimination on the basis of "sex" in federally funded educational programs. Transgender discrimination is typically a straightforward type of "sex" discrimination. A person's employment is conditioned upon presenting as one "sex" rather than another "sex." When a person who is hired as a "female" decides to present as a "male," for example, the person might be fired. Why was the person fired? Because the employer was uncomfortable with the person's presentation of their "sex." Although the plain language of these statutes banned transgender discrimination, it was not until 2020 that this view became entrenched in federal law.

Beginning in 2012, the Obama administration began to think of transgender discrimination as sex discrimination. The EEOC, which has the responsibility to review claims of discrimination that are filed against the federal government, began to rule in favor of transgender plaintiffs under Title VII. Then the EEOC, as well as private plaintiffs, began to file complaints against private employers, using this theory.

The issue of whether Title VII can be used in a case in which the plaintiff alleges she faced discrimination on the basis of her transgender status was before the Supreme Court during the 2019–2020 session. In March 2018, the Sixth Circuit Court of Appeals became the first court of appeals to conclude that bias against a transgendered employee is sex discrimination. The EEOC brought this case on behalf of Aimee Stephens against R. G. & G. R. Harris Funeral Homes.[89] The Supreme Court agreed to hear the case; the Trump administration took a different perspective than the Obama administration on this issue. The Justice Department, which represents the EEOC in the Supreme Court, defended the position of the funeral home. Despite the clear language of Title VII, it argued that it is inconceivable that Congress intended for Title VII to ban transgender discrimination. The public antipathy to transgender people made that idea unthinkable.

Although public sentiment may be moving toward more acceptance of transgender people in the workplace, that acceptance stops at the bathroom. Rigidly sex-segregated bathrooms have been a deeply rooted American belief for decades or even centuries. When the Equal Rights Amendment (ERA) was proposed, one of the key arguments against it was that women would lose the ability to use sex-segregated restrooms. Phyllis Schlafly argued that unisex bathrooms would lead to a unisex society.[90]

It was very important to opponents of the ERA to maintain strict gender roles in society, and the ERA challenged the legitimacy of those norms. And in fact, the proponents of the ERA responded to those arguments by insisting that restrooms would stay sex segregated after the ERA was ratified. The arguments sounded a little like the contemporary marriage debate. ERA proponents reify the importance of sex-segregated bathrooms, just as the proponents of same-sex marriage reify the institution of marriage. ERA proponents could never say they wanted to get rid of sex-segregated bathroom, just as proponents of same-sex marriage could never say they wanted to get rid of state benefits being tied to marriage.

You have to reify bathrooms (or marriage) if you want to have an opportunity to enter them.

As the bathroom debate has morphed into the transgender space, the same fears arise. If someone who is born a male can choose to identify as a woman, and even use a woman's restroom, then the gender-differentiating effect of bathrooms is weakened or lost. After all, the different norms in men's and women's bathrooms have little to do with biology. The stick figure representations of men and women outside the restroom, which always portray the woman in a dress, are the signal that one is entering a deeply sex-differentiated space. Men are expected to urinate in plain sight of other men. Not only do women urinate behind closed doors, but sometimes the entrance to a woman's restroom is set fairly deeply so that no prying eyes can see any women when a door is opened or closed. Women's bodily functions need to be hidden from any men's eyes. By entering a woman's space, the transgender female threatens that social order.

In the litigation involving the use of public bathrooms by transgender people, the relationship between bathrooms and gender norms is very clear. For example, the parents who opposed Gavin Grimm's using the male restroom at their public high school argued that his action might mean that "non-transgender boys would come to school wearing dresses in order to gain access to the girls' restroom."[91] It is hard to believe that these parents really thought boys would wear dresses to gain access to the girls' restroom. But it is plausible to believe that the parents feared that their sons might want to wear a *dress*. A boy or a man in a dress was a horrifying nightmare to them, because they clung so deeply to the importance of gender norms.

Given the public stereotypes against transgender people, it was no surprise that the Trump administration quickly shifted positions from the Obama administration's on the transgender restroom debate. This was a cheap reversal that the Trump administration could make with little or no public outcry. Log Cabin Republicans did not blink an eye as they continued to support Trump despite their supposed concern about people who are transgender. While public polling may show that the American people are more supportive of transgender rights than in the past, that polling may simply reflect people's recitation of what they think is the politically correct position than whether they genuinely want to transform society to help people who are transgender feel more comfortable in daily living, including something as basic as using a public restroom.

The long-term impact of public insults on the public psyche can probably not be overestimated. Although large segments of society may now embrace the entry of same-sex couples into the conservative institution of marriage, that does not mean that they are comfortable working with, living beside, or sharing a bathroom with someone who identifies as transgender. It is easy to articulate support for a group in a survey; it is harder to live those values on a day-to-day basis. Public insults continue to act as a headwind against any reform in this area, and though a statute like Title VII arguably provides them with protection, the dead weight effect makes it unlikely that courts will enforce existing law with teeth.

Many progressive people applauded in June 2020 when the Supreme Court announced its decision in *Bostock v. Clayton County*[92] that Title VII should be understood to ban both sexual orientation and gender identity discrimination. In a 6–3 decision, Justice Gorsuch explained why that conclusion was compelled by the clear language in Title VII banning discrimination "on the basis of sex." He noted that one would not determine whether someone was gay or lesbian or transgender without knowing their sexual identity. In the case of a gay man or a lesbian, one would learn that they are sexually attracted to someone of the same sex; for a transgender person, one would learn that they identify with a gender that is not consistent with the one assigned at birth. Because their status as a gay man, lesbian, or transgender person requires some recognition of their sex, discrimination against them on the basis of that status constitutes discrimination "based on sex." And, Justice Gorsuch concluded, that legal rule is clear even if the original drafters would have been surprised to learn that the statute was interpreted in that way. For the majority, he concluded that the intention of the original drafters is irrelevant when the written text is clear.

That decision is clearly a source of celebration for the LGBTQ+ community because a uniform, federal statute now protects members of the LGBTQ+ community throughout the entire United States of America. No longer can people get married on Sunday and fired on Monday; no longer can people get fired merely for telling an employer that they no longer want to be identified by the sex assigned at birth.

But I urge you to consider the dead weight effect of a potentially positive decision. It has to be there, and of course, it is. The Court is clear about what the decision does *not* do, suggesting that important issues are yet to be resolved in the future. Here is some of the Court's language in response to the defendants' arguments about the dangerous policy precedents set by the *Bostock* decision:

> The employers worry that our decision will sweep beyond Title VII to other federal or state laws that prohibit sex discrimination. And, under Title VII itself, they say sex-segregated bathrooms, locker rooms, and dress codes will prove unsustainable after our decision today. . . . Under Title VII, too, we do not purport to address bathrooms, locker rooms, or anything else of the kind. . . . Separately, the employers fear that complying with Title VII's requirements in cases like ours may require some employers to violate their religious convictions. . . . Because [the Religious Freedom Restoration Act] operates as a kind of super statute, displacing the normal operation of other federal laws, it might supersede Title VII's commands in appropriate cases.[93]

While the majority decision does not purport to resolve issues involving so-called privacy or religious issues, it makes clear that those issues are open and can be resolved in the future. And although the Court claimed to not be resolving these issues, one does not have to look very far to know how they are likely to be resolved. At oral argument, Justice Gorsuch peppered Pam Karlan, who was representing gay plaintiffs, with questions about single-sex bathrooms. She finally had to remind the Court that her client was gay and not transgender and therefore did not raise the gender privacy issues that concerned Justice Gorsuch.[94] Further, the Roberts Court has interpreted religious freedom extremely broadly, especially when the religious claims come from Christians. We already looked at the *Masterpiece Cake Shop* decision; there have been many others in the areas of the Affordable Care Act's mandate for coverage of contraception[95] and the right of states not to fund religious schools with public tax dollars,[96] in which the Court has diluted constitutional or statutory rights to protect Christians from so-called discrimination.

Thus, the Court's assertion that the privacy and religious issues are "open" is disingenuous. Those issues are highlighted in the Court's opinion to suggest to future defendants to be sure to raise them. In fact, the Court chides the defendant in the transgender case for failing to pursue its reli-gious freedom argument and then says: "None of the employers before us today represent in this Court that compliance with Title VII will infringe their own religious liberties in any way."[97] The dead weight was planted firmly. It is there to limit exercises of Title VII in the future.

6 Abortion

When a woman* takes a home pregnancy test in the United States and learns that she is likely to be pregnant, she must bear an onslaught of insults if she chooses to terminate her pregnancy. Outside the walls of the abortion clinic, she is likely to see enlarged and distorted images of fetuses sucking their thumbs, which are designed to cast her as a cruel murderer. In more than a dozen states, she will also be handed a so-called informed consent brochure that is full of distorted fetuses and misinformation about her mental health and cancer risk, intended to scare her into carrying the fetus to term rather than to inform her about genuine medical risks. Only young mothers with robust, healthy babies are ever smiling in these brochures.

In this chapter, I argue that we can better comprehend the success of the antiabortion movement if we understand the dead weight effect of these public insults. They help limit the effectiveness of the constitutional

* While I recognize that some transgender men have become pregnant and that some pregnant people identify as gender nonbinary, I use the term "pregnant woman" in this chapter to signify the historical mistreatment of people who identify as women and have become pregnant. It is, of course, likely that this mistreatment will extend to transgender men and gender nonbinary individuals in the future who become pregnant.

right to choose to terminate a pregnancy. As of June 2020, six states had only one abortion clinic left. After a yearlong battle, the state of Missouri's embattled, sole abortion clinic learned in May 2020 that it could keep its doors open for another year, despite the state's public insult campaign against its operations.[1] Missouri also tried to terrorize women to deter them from having an abortion at that lone clinic. Until publication of an exposé in June 2019 by MSNBC reporter Rachel Maddow, who called the practice a "state-sanctioned sexual assault," Missouri required women to have a medically unnecessary, invasive pelvic exam before they could terminate their pregnancies.[2] As we will see, the dead weight effect on the right to choose to terminate a pregnancy is very powerful and should not be underestimated as abortion clinics become a scarce resource in the United States.

The antiabortion public insult strategy evolved over time. When the Supreme Court decided *Roe v. Wade*, 410 U.S. 113 (1973), the Court was told nothing about the plaintiff's background, how she became pregnant, and why she wanted to terminate her pregnancy. Plaintiff Norma McCorvey was a truly anonymous participant in the lawsuit. She stayed anonymous until the 1980s, when she started attending rallies in support of abortion rights. The legal theory behind the pro-choice litigation strategy was that abortion was a "private" matter, and the courts did not need to know the identity of the woman seeking an abortion.

That "privacy" understanding, however, soon broke down as antiabortion advocates began to use stories and voices to discuss the issue in political and legal circles. In 1984, antiabortion activists produced a film called *The Silent Scream*, in which Dr. Bernard Nathanson narrated a purported abortion procedure in which a "lethal weapon" "dismembers, crushes, destroys" and "tears the child apart," while ominous music is played in the background, ending on a "feverish pitch," described as the fetus's "silent scream."[3] "On major network television, the fetus rose to instant stardom, as *The Silent Scream* . . . was aired at least five different times in one month, and one well-known reporter, holding up a fetus in a jar before 10 million viewers, announced: 'This thing being aborted, this potential person, sure *looks like* a baby!'"[4] Antiabortion advocates also published a book entitled *Aborted Women* in 1987, which provided the stories of twenty women who said they regretted their decision to have an abortion.[5] For example, women who had become pregnant as a result of rape or incest argued that their abortions merely served to hide their sexual abuse rather than provide them with agency in their lives. They were described as "rape hostages," a powerful, insulting, and demeaning image.

Beginning in the 1990s, the plaintiffs in both *Roe v. Wade* and its companion case, *Doe v. Bolton*, 410 U.S. 179 (1973), spoke out publicly *against* the Supreme Court's pro-choice decisions. After supporting the *Roe* decision for decades and quitting her job as marketing director at a Dallas abortion clinic, Norma McCorvey became a religious fundamentalist in 1995 and disavowed *Roe* as well as her lesbian relationships.[6] She joined Operation Rescue for a while but then converted to Catholicism and began traveling around the country speaking out against abortion.[7] She filed an unsuccessful lawsuit in 2003 to invalidate the *Roe v. Wade* decision.[8] As part of that lawsuit, she filed affidavits from nearly one thousand women who stated they had had abortions and suffered long-term emotional damage and impaired relationships as a result of that decision, as well as affidavits from workers at abortion clinics alleging that "women are often herded through their procedures with little or no medical or emotional counseling."[9]

Although less well known, Sandra Cano, who was the plaintiff in *Doe v. Bolton*, also spoke out against the legality of abortions and alleged that she had been misled and coerced during the course of the abortion rights litigation. In a 1989 interview, she claimed that she only sought legal advice for assistance in retaining custody of her children while she was pregnant.[10] She said that when her lawyers gained permission for her to have an abortion when she was about six months pregnant, she fled Georgia for Oklahoma. In 2005, testifying before the Subcommittee on the Constitution of the Senate Judiciary Committee, she said: "How can cunning, wicked lawyers use an uneducated, defenseless pregnant women to twist the American court system in such a fraudulent way? . . . Doe v. Bolton is based on a lie and deceit."[11] Like McCorvey, she unsuccessfully sought to have her case overturned and submitted "affivadits from over one thousand women hurt by abortion."[12]

While pro-choice litigators initially thought abortion cases should be pushed as pure "privacy" matters, they came to change course and accept the importance of voices' briefs in the late 1980s. Professor Linda

Edwards credits abortion rights activist Lynne Paltrow for devising the tactic of filing an amicus brief with women's voices as part of the effort to persuade the Supreme Court not to overturn *Roe v. Wade* in 1986 in *Thornburgh v. American College of Obstetricians and Gynecologists*, 476 U.S. 747 (1986).[13] Paltrow carefully wove excerpts from the letters into her legal argument, documenting the harm to some women when they or a loved one had had to obtain a back-alley, illegal abortion in the 1960s and the relief to other women when they were able to procure a safe, legal abortion, which often enabled them to continue to take care of their children, continue their education, keep their jobs, or avoid an unwanted marriage. Three decades later, in 2016, when *Roe* was again at risk of being overturned, more than one hundred lawyers, law professors, and former judges filed a brief in *Whole Woman's Health v. Hellerstedt*[14] describing women's decisions to terminate their pregnancies.[15] Professor Edwards says that "voices briefs are now *de rigueur*."[16]

While recognizing the difficulty of measuring the impact of any legal strategy, Professor Edwards suggests that the pro-choice voices' briefs may have influenced the statement in the 1992 *Planned Parenthood v. Casey* joint opinion (which was joined by Justice Anthony Kennedy) that women's "suffering is too intimate and personal for the State to insist without more, upon its vision of the woman's role, however dominant that vision has been in the course of our history and culture. The destiny of the woman must be shaped to a large extent on her own conception of her spiritual imperatives and her place in society."[17] Likewise, she credits the antiabortion voices' briefs with encouraging Justice Kennedy to write in the 2007 *Gonzales v. Carhart* majority opinion: "While we find no reliable data to measure the phenomenon, it seems unexceptionable to conclude some women come to regret their choice to abort the infant life they once created and sustained."[18] The Justice Kennedy who joined the *Casey* opinion in 1992 seems to have changed his understanding of the importance of women's charting their own destiny by the time he wrote the *Carhart* opinion in 2007. Professor Edwards credits the antiabortion voices' briefs with assisting that transition. While I recognize the role that such briefs may have played in Justice Kennedy's perspective, it is also likely that he was influenced by the powerful use of the public insult playbook by antiabortion forces. This chapter highlights some of those efforts.

The pro-choice community came to embrace the importance of filling briefs with stories about the positive impact of reproductive choice in women's lives, but the antiabortion movement arguably used the strategy more effectively, drawing on some elements of the public insult playbook.[19] Insults simply may be more effective than success stories. While the pro-choice community sought to tell positive stories of the impact that reproductive freedom had on women's lives, the antiabortion movement sought to vilify women who had abortions as well as their doctors, who were dubbed "abortion doctors" rather than gynecologists. In the quotes from Supreme Court opinions, notice how the Court transforms abortion from a reproductive decision central to a woman's destiny to aborting an "infant life." Instead of being about terminating a pregnancy, it is about terminating a life. The antiabortion movement has largely won this image battle, with Justice Thomas leading the charge with his comparison of contemporary abortion practices with euthanasia[20] and many states rushing to criminalize nearly all abortions in the hope of finally overturning *Roe*. The power of insults has been profound and effective.

Norma McCorvey's own story can provide insights into how the use of narratives can act as a form of coercion. A *Vanity Fair* article by Joshua Prager suggests she felt misused by her pro-choice lawyers and sought to cash in on her fame within the abortion rights movement in the 1980s and early 1990s.[21] Then, McCorvey famously changed sides in 1995. But on her deathbed, during an interview for a documentary, McCorvey indicated that she had switched sides for money. "'I think it was a mutual thing,' she says. 'I took their money, they'd put me out in front of the camera and tell me what to say.' She adds, 'I am a good actress.'"[22] Before McCorvey's deathbed confession, Prager concluded: "But in truth McCorvey has long been less pro-choice or pro-life than pro-Norma. And she has played Jane Roe every which way, venturing far from the original script to wring a living from the issue that has come to define her existence."[23]

McCorvey's experience should certainly give us pause to consider the impact on a person's life when their story becomes political fodder. In the documentary that reports McCorvey's deathbed confession and the ways in which she was paid to support antiabortion positions, Reverand Rob Schenck is quoted as saying: "What we did with Norma was highly unethical."[24] By contrast, Tarana Burke, who coined the phrase "MeToo" in 2006 but who attained sustained public attention in 2017 when the phrase was used by actress Ashley Judd, was more cautious about coming forward as part of the #MeToo movement. She was concerned that these white female actresses would appropriate her term while doing little to assist the Black women she was trying to help in Brooklyn, New York. One would hope that the activists who are seeking to publicize the experiences of people like Norma McCorvey and Tarana Burke would do their utmost to make sure those voices are heard in a way that is respectful and empowering. I return to this theme in chapter 7 when I explore the effectiveness of collective efforts for empowerment, like the #MeToo movement.

Within this book's framework, we can understand reproductive rights as an arena in which the antiabortion movement has deployed public insults as a very effective dead weight. The antiabortion movement has not yet persuaded the Supreme Court to reverse *Roe v. Wade*. Nonetheless, it has used a grassroots campaign to scare and intimidate women from exercising their right to terminate their pregnancies. Efforts to directly ban such intimidation by state courts and legislatures have been struck down by the Supreme Court. Congress's efforts to protect women from harassment at clinics have been largely ineffective.

This chapter looks at two areas in which the antiabortion movement has powerfully deployed public insults to make it more difficult for women to terminate their pregnancies: (1) clinic harassment and (2) draconian informed consent laws. In both cases, the public insult playbook has been very effective as a dead weight on the right to choose to terminate a pregnancy.

ABORTION INTIMIDATION AND HARASSMENT

Clinic harassment, a powerful and emotionally scarring tactic in its own right, has fostered a political climate that has even led to murder. Antiabortion zealots murdered Dr. David Gunn and Dr. George Patterson in 1993; Dr. John Bayard Britton in 1994; Dr. Barnett Slepian in 1998; Dr. George Tiller in 2009; and Colorado Springs police officer Garrett Swasey, along with civilians Ke'Arre Stewart and Jennifer Markovsky, in 2015. The Colorado shooter "told police he dreamed he'll be met in Heaven by aborted fetuses wanting to thank him for saving unborn babies."[25] Other than prosecuting antiabortion activists who have murdered doctors, the legal system has offered no effective remedy against the harassment and intimidation of pregnant women and their doctors.

While most antiabortion activists do not condone murder as a way to end abortions, for decades activists have been using the combination of photography and the internet to intimidate women seeking abortions. As reported by the *Wall Street Journal* in 2002, antiabortion activists photograph women getting out of their cars to enter an abortion clinic and then yell: "You'll have nightmares about this day the rest of your life. . . . Your sin won't be hidden or forgotten."[26] A 2002 *Chicago Tribune* story focused on a woman who had had an abortion and whose photographs, along with her medical records, were published on the website of Missionaries to the Unborn, next to a photograph of Adolph Hitler.[27] The owner of one such internet site, called Abortion Cams, openly stated that his goal was "to deter women from seeking abortions; on the site, he calls women who get abortions 'homicidal mothers' who deserve punishment."[28] He bragged: "We have anecdotal evidence every week that people arrive at the clinic, see the cameras, and turn around and leave. . . . There are people who are deterred because of the knowledge that their shameful acts are going to be exposed."[29]

An example of the kind of imagery used by these groups is a placard frequently used by Missionaries to the Preborn,[30] which is prominently featured on their website. It displays a large handheld sign with the message "THIS IS YOUR NEIGHBOR" with an enlarged image of a fetus huddled with an umbilical cord. In the image, the sign is displayed on a crowded public roadway. A young boy can be seen behind the sign, holding it up. The sign conveys a gripping message that aborting a fetus is killing your neighbor, with the suggestion that the fetus could otherwise become the white boy displayed holding the sign.

In 2015, an antiabortion activist group called Center for Medical Progress released a series of undercover videos that sought to prove that Planned Parenthood engaged in illegal sales of harvested fetal tissue. While that effort did not result in any criminal charges being leveled against Planned Parenthood, it was part of a public campaign to prompt a reaction of visceral horror among the public. In an interview with Ruth Graham in 2015, antiabortion activist Eric Scheidler argues that the "pro-life movement has certainly gotten a huge boost from the videos."[31] Speaking in 2015, he argued that "Planned Parenthood will never really come out from under this scandal." Antiabortion activist Monica Miller agrees about the impact of the Planned Parenthood videos. She says: "The most valuable aspect of the Center for Medical Progress videos is not what the abortion providers say about abortion, rather it's the video of the freshly-killed preborn babies in the back room where technicians are rummaging through the body parts of the babies. It is a glimpse of hell, and the abortion industry will never be able to run from such images!"[32] The campaign to defund Planned Parenthood has achieved notable success since 2015, with the Trump administration defunding it from Title X community health centers in 2019.[33]

Scheidler has led the campaign to display enlarged, distorted images of fetuses on city streets and elsewhere. In the Ruth Graham interview, he explained how he uses events that he calls "Face the Truth" tours, "in which volunteers station themselves at major intersections holding large signs featuring photographs of aborted fetuses. At a typical event, volunteers stand at least 20 feet apart from each other along all four prongs of an intersection, to make sure that no drivers can escape from viewing them." While acknowledging these signs make some people feel uncomfortable, he argues for their use because of their impact. He asserts that it is important to take the risk of offending some people because otherwise it is at the "cost of showing the reality of these things."[34] Jonathan Van Maren has justified this use of what he calls "abortion victim photos" by saying: "The photographic evidence of injustice is not pleasant to look at it, but it is essential that we as a society are consistently reminded that not everyone is accorded the same rights that we are, and that we should not rest until that horrifying inequity is addressed."[35]

Cities and states have sought to restrict the use of these graphic displays or protests even if the protesters are not threatening violence. The courts have struck down many of those measures or interpreted them so narrowly as to make them ineffectual. The suburb of Brookfield, Wisconsin, enacted one of the first measures, in response to picketing outside the home of a doctor who performed abortions. The city banned all picketing "before or about the residence of any individual."[36] In a 6–3 opinion in *Frisby v. Schultz*, 487 U.S. 474 (1988), in which liberal Justices William Brennan, Thurgood Marshall, and John Paul Stevens dissented, the Supreme Court upheld this ordinance, with the narrowing construction that it only applied to picketing targeted at a single residence. Because the picketing was targeted at an individual's home (rather than business), the Court found: "The resident is figuratively and perhaps literally, trapped within the home, and because of the unique and subtle impact of such picketing is left with no ready means of avoiding the unwanted speech."[37] Consistent with this book's thesis, legal tools were available to address the public insult assault when the harassment was directed at one's home or "citadel."[38] Those with the economic privilege of owning a private residence in an upscale suburb can find protection within the law. The ordinance protected the physician from protesters surrounding his home; it did not protect the woman seeking an abortion from any picketing at the health-care center where she obtained it.

In the aftermath of the *Frisby* decision, a Florida state court judge enjoined antiabortion protesters from engaging in protest activities at and near abortion clinics. The case stemmed from a trial court judge issuing an injunction to bar Operation Rescue from trespassing at an abortion clinic.[39] The trial court's decision documented the varied practices used by Operation Rescue to impede women's access to abortions, including the recording of license plate numbers and the jamming of clinic telephone lines, making "it impossible for clinic staff to summon an ambulance to transfer any patient to the hospital should an emergency arise."[40] The injunction forbade protesters from approaching closer than thirty-six feet from the property line; precluded the use of bullhorns and other amplified means of communication "or other sounds or images observable to or within earshot of the patients inside the Clinic"; precluded protesters from physically approaching any person within three hundred feet of the clinic and from coming within three hundred feet of the residences of the employees; and "at all times on all days, from physically abusing, grabbing, intimidating, harassing, touching, pushing, shoving, crowding or assaulting persons entering or leaving work at or using services at the petitioners' Clinic or trying to gain access to, or leave, any of the homes of owners, staff or patients of the Clinic."[41] This injunction was entered after a more narrow one had failed to stop the trespassing and harassment, and after three days of hearings about the impact of the protesters' actions on the women seeking abortions and their health-care providers.

The Florida Supreme Court approved the breadth of the state court injunction, finding that the First Amendment "gives the picketer no boon to jeopardize the health, safety, and rights of others. No citizen has the right to insert a foot in the hospital or clinic door and insist on being heard— while purposefully blocking the door to those in genuine need of medical services. No picketer can force speech into the captive ear of the unwilling and disabled."[42] In addition to *Frisby*, the Florida Supreme Court found that its injunction was consistent with injunctions upheld by numerous federal courts.

Nonetheless, in *Madsen v. Women's Health Center*, 512 U.S. 753 (1994), the US Supreme Court found that *Frisby* could not be used to justify such a broad injunction, where most of its provisions were for the purpose of protecting access to the clinic rather than protection of the homes of the health-care providers. First, the Court assessed the constitutionality of the thirty-six-foot speech-free buffer zone. The trial court had chosen thirty-six feet so as to push protesters across the street, where they could "still be seen and heard from the clinic parking lots."[43] But the Court overturned that aspect of the buffer that extended to surrounding private property. While a buffer to "facilitate the orderly flow of traffic" was permissible, it was not permissible for the buffer to serve the purpose of shielding patients and staff from being bombarded by speech within a few feet of the clinic entrance.

Second, the Supreme Court upheld a "high noise level" restriction during workdays, concluding that "[n]oise control is particularly important around hospitals and medical facilities during surgery and recovery periods" but overturned the "images observable" provision of the state court injunction.[44] The Court found "it is much easier for the clinic to pull its curtains than for a patient to stop up her ears, and no more is required to avoid seeing placards through the windows of the clinic."[45] The Court found that the fact that some patients might find the images "disagreeable" was not a sufficient basis to allow the state to curtail their use under First Amendment doctrine. Thus, the Court emboldened antiabortion activists to continue to use enlarged, distorted images of fetuses around abortion clinics as a tool despite evidence that those images were for the purpose of raising the "level of anxiety and hypertension suffered by the patients inside the clinic."[46]

Finally, the Court overturned a prohibition against picketing, demonstrating, or using sound equipment within three hundred feet of the residences of clinic staff. Distinguishing *Frisby*, the Court concluded that the three-hundred-foot zone was excessive, because it would ban "general marching through residential neighborhoods, or even walking a route in front of an entire block of houses."[47] While it was appropriate to protect the entrance to a single house, the Court found it was not constitutionally permissible to use a three-hundred-foot buffer zone to protect a block of homes. The "citadel" rule turned out to be quite narrow. Doctors' homes, but not the clinics that patients needed to enter, could be protected from aggressive harassment.

Similarly, the US Supreme Court thwarted a New York federal district court judge who tried to enter an effective injunction against abortion protesters outside a clinic. Because Operation Rescue protesters blocked doorways and threatened the safety of entering patients and employees, the federal district court judge put in place a fixed buffer zone around the clinic doorways, driveways, and driveway entrances, as well as a floating fifteen-foot buffer zone around patients as they sought to enter the clinic. This injunction was put in place after the defendants had been cited with contempt on five occasions for violating a more limited injunction, and after the district court held thirty-nine days of hearings. Even though the district court judge tried to accommodate the free speech rights of the protesters by allowing two "sidewalk counselors" to approach the patient within the fifteen-foot buffer zone, the Supreme Court found the floating buffer zone to be unconstitutional in *Schenck v. Pro-Choice Network of Western New York*, 519 U.S. 357 (1997).

Although the district court judge had issued this injunction after hearing thirty-nine days of testimony, the Supreme Court concluded that it violated the First Amendment by "burden[ing] more speech than is necessary to serve the relevant governmental interests."[48] Because the sidewalk was only seventeen feet wide, the Court was concerned that "protesters who wish to walk alongside an individual entering or leaving the clinic are pushed into the street, unless the individual walks a straight line on the outer edges of the sidewalk."[49] The Court also overturned fifteen-foot buffer zones around patient vehicles, because the Court found that it "contradicts the commonsense notion that a more limited injunction . . . would be sufficient to ensure that drivers are not confused about how to enter the clinic and are able to gain access to its driveways and parking lots safely and easily."[50] Although appellate courts usually defer to the factual findings of trial court judges, especially when they have held thirty-nine days of hearings, the Supreme Court decided to apply "common sense" to overturn the floating buffer zones. The Supreme Court was more concerned with whether protesters, who had already been held in contempt of court five times because of their aggressive harassment of clinic patients, might have to step into the street to maintain a mere fifteen-foot floating buffer zone. While a thirty-five-foot fixed buffer was found constitutional in *Madsen*, a mere fifteen-foot floating buffer was not found constitutional in *Schenck*. One can see how the Supreme Court's precedent was narrowing the zone of protection from harassment and violence for women seeking abortion services.

The next case to reach the Supreme Court involved a state legislature trying to proactively protect abortion clinics rather than rely on trespass law and contempt citations to do so. In 1993, before the Supreme Court decided *Madsen* or *Schenck*, Colorado passed a statute that made it unlawful for any person to "knowingly approach" within *eight* feet of another person, without that person's consent, "for the purpose of passing a leaflet or handbill to, displaying a sign to, or engaging in oral protest, education, or counseling with such other person."[51] The law also required protesters to stay at least one hundred feet from any entrance door to a health-care facility. In upholding the statute, the Court noted that the "8-foot restriction on an unwanted physical approach leaves ample room to communicate a message through speech. Signs, pictures, and voice itself can across an 8-foot gap with ease."[52] The eight-foot restriction in no way limited the display of enlarged and distorted photos of fetuses by loud protesters.

Over a vigorous dissent by Justice Antonin Scalia, the Supreme Court in *Hill v. Colorado*, 530 U.S. 703 (2000), upheld the statute, finding that it was a narrowly tailored, content-neutral, time, place, and manner regulation. Justice Scalia's dissent is instructive because it shows the limits that conservatives believe apply to women's right to be free from harassment when seeking to access abortion services. Scalia does not just go after the *Hill* majority opinion; he criticizes the narrow line of cases lead-ing up to *Hill*:

> What is before us, after all, is a speech regulation directed against the oppo-nents of abortion, and it therefore enjoys the benefit of the "ad hoc nullifica-tion machine" that the Court has set in motion to push aside whatever doctrines of constitutional law stand in the way of that highly favored prac-tice [citing *Madsen*]. Having deprived abortion opponents of the political right to persuade the electorate that abortion should be restricted by law, the Court today continues and expands its assault upon their individual rights to persuade women contemplating abortion that what they are doing is wrong. Because, like the rest of our abortion jurisprudence, today's deci-sion is in stark contradiction of the constitutional principles we apply in other contexts, I dissent.[53]

Justice Scalia's dissent drew an explicit connection between the abor-tion protesters and the substantive right itself. Even though the Supreme Court had started to retreat from its absolute protection of abortion in the first trimester of pregnancy in *Planned Parenthood v. Casey*, 505 U.S. 833 (1992) (discussed below), Justice Scalia primarily understood that case law as preventing states from banning abortion altogether. Because states could not ban abortions, he thought it important that antiabortion activists have every available tool to "persuade" women not to obtain an abortion. Although he dissented in *Madsen*, he apparently thought those tools of per-suasion should include blockading clinic doors. Whereas Scalia considered an opinion like *Hill v. Colorado* to reflect an "assault" on the right of people to object to abortions, I see these cases as reflecting the very narrow protec-tions offered to women who are being verbally and physically assaulted by antiabortion activists. Scalia clearly wanted the First Amendment to shield antiabortion activists from any limits on their campaign. It is no surprise that the rights of antiabortion activists to protest have expanded at the same time that state legislatures have increasingly sought to restrict abor-tion rights. While Scalia did not live to see the Supreme Court packed with antiabortion justices, the antiabortion campaign was simultaneously suc-cessful in both the streets and state legislatures. Tying together the protest-ers, the state legislatures, and the courts shows the power of public insults to act as a barrier to the exercise of existing rights while also showing its ability to impose new barriers in the future. *Hill v. Colorado* was the narrowest of victories for women seeking safe access to abortion clinics.

State courts and legislatures were not the only entity trying to limit intimidation and harassment by antiabortion activists. In 1994, upon the recommendation of a task force established by Attorney General Janet Reno, Congress responded to this problem by enacting the Freedom of Access to Clinic Entrances Act of 1994 (FACE).[54] FACE provides a private right of action against anyone who

> by threat of force or by physical obstruction, intentionally injures, intimidates or interferes with, or attempts to injure, intimidate or interfere with, any person because that person is or has been, or in order to intimidate such person or any other person or any class of persons from, obtaining or providing reproductive health services.[55]

By its language, FACE only provides a cause of action when there is a "threat of force" or "physical obstruction." The graphic display of distorted fetuses and aggressive "sidewalk counseling" is not specifically prohibited. Those limitations have helped the statute pass First Amendment scrutiny but also have done little to prevent the intimidation itself.[56] As the Fourth Circuit has said, the statute "does not prohibit protestors from praying, chanting, counseling, carrying signs, distributing handbills or otherwise expressing opposition to abortion, so long as these activities are carried out in a non-violent, non-obstructive manner."[57] The most far-reaching application of this statute, over a vigorous dissent, was its application to "wanted posters" that were circulated with lines drawn through the names of doctors who performed abortion services and who had already been killed or wounded. In context, the district court concluded, and the Ninth Circuit affirmed, that those posters displayed an intent to harm the abortion providers, because three abortion providers had been killed soon after their identities were displayed on previous posters.[58] Thus, FACE could be used to stop chilling death threats but could not be used to stop the broader strategy of displaying larger-than-life images of fetuses to intimidate women from obtaining abortion services.

And what has been the impact of this aggressive antiabortion activism through distorted images of fetuses? While cause and effect are difficult to establish, a wide range of authors have argued that this public insult campaign has had a powerful impact on society's views on abortion.

In 1987, Rosalind Petchesky argued that "antiabortionists in both the United States and Britain have long applied the principle that a picture of a dead fetus is worth a thousand words. Chaste silhouettes of the fetal form, or voyeuristic-necrophilic photographs of its remains, litter the background of any abortion talk."[59] Petchesky traced the image of a fetus as a "curled-up profile, with its enlarged head and finlike arms, suspending in its balloon of amniotic fluid" to its first appearance in a June 1962 issue of *Look* magazine. "In every picture the fetus is solitary, dangling in the air (or its sac) with nothing to connect it to any life-support system."[60]

Petchesky tied this use of fetal images to a public insult campaign against women seeking abortions.

> When legions of right-wing women in the antiabortion movement brandish pictures of gory dead or dreamlike space-floating fetuses outside clinics or in demonstrations, they are participating in a visual pageant that directly degrades women—and thus themselves. Wafting these fetus-pictures as icons, literal fetishes, they both propagate and celebrate the image of the fetus as autonomous space-hero and the pregnant woman as "empty space." Their visual statements are straightforward representations of the antifeminist ideas they (and their male cohorts) support.[61]

Writing in 1987, Petchesky anticipated the use of these distorted visual representations, which figuratively removed the fetus from a pregnant woman's body, to scare women away from seeking abortions and to persuade judges to cut back on women's access to reproductive services.

Similarly, Celeste Condit, who studied rhetorical criticism, argued in 1990 that the enlarged and distorted fetal images have been an effective cornerstone of the antiabortion campaign:

> The pictures—a baby-like fetus, a smiling fetus, a fetus that sucks its thumb. Butchered fetuses—bloody mounds of human tissue hacked arms, mangled legs, crushed skulls. Without these compelling and brutal photographs the American abortion controversy probably would not continue. But the photographs have been widely disseminated throughout the country—passed through church pews, tucked under windshield wipers, flashed on screens in public meetings.[62]

These pictures create "revulsion at killing babies,"[63] leading many members of the public to view the pregnant woman as the enemy of the fetus rather than the person choosing to sustain the fetus's life.

More recently, Australian Kirsty McLaren has argued that these fetal images have created "moral shocks and emotional meanings" which in turn have popularized antiabortion views.[64] She argues that "emotion and visual culture have historically been neglected by social movement studies."[65] She concluded from her study of the use of visual imagery in the antiabortion movement that "visual repertoires are central of expressive politics and provide compelling evidence of how emotions animate and sustain social movement activity."[66] Her arguments underscore the power of public insults; strong emotional responses help sustain social movements.

Linda Myrsiades argued that these fetal images—which are separated from the pregnant woman's uterus—have transformed the pregnant woman to a "danger from which the government must protect the [fetus], enactments of which appear in prosecutions of mothers for foetal abuse."[67] She traced the broad use of these fetal images as being a causal factor in the prosecution of pregnant women in thirty states for not meeting the "standards of a duty of care in the best interest of the child in prosecutions that related to [fetal] rights."[68] While causation is always difficult to prove, her argument is consistent with the evidence presented in this book that public insults (in this instance in the form of visual imagery) can act as a dead weight against the enforcement of basic civil rights. As pregnant women become disembodied from their uterus, they can more easily be viewed as the "danger" from which the state must protect the "unborn child." Women "were constituted as a foetus' worst nightmare, monster mothers who would eat their young and who, therefore, must be regulated and controlled by those with a constitutional interest in foetal rights, that is, the state. In the construction of such regulation and control, the protection of women was partially, if not largely, displaced by protection of the foetus, woman was separated from mother, and the womb from the woman."[69]

The success of the antiabortion movement in influencing how society views abortions can be seen in its impact on pro-choice accounts of women who speak publicly about their decisions to have an abortion. Mallary

Allen did a careful investigation of the pro-choice narratives published on the internet through a website called ImNotSorry.net.[70] She concluded that, beginning in the 1990s, abortion-rights advocates responded to the "growing public disdain for unqualified abortion rights" by emphasizing "abortion as a rare, regrettable option."[71] She argued that this change in pro-choice abortion rhetoric from the 1970s and 1980s, when it was "packaged" as an important civil right, reflected that "abortion rights today are more contentious, especially for advocates, than in the past."[72] In other words, powerful antiabortion rhetoric has transformed abortion advocacy into a more apologetic posture in which the right, itself, can more easily be diluted by the courts and legislatures.

These cultural and legal transformations can only be seen when we include the impact of verbal and visual imagery in our understanding of societal change. In the next part of this chapter, I examine how legal doctrine has bowed to these powerful story lines about pregnant women and thereby limited the ability of pregnant women to choose to terminate their pregnancies without harassment or intimidation.

STATE-IMPOSED UNINFORMED CONSENT

The public insult campaign to scare and intimidate women from choosing to terminate their pregnancies has intruded upon the doctor-patient relationship. In many states, doctors are required to provide women with deeply misleading descriptions of abortions and pregnancies in an attempt to "persuade" them not to terminate their pregnancies. The enlarged pictures of fetuses that are common on the streets in front of clinics are prominently displayed in brochures that many states require women to receive as part of the so-called informed consent aspect of their requested medical treatment. These states typically provide distorted images of fetuses, as if those fetuses live independently outside women's bodies, along with inaccurate statements about the medical risks of abortions compared to childbirth.

While the courts *could* preclude the state from imposing these inaccurate and irrelevant messages on pregnant women as a condition of their obtaining a legal abortion, they have refrained from doing so in recent years. Although there has been a lot of discussion about the impact of *Planned Parenthood of Southeastern Pennsylvania v. Casey*[73] on a state's ability to creative restrictive barriers to abortion services,[74] the impact of that decision on a state's use of so-called informed consent rules to coerce women into continuing their pregnancies has been largely ignored. The *Casey* Court affirmed the right of the state to use informed consent rules to persuade pregnant women not to terminate their pregnancies.[75] Since the 1992 *Casey* decision, there has been a race to the bottom as states try to force physicians and other medical personnel to pummel pregnant women with information in the name of informed consent that really has nothing to do with the traditional concept of consent.[76] Rather than treat pregnant women like patients who are entitled to have appropriate medical information to make an informed decision whether to choose a particular medical procedure, many states treat pregnant women as merely a vessel to reflect their own notion of women's proper destiny as mothers.

Many states insist that women be handed glossy brochures depicting four-week fetuses that are magnified into portrayals of living children.[77] They are told that their decision to terminate their pregnancy is likely to lead to increased risks of breast cancer, depression, and future fertility problem. Childbirth, by contrast, is romantically portrayed as a risk-free, wholly positive experience, consistent with their natural destiny as mothers. Under the guise of informed consent, these publications intrude into a woman's decision-making process by portraying pregnant women as if they are mothers, rather than as women who are entitled to decide whether they want to become mothers. Unsuccessful arguments have been made that such informed consent rules violate women's liberty interest by imposing an undue burden in their path to reproductive freedom and that such rules violate a physician's First Amendment interest by forcing doctors to utter words that are inconsistent with their own views about how to best treat a patient.[78] In these portrayals of pregnancy, the pregnant woman is the villain-mother who is trying to kill her baby.

Alabama,[79] Arizona,[80] Georgia,[81] Indiana,[82] Kansas,[83] Louisiana,[84] North Carolina,[85] North Dakota,[86] Oklahoma,[87] Texas,[88] West Virginia,[89] and Wisconsin[90] require pregnant women who are seeking to terminate their pregnancies to receive a lengthy, glossy, and misleading brochure under the guise of "informed consent."[91] No parallel requirements exist for women who plan to try to take their pregnancy to term. In that instance, physicians merely use their professional expertise to provide informed consent, as relevant to the woman's individual experience. I summarize several of these brochures here to give the reader a sense of their misleading character.

Indiana: The *Abortion Informed Consent* brochure[92] is a fifteen-page glossy publication required by Indiana law.[93] "At least eighteen hours before an abortion, the physician who is to perform your abortion is required to provide you with a color copy of this brochure."[94] By handing the brochure to the patient, the physician is implicitly approving its message. The brochure includes five pages of descriptions and illustrations of the fetus from two to forty weeks' gestation. There are then four pages on the risks of having an abortion, with "death" listed as one of the nonquantified possibilities. Information about assistance with pregnancy, childbirth, and adoption is provided, with no mention of how to access abortion services.

Kansas: The *If You Are Pregnant* brochure[95] is thirty-two pages in length and is required by the Woman's Right-to-Know Act.[96] Its cover features an enlarged photo of a nine-week fetus. It describes the fetus as an "unborn child." It has eleven pages of medical illustrations and describes the fetus from two to forty weeks. Unlike other states, which have descriptions accompanying the photos that use terms like "fetus" or "embryo" or "zygote," Kansas uses the term "unborn child" throughout its brochure. It also magnifies the images, in some cases, to show the skull to make the fetus appear more childlike. It then has eleven pages on the medical risks of abortion. Under the long-term medical risks of abortion, it lists complications with future childbearing and breast cancer. The discussion under the heading "Breast Cancer" is somewhat balanced, but one can imagine that such a heading under the topic of "long-term medical risks" might cause a woman to assume that the breast cancer discussion will be fairly dire. Under the heading "Psychological Risk of Abortion," the state only lists negative effects. Other states, such as Arizona, are more balanced in discussing the possible psychological effects and make statements like, "Women may have both positive and negative feelings after having an abortion." If the woman reaches page 28 of the Kansas brochure, then she may learn of the "medical risks of childbirth" but be reassured that "[c]ontinuing a pregnancy and delivering a baby is usually a safe, healthy process." There is no reference to postpartum depression. And of course, women are told about adoption and childbirth resources but not about any abortion-related resources.

North Carolina: The *A Woman's Right to Know* brochure[97] is twenty-eight pages in length and is required by Session Law 2011-405.[98] It contains three-by-three-inch medical illustrations of the fetus from two to forty weeks. Even though the description, for example, of a six- to eight-week embryo says the embryo is less than one-quarter inch in length, the displayed image is three inches in length (twelve times the actual size of the embryo). Discussion of the abortion procedure does not begin until page 17. The brochure than discusses all the possible medical risks of having an abortion for four pages. The brochure inaccurately says that for women who choose medical abortions, "three of 1000 will have a major complication requiring hospital admission, surgery or blood transfusion."[99] In fact, researchers have found that only one in ten thousand women who have had any kind of abortion make emergency room visits following the abortion, and of those women, half were sent home with no medical treatment at all. Only one in five, of the one in ten thousand, "involved a major complication that required an overnight hospital stay, a blood transfusion or surgery."[100] In other words, the accurate figure would be one in fifty thousand (0.00002) rather than one in ten thousand (0.0001) for *all* kinds of abortions. The brochure than offers a comparison between the risks of abortion and delivery. While acknowledging that the mortality rate for abortion is lower than the mortality rate for childbirth, the brochure emphasizes "that women undergoing abortion should be informed about the subsequent risk of depression [and] . . . [t]here is evidence induced abortion may lead to an increased risk of premature birth in a later pregnancy."[101] The premature birth finding has been widely criticized, but the brochure devotes extensive discussion to the consequences of premature births, such as children born with severe developmental disabilities, without mentioning recent studies that have found no relationship between a history of induced abortion and subsequently giving birth to low-birth-weight babies.[102] The purpose of the discussion is to persuade and confuse rather than offer balanced information to inform consent.

Texas: The *A Woman's Right to Know* brochure is twenty-one pages long.[103] It uses three-by-three-inch illustrations from four to forty weeks' gestation and describes these as images of a "baby." It follows the six pages of illustrations with ten pages of discussion of topics such as "abortion risks" and "abortion procedures and side effects." In the discussion of "mental health risks," there is only discussion of negative feelings, such as "depression or thoughts of suicide."[104] There is also a heading "Breast Cancer Risk," which begins with the sentence: "Your pregnancy history affects your chances of getting breast cancer." While "research" is mentioned, no citations are provided, and the reader is merely told "doctors and scientists are actively studying the complex biology of breast cancer to understand whether abortion may affect the risk of breast cancer."[105] On pages 18 and 19 is a discussion of pregnancy and childbirth. Whereas the abortion discussion includes a photo of a Black woman looking downward in a depressive state, the childbirth discussion includes a photo of a white woman holding a white infant with a big smile on her face.[106] This misleading and inaccurate portrayal of information, with its racial subtext, has continued despite complaints by medical experts and others arguing that "important sections—such as those connecting abortions to the likelihood of breast cancer and infertility—are wrong."[107]

Table 1 summarizes how the states bury relevant medical data in their so-called informed consent brochures and, in most cases, also include inaccurate or misleading information. Rather than providing informed consent to help a woman choose among medical alternatives, these brochures must be considered strident, insulting propaganda that is thrust on women as they contemplate whether to terminate their pregnancies.

Notice the pattern of these state brochures. About one-third of the pages are devoted to medical illustrations of the fetus (which is sometimes called a "baby" or "unborn child"). They then follow these graphic depictions with detailed discussions of the process of having an abortion, sometimes including medically misleading or erroneous information. If a woman wades through all that material, she then will typically see a page or so of positive descriptions of childbirth, with no discussion of the process of childbirth and very limited mention of any health risks. Although phrased as a "woman's right to know," suggesting these brochures are designed to benefit pregnant women in their decision-making process, it is much more likely that these brochures would obscure and confuse that process.

Table 1   Summary of State Brochures

State	No. Booklet Pages	No. Pages Fetal Illustrations	Page Where Pregnancy Information Provided	Inaccurate or Misleading Information
Alabama	33	9	16	Fetus called "unborn child"
Arizona	23	6	16	Fetus called "unborn child"
Georgia	36	14	27	Pregnant woman called "mother."
Indiana	15	5	10	Pregnant woman called "mother" in description of abortion procedures
Kansas	32	11	28	Fetus called "unborn child" throughout; discusses breast cancer risk and suggests that psychological impact is always negative
Louisiana	24	10	22	Fetus called "baby" throughout; discusses breast cancer risk
North Carolina	28	12	21	Overstates medical risks of abortion
Oklahoma	20	6	18	Discusses breast cancer risk
Texas	21	6	18	Discusses breast cancer and mental health risks
West Virginia	17	8	15	Mentions possible future difficulty with becoming pregnant or carrying a pregnancy to term
Wisconsin	28	10	22	Comparison of medical risks of abortion to childbirth inaccurate

The Supreme Court's *Casey* decision opened the door to states mandating certain information as part of the informed consent process, but it is difficult to describe these glossy brochures as furthering that purpose. They do not conform to basic principles of informed consent regarding the way information should be conveyed to inform a patient of various available treatment or health-care options. Rather than explain the genuine medical risks of abortion and childbirth, these brochures inundate women with medically irrelevant information to distort their decision-making process. When patients are considering heart surgery, or even a routine dermatological procedure, they are not given photos of bloody procedures to dissuade them from undergoing medical treatment. Instead, they are presented with materials on the genuine risk of the procedure, often expressed in percentage terms, compared to their potential medical risks if they have no procedure at all. Because these brochures are irrelevant to the standard conception of informed consent, doctors performing abortions have to provide genuine informed consent information to women contemplating these procedures in addition to the state-mandated brochures. Labeling these brochures a part of the "informed consent" process does not change their status as state-required propaganda.

These brochures are created for the purpose of using irrelevant and emotional appeals to cause women to "choose" their natural destiny as mother. The popular press is full of stories about the pressures on young women to become pregnant and have children. These discussions revolve around "when" rather than "if."[108] After conducting a national survey of twelve hundred American women of reproductive age who did not bear children, in 2012 researchers concluded: "Rather than assume that women without children are missing something, society should benefit from valuing a variety of paths for adult women to have satisfying lives."[109] Yet authors such as Ellen Walker find it necessary to write entire books questioning how women can possibly feel "complete" if they do not raise children.[110]

Thus, the appropriate way of understanding these state-mandated "woman's right to know" brochures is that they are just one part of the enormous societal pressure on women to fulfill their purported natural and appropriate destiny by giving birth to a child. By calling the fetus "an unborn child" and sometimes directly calling the pregnant woman a "mother," the state is being clear that the only appropriate ethical decision is for a woman to fulfill her destiny by continuing with her pregnancy to term. Women who terminate their pregnancies are demons.

Can one imagine the outcry if a state decided to replace the medical illustrations of super-sized fetuses on the cover of these brochures with photos of women writhing in pain during childbirth? Or a photo of a woman happily leaving an abortion facility after terminating a pregnancy? Such images are unthinkable because these brochures are really about the state's right to coerce women, not about a woman acquiring balanced and helpful medical information about the medical risks of abortion versus childbirth.

A PATH FORWARD?

Rather than serving as a tool of coercion in women's lives, is it possible for the informed consent process to become a way to provide accurate rather than stereotypical information about pregnancy and abortion, even in conservative states? A recently enacted Ohio statute provides a promising example of informed consent but also shows how the political right can callously undermine such progress.

One challenge for women who receive a prenatal diagnosis of Down syndrome is that they may have stereotypical understandings of what it means to raise a child with that condition. For example, Heather Sachs testified before the Senate Finance Committee in Maryland that she only received a pamphlet entitled *So You've Had a Mongoloid: Now What?*, when she gave birth to her daughter with Down syndrome. She worked in coalition with others to require physicians and health-care providers to deliver accurate, up-to-date information to women who have received a prenatal diagnosis of Down syndrome.[111] As part of this effort, the National Down Syndrome Society, a coalition of individuals and organizations, has drafted what it describes as "pro-information" statutes to help improve the lives of children born with Down syndrome.[112] This accurate information "covers all pregnancy options, including termination, as was required by participating medical groups and understood by the Down syndrome groups."[113] Although the pro-information movement has only had legislative success in a handful of states, many interested individuals have tried to counter negative stereotypes about being the parent of a child with Down syndrome in all states by posting positive images and stories on social media.

In 2014, Ohio was one of the states to pass such a pro-information statute.[114] But then, in 2017, Ohio took steps to stop this pro-information movement in its tracks. Ohio Senate Bill 164[115] made it a felony of the fourth degree for a physician to induce an abortion in a pregnant woman who has had a prenatal diagnosis of Down syndrome. David Perry, the father of a child with Down syndrome who opposed Ohio's law, has explained the implications of the Ohio Down syndrome bill for this national pro-information movement:

> This coalition cannot survive when states like Ohio use Down syndrome as a weapon against reproductive rights. If legislatures make it criminal even to speak about decisions and motivations, how can we urge doctors to help women navigate life as a parent of a child with a genetic condition? If women and doctors have to avoid the conversation for fear of criminal liability, fear and myth will win over information.[116]

This example of the state not living up to its agreement with respect to pregnant women is not surprising, because it reflects how readily states are willing to latch onto a negative and coercive message when the opportunity presents itself. The COVID-19 pandemic, for example, gave states the opportunity to characterize pregnant women as selfish users of unnecessary medical services to argue that all abortions should be prohibited. On March 23, 2020, during the COVID-19 pandemic, Texas banned abortions, characterizing them as "nonessential" medical services. Three days later, Ohio joined the ranks by prohibiting all procedural abortions. By March 27, 2020, Iowa, Alabama, and Oklahoma had taken advantage of the COVID crisis to prohibit all abortion care. Many of these bans have been overturned by the courts, although the situation in Texas has been akin to a game of ping-pong, with access being restricted and then restored. Due to these restrictions, Planned Parenthood reports that clinics in neighboring states have reported a sevenfold increase in patients as Texas women travel across state lines during the pandemic.[117]

The public insult campaign is always lurking in the background, even when the pro-choice community thinks it has attained a workable compromise or even basic access to a constitutional right. Compromises are inherently fragile in an era of vociferous public insults. The dead weight of public insults is also sitting on access to abortion, making it hard for women to fully access that constitutional right.

7 Anita Hill and the #MeToo Movement

In the popular HBO series *Mad Men*, advertising executive Don Draper and his male colleagues engage in casual and rampant exploitation and sexual harassment of the women in their mid-twentieth-century fictional workplace. As Stephanie Coontz reported in 2010 during the show's final season: "Every historian I know loves the show; it is, quite simply, one of the most historically accurate television series ever produced."[1] Yet many women reported to her that they could not watch *Mad Men* because of the way it unflinchingly portrayed the sexism of an era that they, too, had lived through. They did not need to watch *Mad Men* to be aware of the sexist and deeply demeaning nature of the workplace.

Nonetheless, feminists have used the media to encourage public recognition of sexual harassment and the need for effective redress to be available. In fact, Coontz praises *Mad Men* for perceptively portraying the plight of women enduring sexual harassment. Using the media to change public perceptions is a complicated endeavor, but in this chapter I try to look at the arguable gains that have been made since Anita Hill's graphic testimony and the rise of the #MeToo movement. Is there reason to think that this sort of publicity has been an effective counter to the traditional sexual harassment playbook, so well depicted in *Mad Men*?

THE LAW OF SEXUAL HARASSMENT

In theory, the law of sexual harassment should be a promising area to pursue the thesis of this book: that there needs to be recourse against public insults in order to achieve equality for subjugated groups in society, such as women. Catharine MacKinnon's work played a central role in the development of this cause of action;[2] her scholarship has focused on creating *systemic* remedies for women to help them overcome their subordination in society.

MacKinnon saw the experience of sexual harassment as a key component of women's subjugation in society;[3] thus, an effective remedy against sexual harassment should have a positive impact on women as a group. Writing in 1979, before the courts had accepted sexual harassment as a viable legal theory under Title VII, she argued:

> Legal recognition that sexual harassment is sex discrimination in employment would help women break the bond between material survival and sexual exploitation. It would support and legitimize women's economic equality and sexual self-determination at a point at which the two are linked.[4]

In other words, she saw a sexual harassment legal theory as crucial to remedying women's history of economic inequality. It would not simply provide a remedy to one woman at a time but would also structurally change the workplace so that women could attain greater social equality. Women could begin to enter a workplace free of sexual harassment and stop being valued "according to men's perceptions of their potential to be sexually harassed."[5] MacKinnon predicted that a vibrant sexual harassment remedy under Title VII could help remedy the horizontal and vertical discrimination that women face at the workplace.

MacKinnon's theoretical goal was transformative. She hoped Title VII could become a more effective remedy to transform the workplace into a sphere that was more equitable for women.

Given the strength of the power elite, putting this theory into practice, not surprisingly, has not been so simple. While women can bring causes of action under Title VII for sexual harassment, the developing case law has made it very difficult for them to prevail. The women who do succeed seem to reflect a narrow category: white women who are perceived to be heterosexual and have faced flagrant, persistent sexual insults and nonconsensual physical touching. Given the enduring power of race, male, and class privilege, it is not surprising that the legal system is reluctant to hold powerful men liable for sexually harassing behavior unless that behavior seems truly exceptional and violates our norms of protecting "fragile" women from harm, such as when there is a combination of flagrantly sexualized comments and nonconsensual touching. Further, the reported cases show the economic ability of wealthy men to resist even these flagrant claims of sexual harassment. Legal technicalities often delay justice for more than a decade until a plaintiff finally prevails. Sadly, legal redress has fallen far short of gaining women workplaces free of harassment. Studies estimate "that anywhere from almost a quarter to more than eight in ten women" experience sexual harassment at work during their lifetime.[6]

This case law, of course, also exists in the shadow of what has happened to women who have brought sexual harassment claims against prominent men. From Anita Hill to Christine Blasey Ford to the dozens of women who have accused Donald Trump of sexual misconduct,[7] the message is clear. Powerful men will fight back and double down. Do not expect there to be consequences for the men, even if the public believes your allegations. While the #MeToo movement may be urging women to speak publicly about their experiences of rape and harassment, it is not yet clear that there are systemic consequences from this activism. This chapter helps us better understand what positive impact may have resulted from the efforts of Anita Hill and the #MeToo movement to publicize and criticize sexual harassment. Obviously the legal system will not cure the problem of sexual harassment. Political change through movements like the #MeToo movement is likely to be more transformative. But there is the possibility that the legal system may be ready to branch out and not just protect women from a Victorian sense of their place in society. It may be ready to serve as a tool for women to fight back.

THE SEXUAL HARASSMENT PLAYBOOK

The pages of the Supreme Court Reporter can give us a glimpse into how the untrammeled sexual harassment portrayed in *Mad Men* endured in the 1980s and beyond.

The Supreme Court decided its first sexual harassment case in 1986, with Catharine MacKinnon serving as cocounsel. The plaintiff was Mechelle Vinson. Her case was a classic example of someone being victimized with little power to fight back. As a child, she was abused by her father; she married a man at age fifteen to escape that abuse.[8] She also managed to leave her abusive husband at age nineteen and began to work at a bank in Washington, D.C., as a teller. Unfortunately, as a young, impoverished, Black woman, she soon found herself a victim of abuse again. This time, the perpetrator was her boss, Sidney Taylor. Although the abuse began in 1974, Vinson was not able to obtain relief at the US Supreme Court until 1986.[9] Nonetheless, her case was pathbreaking, even if it did little to remedy the abuse in her own life.

The facts of her case are important because they reflect the way the public insult playbook can help a man maintain his power and authority in the workplace over a low-level, Black woman. When Vinson started work, Taylor allegedly told her: "If you don't sleep with me, I'll destroy you." Fearful of losing her job, Vinson submitted; she "estimated that over the next several years she had intercourse with him some 40 or 50 times."[10] Her lawyer described her case as an "allegation of sexual slavery."[11]

But Taylor was not satisfied with having intercourse with Vinson; he also chose to publicly humiliate her in order to maintain his power and authority. He "fondled her in front of other employees, followed her into the women's restroom when she went there alone, exposed himself to her, and even forcibly raped her on several occasions."[12] When he asked her to engage in demeaning work, he would allegedly say to her: "You're an animal, you're nothing, and I'm going to show you you're nothing."[13]

Taylor also allegedly touched and fondled other female employees and made them look at pornography with him to "relax" them.[14] The district court judge did not allow Vinson to enter evidence of how Taylor treated other female employees, because he did not see how Taylor's treatment of other women at the workplace was relevant to the question of whether Vinson, herself, was harassed. The court insisted on treating sexual harassment as a "one-off" event rather than a power regime in which Taylor selected Vinson for harassment as part of his sex-based control of the workplace. It was part and parcel of his treatment of women rather than an exceptional circumstance. By flaunting his power at the workplace,

Taylor was intimidating Vinson so that she would not try to report his egregious behavior.

The district court judge had no understanding of the power dynamics of sexual harassment in the workplace. He refused to allow Vinson to introduce evidence about treatment of other women and then ruled against her because she had not reported Taylor's egregious behavior to management. He did not even consider the strong evidence of how Taylor exerted his authority at the workplace in a way that was designed to intimidate Vinson from complaining. Instead, the district court judge allowed Taylor to introduce evidence of Vinson's so-called provocative clothing. In rebuking Vinson for not filing a formal complaint at the workplace, the judge also suggested that Vinson "asked for it" by wearing provocative clothing. The judge concluded that her participation in the "relationship" was "voluntary" and had nothing to do with her employment opportunities. He found that she "was not the victim of sexual harassment and was not the victim of sexual discrimination" while employed at the bank.[15] He "wouldn't even give the impoverished plaintiff a pro bono transcript, ruling that the case didn't involve any important issues."[16]

In 1980, when the district court judge ruled on Vinson's case, a man like Taylor could expect to engage in that kind of behavior with impunity. He could openly touch and fondle subordinate female employees, threaten them with adverse consequences if they did not submit to his sexual demands, and not be concerned about legal liability. His threat that he would "destroy" Vinson if she sought to complain was credible. Anita Hill did not testify about Clarence Thomas until 1991. Title VII was amended in 1991 to permit compensatory damages for emotional harm. Until that amendment was put in place, women who faced a hostile workplace, but did not quit, could not obtain any financial relief from the courts if they did not face some kind of wage discrimination. And in 1980 the Supreme Court had not yet ruled that sexual harassment claims were even cognizable under Title VII. Vinson had every reason to believe that submitting to Taylor's sexual advances and tolerating an abusive work environment were a necessary predicate to maintaining employment and supporting herself financially. Her lived reality supported MacKinnon's description of how sexual harassment was effective at the workplace to maintain women's gender-based inequality. Until the Supreme Court recognized sexual harassment as a cause of action, judges were implicit in helping to preserve this inequality by rejecting the legitimacy of a claim of sexual harassment.

Nonetheless, Vinson did ultimately achieve a successful outcome at the US Supreme Court. The Court broadly recognized that there are two types of sexual harassment claims: quid pro quo claims and hostile work environment claims. A quid pro quo claim is made when a supervisor directly conditions the grant or denial of favorable treatment at the workplace on acceptance of his or her sexual demands. A hostile work environment claim is made when an individual's conduct at the workplace has the effect of creating an intimidating, hostile, or offensive working environment. In a later case, the Supreme Court clarified that the distinction is between explicit alterations in the terms of conditions of employment and "constructive" alterations due to the creation of a hostile work environment.[17] The court emphasized in both *Vinson* and later cases that a plaintiff must demonstrate that the hostile conditions are "severe or pervasive" to succeed under that legal theory.

In light of these rules, one might have expected Vinson to proceed on a quid pro quo legal theory. After all, she testified that she perceived her continued employment to be dependent on her having intercourse with her immediate supervisor. But how would she prove that? Taylor would deny the threat. Because she did go along with his demands, she could not prove whether the threat was genuine. A hostile work environment, by contrast, was easier to establish because of the ways that Vinson flaunted his harassment. He engaged in blatantly humiliating treatment of all the women at the workplace and publicly displayed his humiliating treatment of Vinson. He was using the public insult playbook effectively to intimidate the women at the workplace. A hostile work environment theory therefore seemed to be the appropriate litigation strategy.

When Vinson had prevailed in the court of appeals, the court saw no reason to create different rules for liability in quid pro quo and hostile work environment cases. Both causes of action, in the opinion of the court of appeals, could proceed without special notice to the employer. But in an opinion authored by Justice Rehnquist, the Supreme Court disagreed. While four members of the Supreme Court were willing to agree with the court of appeals on the liability issue, Justice O'Connor provided the swing vote to side with Rehnquist, creating different liability rules for quid pro quo and hostile work environment claims.[18] Liability existed when a plaintiff could establish evidence of a quid pro quo even if she had not put her employer on notice of the inappropriate behavior by a supervisor. In hostile work environment cases, however, the Court concluded that an employee had to demonstrate that she had put the employer on notice, or that such efforts would be futile. An employer was not expected to simply know the conditions of its own hostile workplace unless the employee had brought it to the employer's attention by filing a complaint, or the plaintiff had to show that such an action would have been futile.

What did those rules mean for Vinson? The employer argued that Vinson's failure to use its established grievance procedures or otherwise put it on notice of Taylor's wrongdoing insulated it from liability, even though Taylor was her supervisor. The Supreme Court refused to accept that argument.[19] In this case, the employer's grievance procedure did not specifically mention sexual harassment and would have required Vinson to complain to her immediate supervisor, Taylor. The evidence therefore suggested that the employer's grievance procedure was not "calculated to encourage victims of harassment to come forward."[20] The case might have met the futility exception for complaining about sexual harassment. We'll never know how the hostile district court judge would have ruled on remand under this rule; the case was settled.

Although Vinson's settlement with the bank is not a matter of public record, it is known that she was blacklisted in the banking industry and never acquired another bank job after filing this lawsuit.[21] Although Title VII protects against workplace retaliation, that kind of blacklisting does not come within the statute's protection.[22] Thus, then and now, it takes tremendous courage for employees to file public complaints against their employers. Even if they "win," their victory could be pyrrhic.

What did this ruling mean for other women in the future? Did they have an adequate remedy when they were the victims of the public insult playbook: an openly hostile workplace, in which women were subjected to sexually demeaning conduct and remarks? Vinson has been praised for her courage in bringing her claim forward and for the apparent success she attained in having the Supreme Court recognize sexual harassment as a legal theory under Title VII. Taylor thought that he was entitled, as a man, to treat women in a sexually demeaning way. When MacKinnon first posited this legal theory in the late 1970s, she was ridiculed as a legal charlatan. After she helped obtain relief for Vinson at the Supreme Court, there must have been some gasps of alarm by men in the workplace. Business as usual had clearly changed. Men could not expect to openly harass women in the workplace and get away with it.

But then there are men such as Roger Ailes and Harvey Weinstein. Did they not get the memo saying that overtly sexually harassing women was now illegal?

In a thoughtful op-ed, Linda Hirshman argues that they did get the memo, but they were told that they would not face legal liability for creating a hostile work environment if their company created an apparently effective complaint procedure. Hirshman argues that the result of the *Vinson* decision was that employers "drew on virtuous-sounding policies and started training programs no one would attend, or which would be the butt of endless workplace humor and resentment . . . 'well-trained people in human resources under[stood] their job as being to protect the company and its powerful executives no matter what.'"[23] At Harvey Weinstein's company, for example, any complaints regarding sexual harassment would be funneled back to *Harvey Weinstein*. In an exposé, Ronan Farrow reported that one of Weinstein's accusers said:

> Weinstein would be informed of anything she told them, a practice not uncommon in businesses the size of the Weinstein Company. Several former Weinstein employees told [Farrow] that the company's human-resources department was utterly ineffective; one female executive described it as "a place where you went to when you didn't want anything to get done. That was common knowledge across the board. Because everything funneled back to Harvey." She described the department's typical response to allegations of misconduct as "This is his company. If you don't like it, you can leave."[24]

Of course, Harvey Weinstein got caught and was eventually sentenced to prison for rape. The public insult playbook ultimately failed him. Nonetheless, but for the intensive efforts of Jodi Kantor, Megan Twohey, and Ronan Farrow to report Weinstein's decades of harassment and sexual assault, he would likely have been able to continue his degradation of women unfettered. Given the immense power of men like Weinstein and Ailes, has the testimony of Anita Hill and the work of the #MeToo movement substantially helped women come forward and seek redress for sexual harassment at the workplace? That is the next question that I consider.

#METOO PUSHES FORWARD

Anita Hill is a household name because of her graphic testimony before the Senate Judiciary Committee in 1991 about the ways in which Supreme Court nominee Clarence Thomas had sexually harassed her for years when she worked for the Equal Employment Opportunity Commission (EEOC). Hill testified that Thomas "repeatedly asked her to go out with him in a social capacity and would not take no for an answer. She said he would talk about sex in vivid detail, describing pornography he had seen involving women with large breasts, women having sex with animals, group sex and rape scenes."[25] He would describe his own "sexual prowess" and "once mentioned a pornographic film whose star was called 'Long Dong Silver,' which turned into an infamous name in American political lore."[26]

Her testimony did not derail Thomas's nomination to the Supreme Court, in part because the politically powerful used the public insult playbook to smear Hill and any senator who would oppose Thomas's nomination. Thomas famously described the Senate hearing as a "high-tech lynching for uppity Blacks who in any way deign to think for themselves, to do for themselves, to have different ideas."[27] As a Black man, Thomas was an unusual person to take advantage of the public insult playbook, but he had support from important figures like Senator Orrin Hatch, who urged Thomas to explain how the accusations played into racist stereotypes about Black men. The all-male, all-white Senate Judiciary Committee reacted skeptically to Hill's testimony, with chairman Senator Joe Biden questioning her on the specific locations of her harassment allegations and asking her to specifically repeat an allegation about Thomas placing pubic hair in a Coke can. Senator Hatch followed up on Biden's questioning by reading an excerpt from *The Exorcist*, which contained the phrase "an alien pubic hair floating around in my gin,"[28] to suggest that Hill had contrived her testimony from that book. Senator Alan Simpson later suggested that Hill was able to pass a lie detector test because she was delusional. With such vivid attacks against Hill and her supporters, it is no surprise that most Americans thought she had committed perjury during her graphic testimony.[29]

Nonetheless, Hill's testimony did generate a broader understanding of the nature of sexual harassment and the lack of legal relief available to employees whose continued employment is not explicitly predicated on submitting to sexual advances. Access to the public airways by an articulate victim of sexual harassment did influence some people's opinions, even if it was not a majority of Americans. Her testimony provided a hint of how one might respond to the public insult playbook. In response to Hill's testimony, Congress enacted a provision in the Civil Rights Act of 1991 that allowed Title VII plaintiffs to recover for emotional distress and punitive damages, while also imposing caps on such relief. Today, someone who experiences sexual harassment as a condition of work can seek up to $300,000 in compensatory and punitive damages under federal law.

Hill's testimony did not end sexual harassment at the workplace or even cause most people to believe her account of her own experience with it. Hill reported that "a lot of people came to me after the hearing and said, 'People aren't going to come forward now,' and some people blamed me for it."[30] Nonetheless, complaints to the EEOC increased by 73 percent in the year after Hill testified, working women's groups like 9 to 5 reported a dramatic increase in phone calls about sexual harassment, and a record number of women ran for Congress.[31]

More than two decades passed, while activists like Tarana Burke (the actual founder of the original MeToo movement) tried to help victims of harassment and sexual assault. Then the dam broke when, on October 5, 2017, Jodi Kantor and Megan Twohey published an article in the *New York Times* detailing three decades of alleged sexual harassment by Hollywood producer Harvey Weinstein, with at least eight financial settlements paid to women.[32] On October 10, 2017, Ronan Farrow published a *New Yorker* exposé in which he reported that thirteen women had told him that Weinstein sexually harassed or assaulted them.[33] On March 11, 2020, a jury found Weinstein guilty of rape and sexual assault, and a judge sentenced him to twenty-three years in prison.[34]

The Weinstein exposé is given credit for spurring the modern #MeToo movement. After actress Alyssa Milano posted on Twitter on October 15,

2017: "If you've been sexually harassed or assaulted write 'me too' as a reply to this tweet," nearly a million people tweeted #MeToo in forty-eight hours.[35] Building on the 2006 work of Tarana Burke, who used the term to help women and girls who were disproportionately African American get support to survive sexual violence,[36] the contemporary #MeToo movement has used the hashtag to bring attention to the pervasiveness of sexual harassment and assault and, in some cases, to hold powerful men (typically white) accountable for their behavior. While Burke primarily engaged in direct action work in her Brooklyn community, the #MeToo movement tried to galvanize the internet as a forum to publicize the prevalence of sexual harassment, assault, and violence against women (and, later, some men).

In the framework of this book, we can understand the #MeToo movement as revealing that the men who harassed and assaulted women felt free to engage in their campaign of harassment and assault because of their protected status as part of the power elite. In a 2018 article, the *New York Times* credited the #MeToo movement with bringing down 201 powerful men, such as producer Harvey Weinstein and television host Charlie Rose; nearly half of them were replaced by women.[37] Noting this transformation in many workplaces, Joan Williams commented: "We've never seen something like this before. Women have always been seen as risky, because they might do something like have a baby. But men are now being seen as more risky hires."[38]

Not all victims of sexual harassment have brought high-profile cases or even been victimized by people who would receive news attention. Low-income workers in difficult work situations are rarely the face of the #MeToo movement, even though Tarana Burke initially founded the movement in 2006 to particularly give voice and assistance to Black women and girls who were survivors of sexual violence.[39] Not surprisingly, Burke, an African American civil rights activist from Brooklyn, received little public attention when she started an activist organization called "Me Too."[40] And at first she insisted that she had no interest in joining the recent social media campaign instigated by predominantly white female actresses. When approached by white actress Michelle Williams to attend the Golden Globes, she said: "Why? I'm trying very hard not to be the Black woman who is trotted out when you all need to validate your work."[41] But she eventually concluded that working with Williams and the other actresses could help create more resources for victims of sexual harassment and sexual assault as well as provide publicity for understanding the scope of the problem. She also understood how access to privilege can help produce positive change. She said: "Inherently, having privilege isn't bad . . . but it's how you use it, and you have to use it in service of other people. . . . Now that I have it, I'm trying to use it responsibly."[42]

Related to this book's thesis, Burke understood how difficult it was for her, as a working-class Black woman in the Bronx, to broaden social understanding of the scope of the problem of sexual harassment and sexual assault. She jokingly remarked at the end of her interview: "But if it [the #MeToo movement] hadn't come along I would be right here, with my fucking Me Too shirt on, doing workshops and going to rape crisis centers. . . . The work is the work."[43] The challenge, of course, is for this kind of collaboration between a Black, working-class, grassroots organizer and privileged, predominantly white female celebrities to have a broad impact on society. Was Burke just used to validate the work of white women, or did the #MeToo movement achieve positive results for a broad cross-section of women?

There is considerable evidence that women of color disproportionately face sexual harassment, although the media only started highlighting this problem when white female celebrities began publicizing their experiences with it. Tanya Kateri Hernández has documented that many of the early precedent-setting sexual harassment cases were brought by African American women.[44] In addition to Vinson, discussed in the previous section, major cases were brought by Paulette Barnes, Diane Williams, Pamela Price, and Willie Ruth Hawkins.

Hernández does an outstanding job detailing the challenges that Vinson faced in suing the bank. The case settled sixteen years after the harassment began and thirteen years after she filed suit. While she was trying to resolve her case, her alleged harasser, Sidney Taylor, was convicted of seventeen counts of embezzling from the bank. In that extraordinary context, one can imagine the bank had an incentive to settle, since his testimony could be undermined by his criminal convictions involving dishonesty.

Hernández seeks to understand why women of color may disproportionately be victims of sexual harassment. She suggests that, like

Vinson, they may be in a precarious economic position that makes it difficult for them to jeopardize their jobs by coming forward with complaints. Furthermore, Hernández argues that when these women do come forward, they are subjected to stereotypical presumptions about them as African American women. Over strenuous objections from her attorney, Vinson, for example, was subjected to stereotypes of lasciviousness, with comments about her sexually revealing clothing and open talk about her sexuality. "The defenses are she deserved it because she asked for it; we know she asked for it; because she is a temptress, a seductress, a lascivious woman."[45] Often the court does not mention the race of the plaintiff, so a reader of the court opinions cannot directly see the racialized subtext. In this and the preceding chapter, I have tried to identify the race or national origin of the plaintiff and have not always been able to do so, even though some of the cases contain direct racialized comments.

Hernández's work highlights the importance of conceptualizing sexual harassment broadly to include all aspects of demeaning conduct. Studies have shown that Black women are criticized at the workplace for being overly sexual or offensive when they wear innocuous clothing like a red dress, tan slacks with a button-down blouse, or sandals.[46] Their low status renders them especially subject to such negative characterizations of their innocuous conduct. They may be treated adversely because of their dress or appearance without even being subjected to sexualized comments or unwelcome touching.

Deborah Brake has argued that we should give the #MeToo movement credit for forcing "people far and wide to take notice of, and try to understand and empathize with, survivors of sexual harassment and abuse. They have deepened our cultural understanding of the injuries of sexual misconduct, with the potential to generate social change to make these harms less common, particularly for younger generations."[47] Nonetheless, Brake has also argued that the law of sexual harassment can never be sufficiently protective of women at the workplace until the legal protections from coworker retaliation are strengthened. She emphasizes that the "too" part of the "me too" movement highlights that sexual harassment is rarely an isolated incident at the workplace. The same people, typically men, harass many people, typically women, at the workplace. It is onerous and challenging to contest workplace sexual harassment. Thus, the women who come forward might seem to others to be isolated victims of harassment or, worse, fabricators of their mistreatment. Because every step toward needed change almost always engenders the dead weight of backlash, it is crucial that those who speak out about sexual harassment have some protections from retaliation. "One 2003 study found that 75 % of employees who spoke out against workplace mistreatment faced some form of retaliation."[48] When Ronan Farrow conducted interviews for his exposé on Harvey Weinstein, he reported that "virtually all of the people [he] spoke with told [him] that they were frightened of retaliation."[49] Brake urges courts to provide stronger protections "from the daggers and darts of coworker hostility."[50] The continued vitality of the public insult playbook makes it even more important for workers to have strong anti-retaliation protection, given their vulnerability to punitive attacks from the public insult playbook.

While Brake is correct that a movement against workplace sexual harassment can only be successful if the complaining parties and their allies have protection against retaliation at the workplace, it is also true that the scope of what is understood to be sexual harassment has to be broadened to provide adequate relief for those who are subjected to it. We need to understand sexual harassment as not necessarily or exclusively about sexually explicit speech at the workplace. We should understand it as part of the demeaning way that women are systematically treated at the workplace, which perpetuates their subordination in society. As I argued earlier in this chapter, courts have often narrowly understood sexual harassment to consist of explicit sexual epithets or unwanted physical touching. But comments hurled at women at the workplace can be demeaning without being explicitly sexual and without being accompanied by an unwanted physical touch.

A simple example may resonate with readers who work in an office setting where meetings are commonplace. While it is true that a woman may be sexually harassed at the workplace through unwanted comments about her appearance and even sexual slurs that are directed at her, women can also be demeaned at the workplace by having their views consistently overlooked or credited to someone else. In 2015, Sheryl Sandberg and Adam Grant coauthored a *New York Times* op-ed in which they commented on the problem they described as "Speaking While Female."[51] "When a woman speaks in a professional setting, she walks a tightrope. Either she's barely heard, or she's judged as too aggressive. When a man says virtually the same thing, heads nod in appreciation for his fine idea. As a result, women often decide that saying less is more." The authors call this the "speaking-up double bind."

Historically, men have been able to speak explicitly at the workplace in ways that demean women. That might include sexualized comments about their appearance. But it also might simply include interrupting them in a way that silences their voices at work. While men control the public airways at the workplace, women are shunted to the silent corner. The public insult playbook at the workplace needs to be understood as part of the larger problem of women playing a subordinate role in the workplace. Only men's voices have been historically valued. And if a woman happens to have what appears to be a good idea, a man will interrupt and take credit for the idea. These are some of the many ways that women are *demeaned* at the workplace. Sexualized comments are just one of many ways that men enact that demeaning treatment of women.

In this chapter, I seek to offer a ray of hope from some courts that have been willing to conceptualize sexual harassment more broadly: by not necessarily requiring an explicit sexual epithet or unwanted physical touching. MacKinnon, who played a significant role in the development of sexual harassment doctrine, has said that the #MeToo movement "has been successful in getting those in power to take sexual harassment claims seriously by believing women and no longer 'devaluing . . . accusers.'"[52] While MacKinnon may be correct that the #MeToo movement has improved women's credibility when they bring forward claims of sexual harassment, we would expect that the increased willingness to take sexual harassment claims seriously would also extend to the courts. This chapter documents some movement in that direction. Although the #MeToo movement, itself, cannot be given direct credit for this expansion of the courts' understanding of sexual harassment, it is likely one explanatory factor among many. As summarized by Jean Sternlight, social movement theorists generally agree that "lawyers and judges both influence and are influenced by 'popular mobilizations' . . . [and that] judges, even more than legislators, can see close-up how people and entities are impacted by various legal interpretations."[53] While it may be too early to document the effect of the #MeToo explosion in 2017, it would be surprising if that social movement has had no impact on judges and juries who have heard allegations of sexual harassment and assault. Further, it is likely that the publicity about claims of sexual harassment would embolden more employees to file complaints; preliminary evidence suggests that effect has occurred.[54]

POST-#METOO CASES

Is there evidence that some women are prevailing in a post-#MeToo era who previously might not have come forward or may have stood little chance of prevailing? And are these women who have access to privileged resources, or are they sometimes women who come from less privileged backgrounds?

Jamillah Bowman Williams and her coauthors have tried to assess the impact of the #MeToo movement. While recognizing that the social media campaign may have been mostly limited to supporting "slacktivists" who participate in a social movement merely by liking or sharing posts, they seek to use empirical evidence to demonstrate that the #MeToo movement has led to positive social change.[55] They posit several encouraging results from the #MeToo movement: (1) legal terms often accompany the use of the #MeToo hashtag, suggesting concern for understanding and changing the current legal landscape; and (2) there has been an increase in social-political and legal change, such as strikes and protests, the Time's Up Legal Defense Fund, additional EEOC sexual harassment charges, new state and federal legislation, more use of tort law as a remedy, and a series of public accusations against government officials. They therefore conclude that "#MeToo is changing our society's collective understanding of sexual harassment and assault and reducing our collective tolerance for it."[56]

While Williams and her coauthors seek to use empirical sources to measure the impact of the #MeToo movement, I decided to try to find some reported legal cases that may have been positively impacted by the #MeToo movement, such as when the court makes reference to the movement. In reading the successful litigation stories that follow, we should also ask ourselves if the positive legal developments have been limited to privileged white women or have reached a broader cross-section of society.

As was true when Hernández wrote her account of the *Vinson* case, the race of the plaintiff is rarely mentioned, although many of the cases do involve women who worked in occupations that are nontraditional for women and were in low-status positions at the workplace. It took tremendous perseverance for them to obtain relief. Nonetheless, they prevailed, and their victories could bode well for future claims or, more importantly, continued changes at the workplace.

Inés Maria Jelú Iravedra (October 15, 2018)

Inés Maria Jelú Iravedra's allegations of sexual harassment fit well into the pattern of elite men who take advantage of their status to harass less powerful women. Jelú Iravedra alleged that she was sexually harassed by Héctor O'Neill-Rosa when she worked for the municipality of Guaynabo, Puerto Rico, as an attorney in the legal division.[57] O'Neill-Rosa was not an employee of the municipality but managed the mayoral campaign of his father, Héctor O'Neill García, who was mayor of the municipality. Although not employed by the municipality, he had a municipal employee identification card that gave him access to its working area, which he frequently visited in the months prior to the general elections. Jelú Iravedra finally felt comfortable filing a complaint when O'Neill García was traveling and not acting as mayor of the municipality. O'Neill-Rosa's former wife and the mother of his five children, who also worked for the municipality, was the person who ultimately received the complaint of discrimination. Following Jelú Iravedra's complaint of sexual harassment, she received unsatisfactory employment evaluations and resigned. In her resignation letter, she said that the sexual harassment forced her to leave her job "for psychiatric illness."[58]

Jelú Iravedra alleged that the sexual harassment occurred inside her office, so no one could have observed it. O'Neill-Rosa responded to her allegations by saying they had had a consensual "sporadic romantic tryst" for about three years, although he admitted they never publicly disclosed their relationship.[59] Jelú Iravedra emphatically denied having had a consensual romantic relationship with O'Neill-Rosa. Taking a page from the public insult playbook, the municipality sought summary judgment, arguing that it "is simply so incredible and contradicted by the record that no reasonable jury could believe [her allegations]."[60]

On October 15, 2018, Judge Aida M. Delgado-Colón ruled in favor of Jelú Iravedra, finding that her allegations of sexual harassment were sufficient to get the case to a jury. This decision was important, because it is well known that plaintiffs often lose sexual harassment cases on summary judgment motions, thereby precluding presentation to a jury.[61]

Obtaining a jury trial was a huge victory for Jelú Iravedra. On November 4, 2019, the jury awarded her $1,011,593.24 in compensatory damages for her mental anguish. In total, the judge awarded her $300,000 in compensatory damages under Title VII (the limit specified by the 1991 Civil Rights Act) and $1,423,186.48 in compensatory damages under Puerto Rican law.[62] That judgment did not include costs, interests, and attorneys' fees.

The municipality's attempt to use the public insult playbook did not work in Judge Delgado-Colón's courtroom. Although Jelú Iravedra had less power than the mayor and his family, she did have a law license, which probably helped her navigate a difficult situation involving both sexual harassment and retaliation. As predicted by Professor Brake, she needed protection from both the act of sexual harassment and retaliation in order to prevail. There is no way to know how the #MeToo movement may have impacted the judge, but it is possible that it made her more willing to believe the allegations and send the case to the jury, given the timing of the case in relation to the #MeToo movement. And it probably didn't hurt that the judge, herself, was a woman who may have empathized with the plaintiff or even had her own experience with sexual harassment.

Xueyan Zhou (January 7, 2019)

Xueyan Zhou's allegations of sexual harassment in her work as a software consultant also fit the pattern of a supervisor taking advantage of a woman's lower status.[63] In this case, her status as a woman who was born in China and was of Chinese ancestry also made her more vulnerable to harassment and retaliation. Like Jelú Iravedra's case, hers needed to survive a motion for summary judgment to go forward. After her sexual harassment and retaliation claims survived the summary judgment motion, the case settled on the eve of a jury trial.[64] Although the terms of the settlement are confidential, one would expect that Zhou obtained some relief.

Zhou's case reflects some increased sensitivity on the part of a judge to the nature of sexual harassment, allowing her case to survive a summary judgment motion. But the case also reflects what can be a narrow understanding of sexual harassment, separating racialized and nonsexually explicit elements from an understanding of how it occurs. Zhou's case presented multiple theories of conduct in violation of Title VII: discrimination based on sex, race, and national origin; sexual harassment; and a retaliatory discharge. The district court judge treated each theory as an independent, separate claim and did not seek to understand how they may have all been connected to account for Zhou's treatment at the workplace.

Zhou alleged that she faced hostility from her supervisor Steve Herold as soon as she was assigned to his team. He threatened to put her on a layoff list before he had even worked with her. When she reported this conversation to Herold's boss, Lester Lynd, he took no helpful action but did relay the conversation to Herold. Thus, she allegedly learned early in her career that complaining about inappropriate conduct is not likely to be helpful.

After the layoff comment, and with Herold aware that supervisor Lynd would not prevent him from making those kinds of threats to Zhou, he began to engage in a sequence of behaviors over the next three to four years that Zhou interpreted as sexual overtures. Although Zhou and Herold were both married, he frequently told her that he was "free" and a "bachelor" when his wife was out of town.[65] Twice, he mentioned that he had had an affair with an employee and graphically explained how the female employee supposedly seduced him by sitting next to him in his office and touching her leg against his. He displayed photos to Zhou of his daughter breastfeeding with her chest exposed and of his wife delivering a child. He also visited her home when he apparently knew her husband was out of town, bringing her a casserole and insisting on staying for dinner until Zhou invited her daughter to meet him.

The district court treated those incidents as the sole evidence of sexual harassment. But another incident revealed her special vulnerability as an Asian American woman. While she was being subjected to sexual harassment by Herold, someone wrote the phrase "Asian Sluts" in the men's restroom along with the first names of Zhou and another woman who was of Chinese ancestry. Zhou complained about this graffiti, which articulated a pernicious stereotype of Asian women as highly sexualized and promiscuous. When it became clear that the company was not actively investigating who had written the graffiti, she also sought to participate in the investigation. Soon after she complained about the graffiti incident, supervisor Lynd encouraged her to seek a transfer to another department. She interpreted that request as retaliation for her complaint. Thus, she had had two experiences that suggested to her that complaints were fruitless; they were ignored or resulted in adverse job action.

But one might also ask: Why was Zhou named by the graffiti artist as an Asian slut? Zhou alleged that Herold spoke to her about his affair with another employee in an environment in which others could overhear the comments. He did not merely sexually proposition her; he let others in the workplace be aware of his sexual interest in her. In an environment in which a supervisor publicly sexualizes a female employee, it is no surprise that she would be the target of that kind of graffiti. When Zhou was fired months after complaining about the graffiti incident, the district court agreed that there was sufficient evidence of retaliation to allow that claim to go to a jury. While that decision is commendable, it would have been even better for the judge to use the graffiti incident as further evidence of the way the public insult playbook worked at that workforce. When a supervisor openly harasses an Asian American worker, it is no surprise that someone who had access to the men's bathroom would post graphic graffiti that also sexualized that employee based on her sex and race. The graffiti was part of the sexualized workplace that Zhou was expected to endure as a condition of maintaining her job.

Further, the district court opinion only considered sexual harassment to be a narrow band of sexualized conduct. Zhou's supervisor's immediate assumption, when she was assigned to his unit, that she would be one of the first employees to be fired in the event of an economic downturn may have been due to her sex and race. While the district court judge did not dwell on the significance of Zhou's Chinese ancestry to her treatment at the workplace, it appears that her English language skills may have also harmed her status at the workplace. The district court case included several quotes from Zhou that are consistent with her self-report that she was born in China and likely learned English as a second language. For example, she said: "I don't feel safe to come work, because if we don't find this person, today they put things on the wall, tomorrow they may physically attack me."[66] Just as Herold might have felt comfortable harassing Zhou, as a lower status employee, Zhou's response to that harassment may have reflected her own sense of her special vulnerability as a female, Chinese immigrant. The district court judge employed seemingly objective rules, like counting how many harassing encounters occurred, to determine if Zhou was a victim of legally actionable sexual harassment under Title VII. The fact that she was "only" subjected to approximately fifteen instances of harassment over a three- to four-year period was not sufficient to constitute "pervasive" sexual harassment unless she was *also* subjected to an explicit sexual proposition. She squeaked by under these rules because the district court judge thought the sexual proposition was implicit. The district court judge said: "On the alleged facts, requiring an explicit proposition in order to find that Herold's conduct was severe would ignore the reality of the alleged behavior and would make a mockery of the anti-harassment laws."[67]

While the district judge is to be commended for understanding that sex is often being solicited without an explicit overture, he missed the larger context in which these actions were occurring. Maybe Herold was not actually sexually propositioning Zhou. Maybe he was just trying to make sure that she retained a demeaned status at the workplace as a Chinese American woman. The so-called objective measures do not view the harassment in the context of the plaintiff's power (or lack of power) in the workplace. Zhou apparently entered the workplace under a race- and sex-based stereotype of incompetence and as easy prey of a supervisor determined to sexualize his female employees. He could demean and demoralize them without an explicit quid pro quo. At every opportunity, he played the public insult playbook well by keeping her in a subordinated position. He would have gotten away with it if the district court judge, Abdul K. Kallon, had not thought there was an implicit sexual proposition.

It is hard to know why Judge Kallon ruled in favor of Zhou when the defendant sought a motion for summary judgment. But, like Zhou, Judge Kallon was born outside the United States (in Sierra Leone) and immigrated to the United States, in his case when he was eleven years old. Although Judge Kallon did not describe Zhou's sexual harassment in a racialized context, it is nonetheless possible that he understood the many ways that she was demeaned at the workplace by her supervisor on the basis of both her race and sex. Judge Kallon himself was arguably a victim of the public insult playbook. Despite having an undergraduate degree from Dartmouth College, a law degree from Penn Law School, and extensive legal experience, his nomination to the court of appeals in 2016 was opposed by his home-state senators, Richard Shelby and Jeff Sessions. Nonetheless, he continues to have a lifetime appointment as a district court judge in the northern district of Alabama. His elite status as a judge could protect him from the full implications of the public insult playbook. Zhou needed recourse to the courts to obtain some protection.

Harassment of Restaurant Workers

Three cases from different parts of the country involving blatant harassment of female restaurant workers may reflect an uptick in activism against such behavior in the restaurant industry. Unlike the plaintiffs in the previous two cases, these women did not work in professions where they would have had access to lawyers. Although none of these cases specifically mention #MeToo in the decisions, they echo themes of the #MeToo movement.

STEAK 'N SHAKE IN OHIO (AUGUST 21, 2019)

Sixteen-year-old Hannah Corbin was hired by a Steak 'N Shake in Newark, Ohio, to work as a server. From the start of her employment, Will McCann and other coworkers allegedly engaged in graphic sexual harassment. "Every day I would go in and they would make a new remark about my butt or my boobs or how thick I was. . . . They would make googly eyes . . . [and] stare at me until I got out of sight."[68] McCann allegedly "smacked her butt" several times and rubbed her neck with his hands. The harassment also took on a racialized character when they learned that Corbin (who is white) had an African American boyfriend. "Referring to the black pants which employees had to wear, they said that they were 'black from the waist down' and asked if this gave them a chance with Corbin."[69] All the employees involved in the harassment were white. Corbin allegedly complained about the harassment when her supervisor, Michael Simon, laughed as McCann harassed her in front of him. When Simon refused to take any action, Corbin asked for the phone number of the company's hotline, which Simon provided to her. Corbin allegedly called the hotline but received no assistance from the company even though Steak 'N Shake had a "Youth at Work Initiative" policy for reporting harassment or discrimination.[70] Frustrated by the company's inaction, she asked to be taken off the regular work schedule and only be assigned pickup work. She alleged that she requested this schedule change because the work conditions had become intolerable.

The case went to trial, and the jury ruled in favor of Corbin, finding her account credible even though no store employees corroborated it. Steak 'N Shake did not even put McCann on the stand, presumably because they were concerned about the image he would project. Steak 'N Shake's corporate policy is to refuse to settle its cases. Thus, it is currently appealing the jury verdict ($51,308) and award of attorney's fees ($92,977), even though it has likely spent many times that figure defending itself in this case.

It isn't possible to give the #MeToo movement credit for Corbin reaching out to a lawyer after she quit her job, because she quit in April 2016, a year before the #MeToo movement gained traction. But pursuing a lawsuit requires a lot of perseverance. Corbin, who was seventeen years old when she quit her job in April 2016, was twenty-one by the time the case was decided by a jury. She was deposed and testified at a trial. The jury of her peers believed her over the claims by the restaurant that Corbin never experienced harassment and never complained about any harassment. Did the #MeToo movement make the jury more willing to believe her testimony?

In order to have the case go to trial, the plaintiff had to survive a summary judgment motion. Judge James Graham, who was appointed to the bench by President Ronald Reagan in the 1980s, presided over the case. He denied the defendant's summary judgment motion on the hostile environment and constructive discharge aspects of the case on August 21, 2019. Was eighty-year-old Graham influenced by the #MeToo movement to take these allegations seriously? There is no way to prove cause and effect, but one can imagine that a changing social climate made it easier for Corbin to achieve some success in this lawsuit.

Unfortunately it is still too early to know if Corbin will ever receive monetary damages for her harm. Steak 'N Shake has appealed the judge's ruling including the award of attorney's fees. Her lawyer has cross-appealed the attorney's fee award, arguing they should have been awarded even more. Because of the slow pace of the civil docket, the court of appeals is not likely to rule for another year or two. The pace of justice is slow, especially when a defendant refuses to settle.

SNAPPERS SPORTS BAR AND GRILL IN HAWAII (JANUARY 7, 2020)

The next example follows a similar timeline. The plaintiffs complained about a hostile work environment at the restaurant at which they worked before #MeToo received a lot of media attention. But their case was heard by a district court judge after #MeToo had gained a foothold.

Unlike in the Corbin case, the employees who alleged that they were subjected to sexual harassment did not have to find a private lawyer to bring their case. The EEOC decided to file suit on behalf of Jessica Root, Nicole Garrett, Michelle Edwards, and Adrienne Akin, each of whom experienced a hostile work environment and, in some cases, retaliation for complaining about the harassment.[71]

Jessica Root alleged that owner Michael Wenzel

- called her a "slut" and "whore";[72]
- ripped her bikini top in front of at least fifty patrons;
- told her that he had dreams about having sex with her;
- told her about sex acts with his wife, including a story about them having sex on a boat; and
- spoke of his sexual fantasies about Kitchen Manager Ashley Harris, the size of her breasts and buttocks, including how he wanted to "do" her by "wrapping her legs around him and fuck the shit out of her."[73]

Michele Edwards alleged that Wenzel

- repeatedly told her to wear shorter shorts so that she would make more tips and threatened to cut her shorts with scissors in the back office if she did not comply;
- talked really close to her face and put his hands around her waist when she went to the back office to talk to him;

- would say things in front of customers like, "This is Hawaii, it's okay for me to kiss you and touch your back, I am just friendly. . . . I like to kiss your cheeks";[74]

- would call her "baby" or "honey" and said, "Honey, just come into the back officer for a bit, I can make it to you"; and

- told her, when she wore sparkly eye shadow, "Maybe you could make more money if you were a stripper because that's the only thing you have going for you."

Nicole Garrett alleged that Wenzel

- told her to wear shorter shorts and flirt with customers to receive higher tips and would exclaim that "the breasts are out" in front of patrons, almost on a daily basis.

Adrienne Akin alleged that Wenzel

- reached into her skirt and inappropriately touched her.

But Michael Wenzel was not the only person who sexually harassed the female employees. His son, Troy Wenzel, who worked at the restaurant as a supervisor, engaged in similar behavior. Further, when patrons engaged in inappropriate behavior, such as groping Nicole Garrett's breasts, Michael Wenzel would refuse to help the women in any way. Because he sexually harassed the employees in front of the patrons, it is no surprise that they thought such behavior was acceptable at the restaurant.

This lawsuit was unusual because of intervention by the EEOC. Rather than the plaintiffs having to find a private attorney to bring their lawsuit, the EEOC filed a lawsuit on their behalf. Remarkably, Snappers did not defend the lawsuit at all. The EEOC eventually secured a default judgment against them. The court awarded a total of $251,652 in compensatory and punitive damages, plus prejudgment interest, for a grand total of $255,302.53.

The company filed for bankruptcy in November 2017, and the EEOC tried to obtain some relief through those proceedings.[75] It is unlikely that the complainants received their full award. Like seventeen-year-old Corbin, the complainants in this case waited years for relief and likely did not attain close to the full value of what the judge awarded.

LUIGI'S ITALIAN RESTAURANT IN KANSAS (MARCH 30, 2020)

Like Snapper Sports Bar, Luigi's Italian Restaurant was in default as to the allegations in the plaintiffs' complaint, but defendant Gianni Topalli did appear at the hearing that the court held to determine the plaintiffs' damages.[76]

Cynthia Bennett and Amanda Meads brought an action against the restaurant. Meads testified that Gianni Topalli, the owner of the restaurant,

- brought up sex constantly,
- made sexual jokes about the food at the restaurant,
- brushed up against her and touched her at work,
- requested to have sex with her,
- implied she would lose her job if she didn't have sex with him, and
- Followed her home and propositioned her.

Bennett testified that Topalli

- subjected her to repeated sexual comments,
- questioned her about her personal sex life,
- called her at home,
- asked her to have sex with him, and
- exposed his genitals to her at the restaurant.

Based on the plaintiffs' testimony, the court awarded about $14,000 to Bennett and about $28,000 to Meads, as well as $10,920 in attorney's fees to their lawyer on March 30, 2020, as part of its default judgment in their favor. Assuming that Topalli pays the default judgment, they will have obtained some financial relief in 2020 for conduct that dated back to 2017. While the court did give them some compensatory and punitive damage relief, the back pay part of the relief was quite modest because the court refused to award money for lost tips and only awarded them three months of front pay, for potential future lost income while looking for a new job, given the unskilled nature of their work. The judge thought they could easily find comparable employment elsewhere after they left the restaurant, without considering that this kind of behavior is likely to recur at a new restaurant. They were not awarded sufficient front pay to retrain and seek work in a less sexist environment.

WHERE DOES THIS LEAVE US?

Some commentators believe the #MeToo movement has raised consciousness of the problem and pervasiveness of sexual harassment at the workplace. And it is possible to find cases in which women prevail in sexual harassment complaints and the judges seem more willing than in the past to accept their testimony as credible and as meeting the legal standards for sexual harassment.

But the fact that women continue to bring these legal cases is some evidence that sexual harassment continues to be a common abusive practice in the workplace. In the case against the Italian restaurant, the owner, who was accused of repeatedly making sexual advances to the two plaintiffs, testified that "he would only have asked plaintiffs for sex 'if I'm drunk but I never drank where I work, so.'"[77] The court interpreted that testimony as showing "a casual indifference to the gravamen of plaintiffs' claims."[78] One has to wonder if defendant Topalli has continued with his pattern of sexual harassment against female waitresses after the default judgment was entered against him.

Further, a close reading of these cases shows how difficult it is to obtain legal redress. Although the #MeToo movement has helped fund some sexual harassment litigation, it appears that the women in these cases were fortunate to find lawyers willing to take their cases on a pro bono basis. Even after years of litigation, the defendant company may go bankrupt, so that only pennies on the dollar will be awarded to the successful plaintiffs and their lawyers.

Sexual harassment may be particularly problematic in the restaurant industry, where studies have shown, for example, that waitresses with blond hair, smaller waists, and larger breasts receive the highest tips.[79] Ninety percent of waitresses report that they experience sexual harassment, and half of these women say the interactions occur weekly. Further, restaurant workers bring nearly 40 percent of the sexual harassment cases filed with the EEOC. Restaurant worker activists argue that the practice of tipping waitresses has led to a pandemic level of harassment of workers in the restaurant industry. Saru Jayaraman comments: "[T]he culture of sexual assault in the restaurant industry isn't an accident, but a direct outcome of the subminimum wage and the fact that the majority of people living off tips are women."[80] The Fair Labor Standards Act embeds the practice of tipping by allowing restaurants to pay servers a mere $2.13 an hour, so that they are dependent almost entirely on tips to survive unless their state has a higher minimum wage.[81] Sixteen states still follow the federal $2.13 rule for tipped workers. "Waitresses in these states are three times more likely than workers in non-tipped wage states to be asked by management to sexualize their behavior and appearance for guests."[82]

Roy Moore apparently understood that he could easily exercise his male privilege of openly harassing young waitresses when he was an Alabama judge. Victoria Beverstock remembers that "he made her and the other waitresses uncomfortable by staring at them and flirting. 'He watched us girls quite openly,' said Beverstock. 'His eyes crawled over our shirt and our backsides. He was so open about it that I would try and handle his order as quickly as possible. When you didn't smile and flirt back with him, give him an opening, he became rude and demanding.'"[83] As a member of the political elite, Moore knew the playbook well. He could openly harass and proposition women for decades with no adverse recourse.

Alabama voters did finally turn against Moore in 2017, when nine women came forward and said that Moore had pursued relationships with them while they were teenagers or young women. He lost the 2017 special election by fewer than twenty-one thousand votes in an election that would have normally been an easy Republican victory.[84] Political pundits gave credit to the #MeToo movement for making it possible for the nine women to come forward and accuse Roy Moore of sexual misconduct. "Women across Alabama wanted their voices, stories and abuses at the hands of men finally heard."[85] A 17 percent gender gap flipped the race to the Democratic column, but of course, white men overwhelmingly supported Moore despite the allegations. It is hard to imagine that Doug Jones's victory against Moore made female restaurant workers in Alabama safer from their clients and bosses who seek to sexualize their workforce, with the $2.13 minimum wage for tipped workers still in force.

Thus, while the #MeToo movement and additional legal resources for women who experience sexual harassment may be of some assistance, others would argue that, at least for restaurant workers, more systemic relief is necessary so that women's wages are not so dependent on their sexualized behavior. Catharine MacKinnon may have been correct that legal relief for sexual harassment has the potential to create structural changes in the workforce, but a structural change to the system of compensating women for their perceived sexual attractiveness may have even more potential for improving women's experiences in the workplace.

8 Black Lives Matter

The subjugation of Black people today has its origins in the brutalization of Black people under slavery and Jim Crow.[1] Southern white men created slave patrols in the early 1700s to stop slaves from escaping or rebelling.[2] Slave masters and their hired overseers, as described by Frederick Douglass, worked under the maxim: "It is better that a dozen slaves suffer under the lash, without fault, than that the master or overseer should seem to have been wrong in the presence of the slave."[3] Slave owners were exonerated for killing their slaves merely because of the slaves' so-called "hostile attitude" or resistance to corporal punishment.[4] Slaves were burned alive at the stake in what Stuart Banner has called "super-capital punishment."[5]

While the Thirteenth Amendment ended chattel slavery, its exception for "a punishment for crime whereof the party shall have been duly convicted" allowed the convict leasing system to maintain Black people's "status as a disenfranchised and involuntary labor force for whites."[6] Black people who had been convicted of petty crimes could be sold at public auctions as if they were still enslaved.[7] Black Codes, enforced from 1865 to 1867 in southern states, created a form of debt slavery, which caused Black people to continue to work in "onerous involuntary labor."[8] Confessions of

Black people falsely accused of crimes were obtained through hangings and whippings of the accused. In 1894, in a trenchant account of the horrors of lynching, Douglass foreshadowed the Black Lives Matter (BLM) movement by prophetically stating: "Their [white people's] institutions have taught them no respect for human life, and especially the life of the negro."[9] In 1935, a Mississippi state court judge reflected on the continued reality of lynching by noting the "signs of the rope on [one defendant's] neck were plainly visible during the so-called trial."[10]

The death penalty replaced public lynchings as a form of public terror in the mid-twentieth century: "[I]n the 1950s in Mississippi, crowds of white onlookers gather at southern courthouses to witness the electrocutions of black men in portable electric chairs that traveled from town to town."[11] Such atrocities were not limited to the South. From the 1970s to the 1990s, the Chicago police "coerced dozens of confessions from suspects by beating them, burning them with radiators and cigarettes, putting guns in their mouths, placing plastic bags over their heads, and delivering electric shocks to their ears, noses, fingers, and genitals."[12] More recently, too many videotapes have captured police murdering Black men with choke holds that are reminiscent of the lynchings of a previous generation.[13]

The BLM movement, which has been described as the largest political/social movement in US history,[14] differs in many important respects from previous civil rights struggles. Rather than use the courts as the primary vehicle for obtaining justice, the BLM movement has embraced an abolitionist strategy. "Defund police" has become the latest expression of this movement. As Amna Akbar writes: "The Vision [for Black Lives] demands shrinking the large footprint of policing, surveillance, and incarceration, and shifting resources into other social programs in Black communities: housing, health care, jobs, and schools."[15]

A tension within the BLM movement, which mirrors disagreements between Frederick Douglass and William Lloyd Garrison in the nineteenth century about the role of the Constitution in obtaining the abolition of slavery, is whether constitutional law has any role at all to play in the abolitionist struggle. In a brilliant piece, Dorothy Roberts advances the two possible paths forward. Like Garrison, one can be "resigned to the *futility* of employing U.S. constitutional law to dismantle the prison industrial complex and other aspects of the carceral state."[16] Alternatively, like Douglass, one can find "*utility* in applying the abolitionist history and logic of the Reconstruction Amendments to today's political conditions in the service of prison abolition."[17] Whether one embraces the first or second theory, it is clear that the BLM movement is *not* primarily about using the courts as a vehicle to advance change.

While I cannot resolve this venerable dilemma about the role of the Constitution in overcoming racial oppression, I can certainly predict that any strategies will face the enormous headwinds and dead weights of public insults. Whether the strategy be political (moving resources) or judicial (arguing that certain practices are illegal or unconstitutional), we can be certain that those who are seeking to perpetuate white supremacy will use public insults to try to weaken these legal or political movements. I hope that anticipating such attacks will strengthen our ability to fashion an effective political/legal strategy. Thus, in this final chapter, I ask how the application of my public insult thesis can add insight to some of the successes and struggles of the BLM movement.

BLACK LIVES MATTER

The "BLM" movement, although decentralized, has embraced the strategy of strongly deflecting public insults while seeking structural reform. I am completing this book as the streets have come alive with protests against the murder of George Floyd on May 25, 2020, by Minneapolis police officers. Despite initial attempts to demonize Floyd as a hardened criminal with a weak heart, who faced an appropriate police response, the state of Minnesota was forced to quickly backtrack and charge officer Derek Chauvin with second degree murder. The last eight minutes and forty-six seconds of Floyd's life became a metaphor for police brutality. "526" was plastered on signs in remembrance of the last seconds of Floyd's life. The city of Minneapolis soon banned the kind of choke hold that killed Floyd. "Defund police" became a widely shared demand for structural reform. In the difficult times of the COVID-19 pandemic coupled with police brutality, it is helpful to recognize that structural reform can sometimes be possible despite the barrage of insults by those with racialized power.

Many Black people understand that power bullies will try to demonize them even after they are murdered. They have written "If they kill me" messages in anticipation of the possibility of this horrific event. For example, in 2016, four years before the murder of George Floyd, one of my Black colleagues at the Moritz Law School, Assistant Dean of Students Darren Nealy, wrote on his Facebook page:

> If they kill me, please seek justice, but do so justly. If they kill me, please help my daughters to grow up in a better world than the one that took their father. If they kill me, please provide a counter-narrative to the time that I got detention in junior high for fighting—I'm sure they'll bring that up. If they kill me, please don't give them any pictures of me at my worst—I'd like to think there aren't many, if any, but they'll probably try to dig those up too. If they kill me, be sure to strongly consider who belongs within the realm of that "they" and avoid blaming the wrong parties. That's all I guess. I'll try not to let them kill me.

Dean Nealy foreshadowed the themes of this book: that we need to anticipate the use of the public insult playbook and neutralize those insults by seeking structural reform.

The BLM movement did not begin with the murder of George Floyd. The hashtag was created in 2013 after the acquittal of George Zimmerman in the shooting of Trayvon Martin in February 2012. The murders of Michael Brown in Ferguson and Eric Garner in New York City in 2014 further strengthened the movement. BLM has used two important strategies that are central to this book's thesis. First, it has anticipated the use of the public insult playbook and been ready to challenge the negative portrayals of the Black victims of police violence. Second, it has sought systemic reform rather than merely individual justice for the friends and family of each slain Black person. Those seeking to use the public insult playbook in defense of white supremacy are being unmasked as bullies, and many white people are becoming increasingly troubled by the impact of racism and more open to the need for transformational reform.

I discuss some of the successful BLM campaigns here chronologically to call out racialized use of power and seek structural reform.

Murder of Laquan McDonald

In 2014, Chicago police received a report that seventeen-year-old Laquan McDonald supposedly fit the description of a man who was breaking into cars and stealing radios.[18] McDonald was walking down the street when he was approached by a police officer, who asked him to stop and show his hands. McDonald pulled out both hands, one of which was holding a small knife, and began walking away from the officer. A few minutes later, while McDonald was running away from the first officer, Officer Jason Van Dyke arrived on the scene. Van Dyke got out of his car, aimed his gun at McDonald, and fired at him as he was moving away. He shot McDonald sixteen times, continuing to shoot after McDonald was lying dead on the street. At no time did the officer or anyone else seek to offer medical assistance to McDonald. There was no evidence that McDonald had committed any crime; his only provocation, which led to his death, was having a small knife in his hand as he walked away from the officers. Yet Van Dyke felt entitled to empty his service revolver, reminiscent of the Jim Crow response to the slightest provocation by Black people.

To justify this murder, the officers at the scene immediately took pages from the public insult playbook. McDonald was described as "lunging" at Van Dyke.[19] His walk was characterized as "menacing" and his use of the knife as "aggressive." He was described as trying to "kill" Van Dyke. Although walking Chicago streets with a small knife in one's hand is not a criminal act, the police reports described McDonald as the "offender." Van Dyke even invented a fanciful story about special knives that can propel bullets, to explain why he kept shooting at McDonald as he lay prone on the ground. Van Dyke perceived McDonald, as a Black man, to have superhuman powers to kill from a prone position on the pavement.[20] And Van Dyke was not alone in this perception; police supervisors officially ruled the shooting a "justifiable homicide."[21] When Van Dyke was eventually put on trial, the defense team argued that the murder was justifiable because McDonald had shown symptoms of "rage, aggression, violent behavior, drug induced psychosis."[22] The Fraternal Order of Police defended Van Dyke throughout the proceedings, arguing that it was a "sham trial and shameful verdict" and that police are forced to fight "crime against this disgusting charade."[23] Nonetheless, McDonald's family obtained a $5 million settlement from the city, and Van Dyke was convicted of second-degree murder and sentenced to nearly seven years in prison.[24]

This supposedly "justifiable homicide" soon turned into a second-degree murder conviction. Further, fallout from the killing helped topple members of the Chicago power elite.

These developments were only possible because of the work of Brandon Smith, a journalist who filed a public records request in May 2015 to get a copy of the video of the Van Dyke shooting of McDonald.[25] Smith had to go to court to get the video, but a judge finally ordered it be released no later than November 24, 2015. Even though Cook County district attorney Anita Alvarez was complicit in the cover-up of McDonald's killing, she rushed to charge Van Dyke with first degree murder within hours of the video's release.

As soon as the video was released, protesters used a "16" mantra (for the number of shots) to challenge the murder and Chicago's leaders' complicity in the cover-up. Protesters shut down several interstates while shouting "16 shots."[26] They also launched a sixteen-hour sit-in at the Cook County building and called for the resignations of both Cook County attorney Anita Alvarez and Mayor Rahm Emanuel.[27] Even after Van Dyke was convicted, Blacks Lives Matter Chicago, the Black Youth Project 100, and the McDonald family came together to help Kim Foxx, who is Black, defeat Anita Alvarez by a wide margin when she ran for reelection in the 2016 Democratic primary.[28] Alavarez had been so ensconced in the Cook County office that she had had no challenger in the 2012 Democratic primary.[29] The hashtag #ByeAnita supported Foxx's campaign. In 2018, Mayor Rahm Emanuel did not seek a third term as Chicago's mayor, with the McDonald murder likely playing a role in that decision.[30]

The McDonald murder shows how difficult it can be to challenge power bullies even when videotape evidence demonstrates that a murder has taken place. Despite reaching a private settlement with the family, city officials initially rallied around the officer and promoted a blatant public misrepresentation of what had occurred. McDonald, as a Black teenager, was described as a hostile threat to an armed police officer. But for the persistent public information request from a journalist, that private settlement would have been the end of the matter. However, when the videotape surfaced, the protesters were not satisfied with a conviction for second-degree murder. They wanted the public officials who had resisted Van Dyke's being charged for murder to be held responsible for their actions. They turned to electoral politics to make that happen.

This series of events is a valuable, although complicated, example of how social movements can be effective in undermining the public insult playbook while trying to avoid being co-opted by a conservative message. The prosecution of Van Dyke, while delayed, played into the tough-on-crime mentality that conservatives often support. Although Van Dyke is white, the push to convict him arguably reinforces the pattern identified by Gruber of using the "criminal law as the solution to too many problems, and maintaining horrific prison conditions."[31] After Van Dyke was imprisoned, he was beaten in prison and had to be moved to another facility for his safety.[32] While Van Dyke deserved to be held accountable for the murder of McDonald, it would have been a limited victory by local activists if his conviction and mistreatment in prison were the end of the story.

But they weren't. Local activists pushed hard to defeat Alvarez because of her record of overcriminalizing Black people and not holding white officers responsible for police brutality. Kim Foxx, a Black woman, was supported by local activists and beat Alvarez in the Democratic primary. Following a more progressive path, she seeks to be "smart on crime" rather than "tough on crime."[33] She embraces bail reform because she understands that "the current cash bail system unfairly punishes poor people."[34]

Not surprisingly, Foxx has had to work in the context of power bullies who are going to continue to use the public insult playbook to go after her. She often recounts an incident in which she won a school election against a white student and some teachers suggested there should be a revote because the result was unimaginable. And she remembers complaining a few years ago about a staffer in the state attorney's office who liked to look up women's skirts and openly discuss oral sex with young female employees. More recently, a suburban elected official circulated an email in which he criticized one of Foxx's guidelines, saying, "I called the cunt to complain."[35] As a survivor of two incidents of sexual assault as a child, she has learned to overcome any obstacles.

Foxx has pushed hard against sexism and racism. She speaks about race and gender equality issues at meetings of the Illinois State's Attorneys Association, where she is the only Black member and one of fewer than a dozen women.[36] She tries to fight sexual harassment in government work-places by conducting sexual harassment workshops in her own office and then suggesting that judges do the same. Rather than seeing legal action by victims as the solution to deep-seated problems of racial and sexual bias, she is trying to put a brake on the underlying racist and sexist behaviors themselves. She has also faced criticism for some of her decisions, such as dropping all sixteen counts of felony disorderly conduct against former *Empire* actor Jussie Smollett.[37] Some advocates are pressing her to make even deeper reforms and claim there is still "too much emphasis on winning at all costs and not enough on holding cops accountable for misconduct."[38] It may be unrealistic to expect someone who has to retain her job by being reelected to pursue a truly radical vision of reform. But the Foxx story is certainly evidence of how social and political work can help lessen the power of public insults. The suburban politician who called her a cunt because of her stance on shoplifting did not succeed in getting her to change her position on that issue. As she has said: 'You will never, ever, ever, ever, ever hear me apologize for being unapologetically African American."[39] That kind of personal fortitude has helped her defeat the public insult playbook for decades.

Murder of Ahmaud Arbery

The murder of Ahmaud Arbery in February 2020 is another example of videotaped evidence making it impossible for the power bullies to use a campaign of falsehoods to cover up a murder. And again, it is a story of how activists have exposed lies as they fought for structural reform.

The murder of twenty-five-year-old Ahmaud Arbery by the father-son team of Gregory McMichael and Travis McMichael, along with the assistance of William Bryan Jr., is probably familiar to many readers. Arbery, a former high school football standout who liked to stay in shape, was out jogging in a coastal South Georgia neighborhood near his home when the McMichaels decided to pursue him with a .357 magnum and a shotgun.[40] Travis fatally wounded Arbery with three shots from his shotgun. They then lied about the incident, claiming it was in response to a "string of burglaries."[41] After Arbery's death, a detective contacted Wanda Cooper-Jones, his mother, and told her "that Arbery had been involved in a burglary and that the homeowner confronted him and shot him after a tussle."[42]

County prosecutor George Barnhill, despite recusing himself from the case, sent an email to the Georgia attorney general falsely stating that his office had "video of Arbery burglarizing a home immediately preceding the chase and confrontation."[43] He claimed that the McMichaels had "solid firsthand probable cause" that indicated Arbery was involved with a burglary, despite the fact that no such evidence existed. Barnhill went on to claim that Arbery's prior convictions and mental health record supported the theory that he was an aggressor,[44] in a typical pattern of treating all Black men as dangerous. Despite having a video of the incident, filmed by Bryan, the police department initially took no steps to investigate the murder. But on May 5, 2020, when the video surfaced, the situation rapidly changed. Protests and marches were held, and the Georgia Bureau of Investigation arrested the McMichaels two days later. On May 21, 2020, William Bryan Jr. was also arrested for attempting to use his car to "confine and detain" Arbery.[45]

At this time, it is unclear if the protests against the treatment of the Arbery case will have any lasting consequences in Georgia. Republican governor Brian Kemp called the video "horrific." Former Georgia Republican senator Kelly Loeffler claimed to be "deeply concerned" with the video, while former Georgia Republican representative Douglas Collins said the killing "looks like a criminal act."[46] Protestors have demanded the resignation of county prosecutors but, unlike in Chicago, no resignations have occurred. Will the consequences for the McMichaels cause the next white vigilante to stay home?

One of the many horrific aspects of the Arbery murder is that the white people involved in the murder, as in the murder of George Floyd in Minneapolis and the unwarranted harassment of birdwatcher Christian Cooper in Central Park, did not fear being videotaped. Bryan apparently leaked the video in the expectation that it would *assist* the McMichaels. The officer who murdered George Floyd knew he was being watched and videotaped by an array of people, yet he continued to suffocate Floyd. And, as I discuss later, Central Park birdwatcher Amy Cooper was seemingly unconcerned that Christian Cooper was videotaping her, while she emphasized that he was an "African American" several times in her fake report to the police. The viral nature of social media proved their assumptions to be wrong. The public immediately turned against them, and they faced a range of consequences.

The Murder of Breonna Taylor

Though initially overlooked by activists, newfound attention to Breonna Taylor's murder has led them to discuss the ways in which Black women are brutalized by the police.

At 12:43 a.m. on May 13, 2020, plainclothes police officers, with a "no-knock" warrant, used a battering ram to enter the apartment of twenty-six-year-old Atlanta emergency medical technician (EMT) Breonna Taylor, who was asleep with her boyfriend, Kenneth Walker, a licensed gun owner.[47] The warrant was based on a package that a former boyfriend had mailed to her home two months earlier, which the police thought might contain narcotics. Assuming the intruders were criminals, Walker fired his pistol and shot one officer in the leg. The police responded by shooting twenty-two bullets, eight of which fatally wounded Taylor. No drugs were found at the scene.

Police immediately deployed the public insult playbook. The original police report described Walker as the shooter. He was arrested for the attempted murder of a police officer and first degree assault even though, in his 911 call, he said "somebody kicked in the door and shot my girlfriend."[48] The officers were not wearing body cameras, and no one who witnessed the incident took a video. When Walker, who is also Black, was released on home incarceration, the police union wrote in a Facebook post: "This man violently attacked our officers. . . . Not only is he a threat to the men and women of law enforcement, but he also poses a significant danger to the community we protect!"[49] There was no video to go viral, as there have been in so many other similar episodes, and the incident did not garner much immediate attention. A grand jury indicted Walker, although charges against him were eventually dismissed.[50]

Rather than hearing the truth from the police, Tamike Palmer, Taylor's mother, had to piece together the truth from a conversation with Walker. Walker called her during the murder, after midnight, saying he thought the police had shot Taylor.[51] When she rushed to Taylor's apartment, and then the hospital, she was given inaccurate information about Taylor's status and who had shot her. While withholding the fact that Taylor was dead, the police insinuated that Walker had shot her.[52]

Taylor's family refused to accept the police department's attempt to place the blame on Taylor and Walker. They filed a lawsuit against the Louisville police for wrongful death, excessive force, and gross negligence. Louisville mayor Greg Fischer, who is a white Democrat, initially provided a vague response to the murder of Taylor. He merely suggested that the needs of the police and residents "must be weighed by our justice system as the case proceeds."[53]

Criticism of Fischer grew in the wake of the Floyd murder on May 25, 2020. Then, on June 1, 2020, David McAtee, a Black owner of a popular barbecue restaurant, was killed by Louisville police and the National Guard. Local Black leaders began to call for Fischer to resign, and the Fairness Campaign withdrew its support of him.[54]

While Fischer has not resigned, publicity about this incident has had some consequences. The hashtag #SayHerName, which was launched in 2014 by the African American Policy Forum, began trending in late May 2020 as a way to bring attention to the ways in which Black women are victims of police brutality and systemic racism, but do not receive the same attention or publicity as their male counterparts.[55] In the days leading up to what would have been Taylor's twenty-seventh birthday, the hashtag #BirthdayforBreonna began trending on Twitter, asking for financial support for her family and for charges to be brought against the officers responsible for her death.[56] The Louisville city council adopted "Breonna's law" unanimously, banning the use of no-knock warrants except in cases involving "murder, hostage taking, kidnapping, terrorism and human or sexual trafficking," and mandating that body cameras be used even during those situations.[57] The proposed Justice in Policing Act in Congress would place a federal ban on no-knock warrants in drug cases and withhold funding from states and cities until they did the same.[58]

Amy Cooper's 911 Call

Amy Cooper's interaction in Central Park with Christian Cooper on May 25, 2020, the same day that George Floyd was murdered in Minneapolis, is both a strong example of the public insult playbook at work and of its being effectively thwarted. Contrary to park rules, Amy Cooper was walking her dog unleashed while Christian Cooper was trying to engage in birdwatching. During their verbal dispute, Christian Cooper began videotaping their exchange. Christian Cooper was largely silent, while Amy Cooper can be heard saying: "I'm taking a picture and calling the cops. I'm going to tell them there's an African American man threatening my life."[59]

As a white woman, Amy Cooper knew she could unleash "African American" as an insult to threaten Christian Cooper, who is Black, and marshal the police to her side. In the space of a minute, she used the term "African American" three times in her call to the police to make a false accusation against a Black man.[60]

But Amy Cooper miscalculated. The police refused to intervene, and the recorded moment soon went viral when Christian's sister, Melody Cooper, posted a video of the incident that afternoon on social media. By the next day, May 26, she had been terminated from her job, and thousands of people who viewed the video had criticized her racialized response, while national protests began to challenge the George Floyd murder. In an attempt to broaden this incident, the term "Karen" was pushed out by many people on social media as a shorthand for white women who make false accusations against Black men. One might say this episode had a happy ending; the perpetrator did not get away with her public insults. But we all know that a police officer like Derek Chauvin, who murdered George Floyd at 8:00 p.m. on the same day, could have answered the 911 call, with catastrophic consequences for Christian Cooper.

The response by the police and broader community to Cooper's attempt to use the public insult playbook shows how much has changed in a short period of time. Rather than assume that Christian Cooper was a danger to the community, people immediately began to see the racist trope that Amy Cooper was trying to use on her behalf. In her public apology, Amy Cooper even recognized how her white privilege played out in her interaction with Christian Cooper and the police. She said: "When I think about the police, I'm such a blessed person. I've come to realize especially today that I think of [the police] as a protection agency, and unfortunately, this has caused me to realize that there are so many people in this country that don't have that luxury."[61]

Amy Cooper's recognition that police protection is a "luxury" for many people has now become a widespread perspective in US society. A *Wall Street Journal/NBC News* poll released in early June 2020 found that a majority of Americans were more troubled by the actions of the Minneapolis police that led to Floyd's death than by violence at some protests. A majority of Americans began to support limits on police power, such as banning neck restraints and requiring the use of de-escalation tactics. The favorability ratings for the police also plunged by 10 percent in one week, days after Floyd's death.[62]

Further, consistent with the larger themes of the BLM movement, Christian Cooper chose not to be involved in the prosecution of Amy Cooper.[63] He seemed to be sympathetic to the larger goal of the BLM movement to defund the police and abolish incarceration and did not want to contribute to the overpolicing problem in our society by subjecting Amy Cooper to criminal sanctions. Thus, at the same time, we see an absence of public insults hurled at Christian Cooper and a modest move forward in publicizing the inappropriateness of criminal responses to social problems.

George Floyd

On May 25, 2020, a teenage employee at Cup Foods in Minneapolis called 911 because he thought a customer had bought a pack of cigarettes with a counterfeit $20 bill.[64] When two police officers arrived, George Floyd was sitting with two other people in a car parked around the corner.[65] One of the officers, Thomas Lane, approached the car, pulled out his gun, and ordered Floyd to show his hands. Although this aspect of the arrest has not received much attention, we can see that the police immediately escalated a possible counterfeit currency episode into one with potential deadly force. The officers then handcuffed Floyd while he was acting compliantly, repeatedly apologizing to the officers. Floyd only became uncooperative when the officers tried to put him in their squad car, stating that he felt "claustrophic." A second police car arrived, and the officers struggled to push Floyd into the vehicle. At this point, he told them for the first time that he couldn't breathe. A third and final police car then arrived on the scene, carrying Derek Chauvin.

Chauvin pulled Floyd from the original police car out into the street. He put his knee on George Floyd's neck, while several other officers held their knees on Floyd's back.[66] Floyd started crying out, saying that he couldn't breathe. Bodycam footage showed Floyd saying more than twenty times that he could not breathe. He also pleaded for his mother, begging "please, please, please." At one point, Floyd gasped, "You're going to kill me, man." Chauvin replied: "Then stop talking, stop yelling. It takes heck of a lot of oxygen to talk." Floyd cried: "Can't believe this man. Mom, love you. Love you. Tell my kids I love them. I'm dead."[67]

Although one officer called for an EMT, the officers remained on top of George Floyd. After five minutes of restricted air, Floyd appeared to go unconscious. The EMTs arrived within two minutes and checked for Floyd's pulse but couldn't find one. During their examination, Chauvin kept his knee on Floyd's neck. Finally, one of the EMTs motioned that Chauvin needed to move so they could carry Floyd into the ambulance. Chauvin finally got up, after kneeling on Floyd's neck for eight minutes and forty-six seconds, three of which came after Floyd fell unconscious. Less than an hour later, Floyd was pronounced dead at a nearby hospital.

Through a combination of security camera footage and bystander videos, the majority of this encounter was filmed, and it was posted on social media. Unlike in the cases of Ahmaud Arbery and Laquon McDonald, third-party citizens controlled the majority of footage, and the video of George Floyd's death went viral the very night he was killed. On May 26, protests began in Minneapolis, and the four officers involved in the arrest were fired.[68] By May 28, protests were occurring in dozens of cities across the country. Finally, on May 29, Derek Chauvin was charged with third degree murder. Later, on June 2, the charges were raised to second degree murder, and the three other officers involved in George Floyd's death were charged with aiding and abetting second degree murder.[69]

Several of the protests, which all began peacefully, included some property damage. As both an instigation and response to these protests, police outfitted in military equipment and riot gear responded with violence. Tear gas was shot into crowds in seemingly every major city, including San Diego, Orlando, Detroit, Minneapolis, Washington, D.C., Columbus, New York, Denver, and Dallas, among others.[70] Dozens of other viral videos surfaced, showing police driving into crowds, police in full riot gear assaulting journalists and seemingly innocent protesters, and police smashing car windows and violently pulling citizens from their vehicles.[71] Finally, in Louisville, the same city where Breonna Taylor had been killed, African American man David McAtee was shot and killed by police; none of the officers involved had their body cameras on at the time.[72] While the political right has tried to describe the protesters as looters and rioters, it is more accurate to describe the police response itself as a riot, with the deliberate infliction of harm on peaceful protesters.

Not surprisingly, the political right tried to hurl public insults against George Floyd. In a video, which received millions of views on Twitter and Facebook, right-wing personality Candace Owens claimed that the Black community was defending the "bottom denominator" in their society in George Floyd.[73] In that same video, Owens listed Floyd's entire history of interactions with the police and justice system. Owens doubled down on her comments in a video interview with right-wing radio host Glenn Beck, claiming: "The fact that he [Floyd] has been held up as a martyr sickens me." Beck pointed out that Floyd had a "very long criminal record." This interview was later retweeted by President Trump.[74]

Insults were also levied against the protesters. President Trump tweeted that the protesters were "THUGS" and claimed "when the looting starts, the shooting starts."[75] The word "thug" has been identified as a code word, almost exclusively used to paint Black men as violent or criminal.[76] The phrase "when the looting starts, the shooting starts" was coined by a racist police chief in Miami who has been accused of inciting some of the violent race riots in the city during the late 1960s.[77] Twitter later restricted Trump's tweet from being retweeted or commented on, claiming that it glorified violence.

Senator Tom Cotton doubled down on this rhetoric, saying the government should do "whatever it takes to restore order," and that there was "[n]o quarter for insurrectionists, anarchists, rioters, and looters."[78] Similarly, Senate majority leader McConnell said: "It's already gone on for entirely too long. I hope state and local authorities will work quickly to crack down on outside agitators and domestic terrorists and restore some order to our cities."[79] These public insults encouraged police to view the protesters as the enemy. American cities and civilians were being referred to using military lingo, dangerously blurring the line between police and military. Not surprisingly, this blurring of police and military was heightened when President Trump called in federal troops to supposedly protect federal monuments in Portland, Oregon.[80]

Another angle of public insults against the protests was to paint the protesters as opportunistic criminals who had hijacked the "true" movement. Tucker Carlson of Fox News showed video of the Minnesota protests and called them "criminal mobs," while Sean Hannity claimed that the protesters were "exploiting" George Floyd's death.[81] Attorney General William Barr echoed these talking points, claiming that "[g]roups of outside radicals and agitators are exploiting the situation to pursue their own separate, violent and extremist agenda," while also blaming supposed far left group Antifa for the violent escalation. This happened close to when President Trump announced he would attempt to label Antifa a terrorist organization. Despite this allegation, the evidence suggests that any infiltration came from far right and white supremacy groups.[82]

The George Floyd protests have produced massive gatherings in every single state in the nation. This movement is not centralized, although it is well supported by BLM groups across the country. Despite the public insults, there may be evidence that these protests could lead to lasting change. In Louisville following the killing of David McAtee and the failure of the officers involved to have their body cameras on, the mayor fired the city's police chief.[83] After initially charging Derek Chauvin with third degree murder and withholding charges from the other three officers involved, Minnesota attorney general Keith Ellison raised Chauvin's charge to second degree murder and pressed charges against the officers involved. This happened following days of nationwide protesting and petitioning for such action.

While some moderates on the left complain that the "defund police" mantra is too radical and likely to play into the hands of the political right, the BLM movement has achieved significant change at local and state government levels. On June 12, 2020, New York became one of the first states to ban the use of choke holds and to repeal a half-century-old law that kept police disciplinary records secret. On the same day, the New York City Council made $1 billion in cuts to the Police Department's $6 billion budget. California governor Gavin Newsom called for an immediate end to the use of "strangleholds" by police. The District of Columbia

Council unanimously passed measures that prohibited the use of chemical irritants, riot gear, and stun grenades on demonstrators. The Iowa legislature banned choke holds and empowered the state attorney general to investigate police misconduct.[84]

To be successful, these actions often had to push past logjams to reform that had persisted for a long time. For example, New York police unions successfully stopped a package of reforms that had quickly been passed by the state legislature in June 2020, in the wake of the mass upsurge against police violence. Rather than police unions controlling a message of public insults against alleged Black rioters, BLM activists have been able to take control of the public narrative and press for structural reforms targeting police misconduct.

In the pathbreaking book *Stamped from the Beginning*, Ibram Kendi reminds us that both anti-racist and pro-racist ideologies have long existed in the United States.[85] Thus, it should be no surprise that hours after Democrats unveiled the Justice in Policing Act, President Trump tweeted: "The Radical Left Democrats want to Defund and Abandon our Police."[86] We can depend on the political right to continue to use the public insult playbook to create headwinds to reform and to drag down any change with dead weights. Their tactics are not going to disappear even if progressives gain majority support for their reforms. At this point, however, it is possible that the political right has overplayed its hand, so that progressives shrug at these public insults rather than really worrying that they are gaining traction. It is possible that proponents of structural reform have had a meaningful impact on the views of a majority of Americans despite the public insult playbook.

LESSONS FOR OTHER MOVEMENTS?

There is no easy way for progressives to counter the public insult playbook. While some have proclaimed that the #MeToo movement has increased the visibility of the important issue of sexual harassment and sexual assault, others argue that women's lived experiences have largely gone unchanged, especially for women in workplaces such as the restaurant industry, where flaunting their sexuality is considered a prerequisite to getting good tips or favorable treatment by the boss. We can certainly point to some famous men who have been brought down by the #MeToo movement, but Aya Gruber cautions us to remember that a feminist cause should not proclaim success by fueling the mass incarceration movement. She says that a basic tenet of modern feminist thought should be: "Criminal law is a last, not first, resort."[87]

Jasmine Harris has suggested that the disability rights movement has been hampered by its reliance on privacy jurisprudence to advance its rights; she urges people with disabilities to be more public about their status and efforts. She notes that the DREAMers, original MeToo movement, and early LGB movement appropriated the schema of the "closet" and "coming out" to generate broader support for their movements.[88] The early gay rights movement pressed for lesbian and gay visibility to counter the effects of "Don't Ask Don't Tell" and the Defense of Marriage Act. Despite the legal perils of revealing their immigration status, undocumented immigrants have gone public to change the "shadow" narrative. The #MeToo movement has challenged nondisclosure agreements and is pressing Congress to restrict the use of mandatory arbitration to resolve sexual harassment disputes. While these movements have not achieved total victory, they have succeeded in countering some of the effects of the public insult playbook.

Of course, much work lies ahead. Harris observes that "publicity as a strategic communications campaign has not yet happened in disability rights."[89] That observation may be an overstatement, because some members of the disability community have sought to engage in public information campaigns to shatter prejudices and stereotypes. For example, a national campaign has successfully sought to eliminate the use of the term "retarded" in federal, state, and local policy. Maryland first eliminated the R-word from the health and education code based on advocacy by the family of Rosa Marcelino;[90] in 2010, President Obama signed into law a bill that would ban such language at the federal level, after a grassroots campaign to "Spread the Word" was successful.[91] Celebrities and politicians who are caught saying the R-word often face immediate backlash and are forced to issue apologies or face adverse consequences. Recent examples of this include Kim Kardashian,[92] Giants cornerback Janoris Jenkins,[93] and Senator Kevin Kramer of North Dakota.[94] Netflix documentaries like *Crip*

Camp[95] may also be increasing disability visibility. Nonetheless, as is well documented by Doron Dorfman, many members of society view people with disabilities who seek accommodations as fraudsters or shirkers.[96] That perception may be perpetuated through the closeting of invisible disabilities.

Whether or not the reader believes that too little work has gone into public discussion of the effects of disabilities on people's lives, it is clear that community activists do have the strength and ability to overcome the dead weights and headwinds of the public insult playbook. From Harvey Milk's early call for the gay rights community to come out of the closet, to Anita Hill's courage in testifying before the US Senate about graphic sexual harassment, to DREAMers who risk deportation by speaking about their life circumstances, we have evidence that the public insult playbook can be countered through the steady work of consistent organizing and the valor of activists willing to speak out, even at great personal cost. Their work can help us achieve progressive, structural change.

The BLM movement has offered us an effective example of a response to the public insult playbook. It has quickly responded to the lies and irrelevancies that have been postulated as an excuse to murder Black people. It has pushed hard for structural reform rather than merely justice for the family or friends of one victim. It did not declare victory when the murder charge against Derek Chauvin was raised to second degree murder. Instead, BLM continued to call for transformative change. Its rallying cry has been echoed and amplified by the millions around the world who demonstrated in solidarity.

The message of this book has been that we cannot achieve effective structural reform without accounting for the power of the public insult playbook. As Kendi reminds us in documenting the pervasiveness of racist ideology, power bullies will always go to the public insult playbook to attack progressives. BLM has shown us the effectiveness of anticipating those insults and quickly pushing for structural reform. It hasn't been easy. A lot of people have had to die for this strategy to achieve any positive results. It has taken an international multiracial community, which has been willing to take to the streets even during the COVID-19 pandemic, to achieve this progress. Despite racism's persistence, it is possible for progressives to counter the public insults and seek to advance structural reforms.

. . . . .

Ending on a positive note, I'd like to share the example of Representative Alexandria Ocasio-Cortez (AOC), who spoke on the floor of the House of Representatives to reply to two public statements by Representative Ted Yoho in summer 2020. On the steps of the House of Representatives, on July 21, 2020, Yoho had called AOC "disgusting"; had told her, "You are out of your freaking mind"; and was overheard by a reporter saying that she was a "fucking bitch." A day later, he then gave a nonapology on the floor of the House, in which he said that he could not be considered disrespectful toward women because he had been married for forty-five years and had two daughters.[97]

On July 23 AOC gave a ten-minute speech on the House floor.[98] First she put Yoho's comments in the context of many women's lives. In a calm and measured tone, she powerfully explained the power of insults in women's lives:

> I have worked a working-class job. I have waited tables in restaurants. I have ridden the subway. I have walked the streets in New York City. And this kind of language is not new. I have encountered words uttered by Mr. Yoho and men uttering the same words as Mr. Yoho while I was being harassed in restaurants. I have tossed men out of bars that have used language like Mr. Yoho's and I have encountered this type of harassment riding the subway in New York City. This is not new. And that is the problem. Mr. Yoho was not alone. He was walking shoulder to shoulder with Representative Roger Williams. And that's when we start to see this issue is not about one incident. It is cultural. It is a culture of lack of impunity, of accepting of violence and having language against women, an entire structure of power that supports that.
>
> Because not only have I been spoken to disrespectfully, particularly by members of the Republican Party, and elected officials in the Republican Party, not just here, but the President of the United States last year told me to go home, to another country, with the implication that I don't even belong in America. The Governor of Florida, Governor Desantis, before I was sworn in, called me a "whatever." That . . . dehumanizing language is not new, and what we are seeing is that incidents like these are happening in a pattern. This is a pattern of an attitude towards women and dehumanization of others.

In a few short minutes, she showed how men use the power of insults to dehumanize women in all walks of life: on the subway, in the streets, in a restaurant, in the halls of Congress, and even in the White House. Further, she tied Yoho's misogyny to insults leveled against immigrants. She portrayed the public insult playbook as a tool against disadvantaged people in society generally, not merely her specifically.

But then, in an equally powerful few minutes, she sought to rally people not to accept Yoho's insults and, in particular, not to allow Yoho to hide behind his wife and daughters to deflect the inappropriateness of his insults. AOC was angrier about Yoho's attempt to co-opt his relationship with his wife and daughters as an excuse for his vile behavior than about the initial insult itself. In that same measured tone, which has been a hallmark of her effectiveness as a public speaker, she said:

> Yesterday, Representative Yoho decided to come to the floor of the House of Representatives and make excuses for his behavior. And that I could not let go. I could not allow my nieces, I could not allow the little girls that I go home to, I could not allow victims of verbal abuse and worse to see that—to see that excuse and to see our Congress accepted as legitimate and accept it as an apology and to accept silence as a form of acceptance. I could not allow that to stand which is why I'm rising today to raise this point of personal privilege. And I do not need Representative Yoho to apologize to me. Clearly, he does not want to. Clearly when given the opportunity he will not. And I will not stay up late at night waiting for an apology from a man who has no remorse over calling women and using abusive language towards women. But what I do have issue with is using women, wives and daughters as shields and excuses for poor behavior. Mr. Yoho mentioned that he has a wife and two daughters. I am two years younger than Mr. Yoho's youngest daughter. I am someone's daughter too. My father, thankfully, is not alive to see how Mr. Yoho treated his daughter. My mother got to see Mr. Yoho's disrespect on the floor of this House towards me on television. And I am here because I have to show my parents that I am their daughter and that they did not raise me to accept abuse from men. Now, what I am here to say is that this harm that Mr. Yoho levied, . . . tried to levy against me, was not just an incident directed at me, but when you do that to any woman, what Mr. Yoho did was give permission to other men to do that to his daughters. He—in using that language in front of the press, he gave permission to use that language against his wife, his daughters, women in his community, and I am here to stand up to say that is not acceptable.

I do not care what your views are. It does not matter how much I disagree or how much it incenses me or how I feel that people are dehumanizing others. I will not do that myself. I will not allow people to change and create hatred in our hearts. And so what I believe is that having a daughter does not make a man decent. Having a wife does not make a man decent. Treating people with dignity and respect makes a decent man. And when a decent man messes up, as we all are bound to do, he tries his best and does apologize. Not to save face, not to win a vote. He apologizes genuinely to repair and acknowledge the harm done so that we can all move on.

Lastly, what I want to express to Mr. Yoho is gratitude. I want to thank him for showing the world that you can be a powerful man, be married and accost women. You can take photos and project an image to the world of being a family man and accost women without remorse and with a sense of impunity. It happens every day in this country. It happened here on the steps of our Nation's Capitol. It happens when individuals who hold the highest office in this land admit, admit to hurting women and using this language against all of us.

AOC sought to help the listener understand how Yoho was yielding power as he used the public insult playbook. He was legitimizing the right of all men to speak disrespectfully to women. She urged the listener to resist the power bullies and seek to create a society in which such verbiage is not acceptable. She helped the listener to understand that Yoho insulted "all of us" when he uttered his deeply misogynist language. She understood that the public insult playbook is not merely a personal attack; it is a tactic to sustain power over disadvantaged members of society.

AOC ended her speech by thanking her colleagues for joining her to listen to her speech. I end this book by thanking my readers for joining me on this journey to better understand the public insult playbook. The public insult playbook is not going away, but we can improve our ability to anticipate and respond to it, as we seek structural reform.

Notes

INTRODUCTION

1. Ruth Colker, *The Disability Pendulum* 41 (2005).
2. *See* 42 U.S.C. § 12211.
3. *See* § 12188(a)(2) (injunctive relief provision).
4. *See* John Wodatch, "Are Some People Taking Advantage of the Disability Access Laws?," *CBS News*, Dec. 8, 2016, www.cbsnews.com/video/are-some -people-taking-advantage-of-disability-access-laws/.
5. *See* Jasmine Harris, "The Privacy Tug of War in Disability Right Law," 169 *U. Penn. L. Rev.* (forthcoming May 2021).
6. C. Wright Mills, *The Power Elite* (1959).
7. Charles Lawrence, Mari Matsuda, Richard Delgado & Kimberlè Crenshaw, *Words That Wound: Critical Race Theory, Assaultive Speech, and the First Amendment* 2 (1993).
8. *Id.* at 67.
9. *Id.* at 89–110.
10. *Id.* at 89.
11. *See* Tom Hays and Larry Neumeister, "Violence in Charlottesville Leads to Soul-Searching," *APNews*, Aug. 23, 2017, www.apnews.com/8eaa68a33ab 84477a938b0d2490419e7 ("After the 1978 furor over the neo-Nazi rally in Skokie, which never actually got off the ground, the ACLU stood firm even as it received hate mail and hundreds of members quit.").

12. *See* "ACLU Case Selection Guidelines: Conflicts between Competing Values or Priorities," www.aclu.org/sites/default/files/field_document/aclu_case_selection_guidelines.pdf.

13. *See* Wendy Kaminer, "The ACLU Retreats from Free Expression," *WSJ*, June 20, 2018, www.wsj.com/articles/the-aclu-retreats-from-free-expression-1529533065.

14. Aya Gruber, *The Feminist War on Crime: The Unexpected Role of Women's Liberation in Mass Incarceration* 17 (2020).

CHAPTER 1. INSULTS: A POWER TOOL FOR POWER BULLIES

1. Peter Feuerherd, "The First Ugly Election: America, 1800," *JSTOR Daily*, July 4, 2016, https://daily.jstor.org/first-ugly-election-america-1800/.

2. Peter Carlson, "Pistols at Dawn," *American History Magazine* 32, 33 (February 2011), www.historynet.com/pistols-at-dawn.htm.

3. *Id.* at 34.

4. *Id.* at 34.

5. *Id.* at 35.

6. *Id.* at 36.

7. *Id.* at 36.

8. *See* Joanne B. Freeman, *The Field of Blood: Violence in Congress and the Road to Civil War* 218–34 (2019).

9. *See* Owen M. Fiss, "Foreword: The Forms of Justice," 93 *Harv. L. Rev.* 1, 2 (1979).

10. "Ferguson Police Say Michael Brown Was Suspect in Robbery," *Fox News*, Aug. 15, 2014, updated Nov. 29, 2015, www.foxnews.com/us/ferguson-police-say-michael-brown-was-suspect-in-robbery.

11. Ezra Klein, "The Police Are the Issue in Ferguson, Not Michael Brown's Character," *Vox*, Aug. 14, 2014, www.vox.com/2014/8/15/6005861/michael-brown-darren-wilson-ferguson-shooting.

12. *See* Ciara Nugent & Billy Perrigo, "'The Edge of an Abyss': How the World's Newspapers Are Responding as the U.S. Descends into Chaos," *Time*, June 2, 2020, https://time.com/5846698/world-reactions-george-floyd-protests/.

13. *Id.*

14. *See* Jose A. DelReal, "Trump Draws Scornful Rebuke for Mocking Reporter with Disability," *Wash. Post*, Nov. 26, 2015, www.washingtonpost.com/news/post-politics/wp/2015/11/25/trump-blasted-by-new-york-times-after-mocking-reporter-with-disability/?utm_term=.dd86e1145860 (discussing response to Trump mocking Kovaleski).

15. *See* Irin Carmon, "Donald Trump's Worst Offense? Mocking Disabled Reporter, Poll Finds," *NBC News*, Aug. 11, 2016, www.nbcnews.com/politics /2016-election/trump-s-worst-offense-mocking-disabled-reporter-poll-finds -n627736 (providing polling on response to Trump mocking Kovaleski).

16. Lauren Carroll, "Fact-Checking Trump's Claim That Thousands in New Jersey Cheered When World Trade Center Crumbled," *Politifact*, Nov. 22, 2015, www.politifact.com/truth-o-meter/statements/2015/nov/22/donald-trump/fact -checking-trumps-claim-thousands-new-jersey-ch/.

17. *See* Linda Qiu, "Donald Trump's Top 10 Campaign Promises," *Politifact*, July 15, 2016, www.politifact.com/truth-o-meter/article/2016/jul/15/donald -trumps-top-10-campaign-promises/ (listing Trump's campaign promises).

18. Carroll, "Fact-Checking Trump's Claim That Thousands in New Jersey Cheered When World Trade Center Crumbled."

19. *See* DelReal, "Trump Draws Scornful Rebuke for Mocking Reporter with Disability."

20. *Id.*

21. *See* Glenn Kessler, "Donald Trump's Revisionist History of Mocking a Disabled Reporter," *Wash. Post*, Aug. 2, 2016, www.washingtonpost.com/news /fact-checker/wp/2016/08/02/donald-trumps-revisionist-history-of-mocking-a -disabled-reporter/?utm_term=.ee7e42b0de31.

22. *See* Qiu, "Donald Trump's Top 10 Campaign Promises."

23. *See* Miriam Valverde, "DACA Remains, but Trump Administration Eliminated DAPA," *Politifact*, Jan. 11, 2019, www.politifact.com/truth-o-meter /promises/trumpometer/promise/1443/terminate-barack-obamas-immigration -executive-orde/.

24. *See* Kessler, "Donald Trump's Revisionist History of Mocking a Disabled Reporter."

25. Daniel Victor and Giovanni Russonello, "Meryl Streep's Golden Globes Speech," *N.Y. Times*, Jan. 8, 2017, www.nytimes.com/2017/01/08/arts/television /meryl-streep-golden-globes-speech.html?module=inline.

26. *See* Liz Spayd, "Not 'She Said, He Said': Mockery, Plain and Simple," *N.Y. Times*, Jan. 10, 2017, www.nytimes.com/2017/01/10/public-editor/trump-streep -golden-globes.html.

27. Valverde, "DACA Remains, but Trump Administration Eliminated DAPA."

28. *See* Gerald N. Rosenberg, *The Hollow Hope: Can Courts Brings about Social Change?* 12 (2008) (contrasting the failure of the civil rights campaign in Albany, Georgia, with later successes)..

29. Jill Lepore, *These Truths: A History of the United States* 256 (2018).

30. *Id.* at 256.

31. Michele Wellsby et al., "Some Insults Are Easier to Detect: The Embodied Insult Detection Effect," 1 *Frontiers in Psychol.* 1, 3 (2010).

32. José Mateo & Francisco Ramos Yus, "Towards a Cross-Cultural Pragmatic Taxonomy of Insults," 1 *J. Language Aggression & Conflict* 87, 88 (2013).

33. *See* Michael S. Rosenwald, "'A High-Tech Lynching': How Brett Kavanaugh Took a Page from the Clarence Thomas Playbook," *Wash. Post*, Sept. 27, 2018, www.washingtonpost.com/history/2018/09/25/high-tech-lynching.

34. History News Network, "A High-Tech Lynching," Columbian College of Arts & Sciences, The George Washington University, Sept. 25, 2018, https://historynewsnetwork.org/article/170071.

35. William L. Benoit & Dawn M. Nill, "A Critical Analysis of Judge Clarence Thomas' Statement before the Senate Judiciary Committee," 49 *Comm. Stud.* 179, 180 (1998).

36. *Id.* at 191.

37. *Id.* at 191.

38. *Id.* at 189.

39. *Id.* at 190.

40. *See* Irin Carmon, "Did Arlen Specter Ever Apologize to Anita Hill," *Salon*, Oct., 15, 2012, www.salon.com/2012/10/15/did_arlen_specter_ever_apologize_to_anita_hill/.

41. Quoted in *id.*

42. William Welch, "Thomas Presided over Shift in Policy at EEOC, Records Show," *APNews*, July 25, 1991, https://apnews.com/b419883e871b5117649d1f3fdacf6f95.

43. Rosenwald, "'A High-Tech Lynching.'"

44. Dylan Scott, "Brett Kavanaugh's Senate Testimony, Explained in 7 Moments," *Vox*, Sept. 27, 2018, www.vox.com/policy-and-politics/2018/9/27/17911652/brett-kavanaugh-senate-testimony-christine-blasey-ford.

45. Sheryl Gay Stolberg, "Kavanaugh Is Sworn in after Close Confirmation Vote in Senate," *N.Y. Times*, Oct. 6, 2018, www.nytimes.com/2018/10/06/us/politics/brett-kavanaugh-supreme-court.html.

46. Scott, "Brett Kavanaugh's Senate Testimony, Explained in 7 Moments."

47. Associated Press, "The Thomas Confirmation Hearing; How the Senators Voted on Thomas," *N.Y. Times*, Oct. 16, 1991, www.nytimes.com/1991/10/16/us/the-thomas-confirmation-how-the-senators-voted-on-thomas.html.

48. Sheryl Gay Stolberg & Nicholas Fandos, "Brett Kavanaugh and Christine Blasey Ford Duel with Tears and Fury," *N.Y. Times*, Sept. 27, 2018, www.nytimes.com/2018/09/27/us/politics/brett-kavanaugh-confirmation-hearings.html.

49. Julia Jacobs, "Anita Hill's Testimony and Other Key Moments from the Clarence Thomas Hearings," *N.Y. Times*, Sept. 20, 2018, www.nytimes.com/2018/09/20/us/politics/anita-hill-testimony-clarence-thomas.html.

CHAPTER 2. HEADWINDS, DEFLECTIONS, AND DEAD WEIGHTS

1. *See, e.g.,* Frances Fox Piven & Richard A. Cloward, *Poor People's Movements: Why They Succeed, How They Fail* (1977); Mark Engler & Paul Engler, *This Is an Uprising: How Nonviolent Revolt Is Shaping the Twenty-First Century* (2016); and Gerald N. Rosenberg, *The Hollow Hope: Can Courts Bring about Social Change?* (2008).

2. Engler & Engler, *This Is an Uprising.*

3. *Id.* at 214.

4. *Id.* at 216.

5. *Id.* at 216.

6. *Id.* at 219.

7. *Id.* at 219–23.

8. *Id.* at 219.

9. *Id.* at 223.

10. *Id.* at 223.

11. Representing Wisconsin's Fifth District, web.archive.org/web/2018122 1231320/https:/sensenbrenner.house.gov/issues/immigration (accessed Mar. 22, 2021). *See also* Congressman Sensenbrenner Statement on the End of the DACA Program, Sept. 5, 2017, web.archive.org/web/20200118182832/https: /sensenbrenner.house.gov/press-releases-statements?ID=B49BEF18-C222-4193 -BB17-91343C23785A (supporting the ending of the DACA program) (accessed Mar. 22, 2021).

12. *See* Meredith Hoffman, "Whatever Happened to Arizona's Minutemen?," *Vice,* Mar. 22, 2016, www.vice.com/en_us/article/xd7jmn/what-happened-to -arizonas-minutemen.

13. *See* Mary Lee Grant & Nick Miroff, "U.S. Militia Groups Head to Border, Stirred by Trump's Call to Arms," *Wash. Post,* Nov. 3, 2018, www.washingtonpost .com/world/national-security/us-militia-groups-head-to-border-stirred-by -trumps-call-to-arms/2018/11/03/ff96826c-decf-11e8-b3f0-62607289efee _story.html?utm_term=.bd169eefbfdf.

14. *See* Kayla Epstein, Lindsey Bever & Eli Rosenberg, "An Armed Militia Was 'Detaining' Migrants at the Border: The FBI Arrested Its Leader," *Wash. Post,* Apr. 22, 2019, www.washingtonpost.com/immigration/2019/04/21/an-armed -militia-was-detaining-migrants-border-fbi-arrested-its-leader/?utm_term= .1917fd5c7379 .

15. Engler & Engler, *This Is an Uprising,* at 223.

16. *Id.* at 223.

17. *Id.* at 223.

18. *See* Janet I. Tu & Lornet Turnbull, "Minutemen Watch U.S.-Canada Border," *Seattle Times*, Oct. 4, 2005, www.seattletimes.com/seattle-news/minute men-watch-us-canada-border/ (describing goals of Minutemen to deter illegal immigration and report employers who hire illegal immigrants); and "Minutemen, Other Anti-Immigrant Militia Groups Stake Out Arizona," Southern Poverty Law Center, June 27, 2005, www.splcenter.org/fighting-hate/intelligence -report/2005/minutemen-other-anti-immigrant-militia-groups-stake-out -arizona-border (describing tactics of vigilante militias).

19. *See* Lazaro Zamora, "Obama's Immigration Executive Actions: Two Years Later," BiPartisan Policy Center, Dec. 9, 2016, bipartisanpolicy.org/blog/obamas -immigration-executive-actions-two-years-later/.

20. *See* Steve Almasy & Darran Simon, "A Timeline of President Trump's Travel Bans," *CNN*, Mar. 30, 2017, www.cnn.com/2017/02/10/us/trump-travel -ban-timeline/index.html.

21. "The Dream Act, DACA, and Other Policies Designed to Protect Dreamers," American Immigration Council, Sept. 3, 2019, www.americanimmigration council.org/research/dream-act-daca-and-other-policies-designed-protect -dreamers

22. *Id.* at 3.

23. Max Greenwood, "Poll: Nearly 9 in 10 Want DACA Recipients to Stay in US," *The Hill*, Jan. 18, 2018, https://thehill.com/blogs/blog-briefing-room/news /369487-poll-nearly-nine-in-10-favor-allowing-daca-recipients-to-stay.

24. Samuel Chamberlain, "Thousands of DACA Recipients with Arrest Records, Including 10 Accused Murderers, Allowed to Stay in US," *Fox News*, June 18, 2018, www.foxnews.com/politics/thousands-of-daca-recipients-with -arrest-records-including-10-accused-murderers-allowed-to-stay-in-us.

25. Reva B. Siegel, "Constitutional Culture, Social Movement Conflict and Constitutional Change: The Case of the De Facto ERA," 94 *Calif. L. Rev.* 1323 (2006).

26. Robin West, "Constitutional Culture or Ordinary Politics: A Reply to Reva Siegel," 94 *Calif. L. Rev.* 1465 (2006).

27. *See, e.g.,* Piven & Cloward, *Poor People's Movements*; Engler & Engler, *This Is An Uprising*; and Rosenberg, *The Hollow Hope*.

28. *See* Joan Williams, *Unbending Gender: Why Family and Work Conflict and What to Do about It* 147 (1999).

29. For a description of the range of approaches that have been suggested by the political left, *see* Conor Friedersdorf, "Why Can't the Left Win?," *Atlantic*, May 4, 2017, www.theatlantic.com/politics/archive/2017/05/why-cant-the-left -win/522102/.

30. *See* Jessica Taylor & Ayesha Rascoe, "Republicans Seize on 'Angry Mob' Mantra to Keep Their Midterm Base Fired Up," *NPR*, Oct. 10, 2018, www.npr

.org/2018/10/10/656396084/republicans-seize-on-angry-mob-mantra-to-keep
-their-midterm-base-fired-up.

31. *See* Eli Rosenberg, "'Grow Up': Orrin Hatch Waves Off Female Protestors Demanding to Speak with Him," *Wash. Post*, Oct. 5, 2018, www.washingtonpost .com/politics/2018/10/05/grow-up-orrin-hatch-waves-off-female-protesters -demanding-speak-with-him/?utm_term=.803ce1eb6dbd.

32. *See* Robert Barnes & Emily Guskin, "More Americans Disapprove of Kavanaugh's Confirmation Than Support It, New Poll Shows," *Wash. Post*, Oct. 12, 2018, www.washingtonpost.com/politics/more-americans-disapprove-of-kavanaughs -confirmation-than-support-it-new-poll-shows/2018/10/12/18dbf872-cd93 -11e8-a3e6-44daa3d35ede_story.html?utm_term=.1dc57ff6be77.

33. U.S. Const. Art. II, § 2, cl. 2.

34. *See* Andrew Prokop, "Why the Electoral College Is the Absolute Worst, Explained," *Vox*, Dec. 19, 2016, www.vox.com/policy-and-politics/2016/11/7 /12315574/electoral-college-explained-presidential-elections-2016.

35. *See* Melanie Zanona & Scott Wong, "Democrats See Hypocrisy in GOP Attacks on 'Liberal Mob,'" *The Hill*, 2018 WL 499690 (Oct. 10, 2018); and Kyle Balluck, "Trump Praises McConnell: He 'Stared Down the Angry Left-Wing Mob' to Get Kavanaugh Confirmed," *The Hill*, 2018 WL 4951210 (Oct. 14, 2018).

36. *See* Jill Lepore, *These Truths: A History of the United States* 256 (2018) (quoting Virginian George Fitzhugh).

37. For a discussion of how Justice Ginsburg has attempted to depart from this model of formal equality, *see* Shira Galinsky, "Returning the Language of Fairness to Equal Protection: Justice Ruth Bader Ginsburg's Affirmative Action Jurisprudence in Grutter and Gratz and Beyond," 7 *N.Y.C. L. Rev.* 357 (2004).

38. 418 U.S. 717 (1974).

39. 448 U.S. 297 (1980.

40. Isaac Saidel-Goley & Joseph William Singer, "Things Invisible to See: State Action & Private Property," 5 *Tex. A & M L. Rev.* 439 (2018).

41. *See* "Barriers to Equity in Education," www.scholastic.com/teacher principalreport/barriers-to-equity.htm (accessed May 30, 2019).

42. *See* Cindy Long, "Stop Blaming Teachers: Those Who Scapegoat Teachers May Have Much to Gain, but Students Have Much More to Lose," National Education Association, www.nea.org/tools/53524.htm (accessed May 20, 2019).

43. 505 U.S. 833 (1992).

44. The controlling opinion said: "The underlying constitutional issue is whether the State can resolve these philosophic questions in such a definitive way that a woman lacks all choice in the matter, except perhaps in those rare circumstances in which the pregnancy is itself a danger to her own life or health, or is the result of rape or incest." *Id.* at 850.

45. *Id.* at 852.

46. Box v. Planned Parenthood of Indiana and Kentucky, 139 S. Ct. 1780 (2019).

47. Gonzales v. Carhart, 550 U.S. 124,159 (2007) (Kennedy, J.)

48. *See* John Haltiwanger, "A State Legislature That Is 85% Male Passed the Most Extreme Abortion Ban in the United States since Roe v. Wade," *Business Insider*, May 15, 2019, www.businessinsider.com/alabamas-85-male-legislature -passed-most-extreme-abortion-ban-since-roe-v-wade-2019-5.

49. *See* Engler & Engler, *This Is an Uprising* (describing conditions under which nonviolent revolt, rather than more mainstream tactics, can help attain change).

50. *See* 42 U.S.C. §§ 12181-12189.

51. *See* Winnie Hu, "For the Disabled, New York's Sidewalks Are an Obstacle Course," *N.Y. Times*, Oct. 8, 2017, www.nytimes.com/2017/10/08/nyregion /new-york-city-sidewalks-disabled-curb-ramps.html; and Disability Rights Advocates, "Court Report Confirms Dismal State of Sidewalks for Disabled New Yorkers," Aug. 10, 2017, https://dralegal.org/press/court-report-confirms-dismal -state-sidewalks-disabled-new-yorkers/.

52. *See* Matt Vasilogambros, "How Voters with Disabilities Are Blocked from the Ballot Box," PEW, Feb. 1, 2018, www.pewtrusts.org/en/research-and-analysis /blogs/stateline/2018/02/01/how-voters-with-disabilities-are-blocked-from-the -ballot-box.

53. *See* Vilissa Thompson, "(In)Accessible Rooms: The Biggest Lie Told by the Hotel Industry," Ramp Your Voice, Jan. 12, 2017, http://rampyourvoice.com/2017 /01/12/inaccessible-rooms-biggest-lie-told-hotel-industry/.

54. *See* David Perry, "Restaurants Haven't Lived Up to the Promise of the Americans with Disabilities Act," *Eater*, May 31, 2017, www.eater.com/2017/5/31 /15701042/american-disabilities-act-restaurants-compliance.

55. Conversation with Arlene Mayerson, Jan. 5, 2019, New Orleans, LA.

56. *See* Kitty Cone, "Short History of the 504 Sit In," Disability Rights Education & Defense Fund, https://dredf.org/504-sit-in-20th-anniversary/short -history-of-the-504-sit-in/ (accessed Dec. 11, 2018).

57. *See* Douglas Crimp, "Before Occupy: How AIDS Activists Seized Control of the FDA in 1988," *Atlantic*, Dec. 6, 2011, www.theatlantic.com/health/archive /2011/12/before-occupy-how-aids-activists-seized-control-of-the-fda-in-1988 /249302/.

58. *See* Maya Rhodan, "Protestors Got Dragged Out of a Hearing on the Republican Health Care Bill," *Time*, Sept. 25, 2017, http://time.com/4956397 /graham-cassidy-republican-health-care-protests/.

59. *See* Colin Deppen, "Why People with Disabilities Are Protesting Like Hell," *HuffPost*, Oct. 11, 2018, www.huffingtonpost.com/entry/people-with -disabilities-protest_us_5baa3d65e4b07dc0b87e1264.

60. *See, e.g.,* Evan Gibbs, "Stopping Drive-By Lawsuits," *Above the Law*, Oct. 2, 2017, https://abovethelaw.com/2017/10/stopping-drive-by-lawsuits/.

61. *See* Michael E. Waterstone, "The Costs of Easy Victory," 57 *Wm. & Mary L. Rev.* 587 (2015).

62. *Id.* at 591.

63. *Id.* at 605.

64. *Id.* at 591.

65. *Id.* at 599.

CHAPTER 3. DRIVE-BY LITIGATORS OR ACCESSIBILITY HEROES?

1. *See* David M. Perry, "Did Trump Call Sessions 'Retarded'?," *Pacific Standard*, Sept. 14, 2018, https://psmag.com/news/did-donald-trump-call-jeff-sessions-retarded.

2. *Id.*

3. *See* Rebecca Cokley, "Calling Trump Unwell Doesn't Hurt Trump: It Hurts Disabled People," *Wash. Post*, June 16, 2020, www.washingtonpost.com/outlook/2020/06/16/mock-trump-hurts-disabled/.

4. Jay Ruderman, "When Will Disability Slurs Become Taboo?," *HuffPost*, Apr. 5, 2015, www.huffpost.com/entry/when-will-disability-slur_b_6593458 (the article incorrectly listed Rand Paul as representing New Hampshire).

5. *See* "Who We Are," Civil Rights and Education Enforcement Center, https://creeclaw.org/who-we-are/ (accessed May 31, 2019).

6. *See* Yates v. Sweet Potato Enterprises, 2017 WL 6520747, Case No. 11-cv-01950-LB (N.D. Calif. Sept. 21, 2017).

7. Yates v. Sweet Potato Enterprises, 2013 WL 4067783, Case No. C11-01950 SBA (N.D. Calif. Aug. 1, 2013).

8. Amy Robertson, "Prior Litigation: Admissible; Evidence of Life with a Disability: Inadmissible," *Thought Snax* (blog), July 17, 2013, thoughtsnax.com/2013/07/17/prior-litigation-admissible-evidence-of-life-with-a-disability-inadmissible/.

9. *Id.* at *2.

10. *Id.* at *3.

11. *See* Brief of *Amici Curiae* National Association of Convenience Stores et al., Steak 'N Shake v. Mielo & Heinzl, No. 17-2678 (filed Nov. 20, 2017).

12. *Id.* at 15.

13. Amy Robertson, "ADA Defense Lawyers Prolong Litigation and Postpone Access: A Case Study of Litigation Abuse," Civil Rights Education and

Enforcement Center, Feb. 27, 2018, https://creeclaw.org/ada-defense-abuse-a
-case-study/.

14. *See* William B. Rubenstein, "On What a 'Private Attorney General' Is—and
Why It Matters," 57 *Vand. L. Rev.* 2128 (2004) (describing various forms of the
private attorney general model).

15. Only injunctive relief is available under ADA Title III. *See* 42 U.S.C. §
12188(a)(1); 28 C.F.R. § 36.501(a).

16. *See* John F. Vargo, "The American Rule on Attorney Fee Allocation: The
Injured Person's Access to Justice," 42 *Am. U. L. Rev.* 1567 (1993).

17. John C. Coffee Jr., "Rescuing the Private Attorney General: Why the Model
of the Lawyer as Bounty Hunter Is Not Working," 42 *Md. L. Rev.* 215 (1983).

18. *Id.* at 216 n.1 (citing Associated Industries of New York State, Inc. v. Ickes,
134 F.2d 694, 704 (2nd Cir. 1943)).

19. *Id.* at 217.

20. *Id.* at 218.

21. *See, e.g.,* BTZ, Inc. v. Great Northern Nekoosa Corp., 47 F.3d 463, 466 n.3
(1st Cir. 1995); In re General Motors Corporation Pick-Truck Fuel Tank Products
Liability Litigation, 55 F.3d 768 (3rd Cir. 1996)

22. Michael Selmi, "The Price of Discrimination: The Nature of Class Action
Employment Discrimination Litigation and Its Effects," 81 *Tex. L. Rev.* 1249,
1331–32 (2003).

23. Michael Waterstone, "A New Vision of Public Enforcement," 92 *Minn. L.
Rev.* 434 (2007).

24. *Id.* at 442.

25. *Id.* at 443.

26. Omnibus Consolidated Rescissions and Appropriations Act of 1996, Pub.
L. No. 104-134, 504(a), 110 Stat. 1321, 50 (1996) (precluding Legal Services Corporation from pursuing class action litigation).

27. *Id.* at 497.

28. *Id.* at 497.

29. *See* Samuel R. Bagenstos, "The Perversity of Limited Civil Rights Remedies: The Case of 'Abusive' ADA Litigation," 54 *UCLA L. Rev.* 1 (2006).

30. *See* Grace Segers, "Feds Holding 12,800 Migrant Children in Detention
Centers, Report Says," *CBS News*, Sept., 13, 2018, www.cbsnews.com/news/feds
-holding-12800-migrant-children-in-detention-centers-report-says/.

31. *See* Erica L. Green, Matt Apuzzo & Katie Benner, "Trump Officials
Reverse Obama's Policy on Affirmative Action in Schools," *N.Y. Times*, July 3,
2018, www.nytimes.com/2018/07/03/us/politics/trump-affirmative-action-race
-schools.html.

32. *See* Inae Oh, "Trump Threatens 'Maximum Criminal Penalties' in Possible
Attempt to Suppress Votes," *Mother Jones*, Nov. 5, 2018, www.motherjones.com
/politics/2018/11/trump-voter-fraud-midterms-threat/.

33. *See, e.g.,* Department of Fair Employment and Housing v. Law School Admission Council, Inc., No. 12-cv-01830-JCS, 2018 WL 1156605, at n.4 (N.D. Cal. March 5, 2018) (observing that Department of Justice failed to take a position on a contempt motion in a case in which it was one of the original plaintiffs).

34. *See* State Board of Tax Commissioners v. Town of St. John, 751 N.E.2d 657, 662 (Ind. 2001) (denying taxpayer's request for attorney's fees after state's real property assessment scheme declared unconstitutional; expresses concern about "bounty hunters"); Stephenson v. Bartlett, 177 N.C. App. 239, 244 (Ct. Appeals 2006) (rejecting attorney's fees due to concern about "bounty hunters" in public interest litigation); League of Women Voters of Florida v. Detzner, 188 So.3d 68, 72 (Dist. Ct. App. Fla. 2016) (expressing concern about "bounty hunters" in rejecting argument for attorney's fees); Consumer Defense Group v. Rental Housing Industry Members, 137 Cal App.4th 1185, 1189 n.1 (Ct. Appeal, 4th Dist., Div. 3, Cal. 2006) (lawsuit against apartment owners for failure to warn consumers of exposure to carcinogens in violation of Proposition 65; awarding of attorney's fees to plaintiffs found to be "objectively unconscionable"; "At oral argument, Anthony G. Graham proudly proclaimed that he was a 'bounty hunter. The statute was created for me.' We will have more to say about exactly who Proposition 65 was created for later, but it wasn't bounty hunters.").

35. *See* H.R. 4498, 100th Cong. § 405 (1989).

36. Fair Housing Act of 1968, 42 U.S.C. § 3602(h).

37. *See* 42 U.S.C. § 2000a (prohibition against discrimination or segregation in places of public accommodation).

38. *See* 42 U.S.C. § 12188(a)(2) (providing for injunctive relief in private suits by affected parties).

39. 135 Cong. Rec. 19,803 (1989).

40. *Id.*

41. Conversation with Arlene Mayerson, Jan. 5, 2019, New Orleans, LA.

42. "What's a 'Drive-By Lawsuit'?," *60 Minutes*, Dec. 4, 2016, www.cbsnews .com/news/60-minutes-americans-with-disabilities-act-lawsuits-anderson -cooper/.

43. *Id.*

44. *Id.*

45. *See* Robyn Powell, "Here's What 60 Minutes Got Wrong about the ADA: Everything," *Yahoo!*, Dec. 12, 2016, web.archive.org/web/20161213172242/http: /www.yahoo.com/news/heres-60-minutes-got-wrong-220018024.html.

46. *See* "Disabled Viewers Criticize 60 Minutes Store," *60 Minutes*, Dec. 8, 2016, https://www.cbsnews.com/news/disabled-viewers-criticize-60-minutes -story/.

47. *See* "Flake Introduces Bill to Stop Abuse of ADA," press release, Sept. 29, 2016, www.flake.senate.gov/public/index.cfm/2016/9/flake-introduces-bill-to -stop-abuse-of-ada.

48. *See* John McMickle, "'Drive-By' Lawsuits under Disabled Statute Costing Economy," *The Hill*, Nov. 13, 2017, https://thehill.com/opinion/finance/360079 -drive-by-lawsuits-under-disabilities-statute-costing-economy.

49. *See* Ken Barnes, "Congress Should Take Action on ADA 'Drive-By' Lawsuits," *Forbes*, Dec. 14, 2017, www.forbes.com/sites/realspin/2017/12/14/congress -should-take-action-on-ada-drive-by-lawsuits/#58b568e6f6fa.

50. *See* Katherine Pearson, Director of Accessibility Rights, commentary, Equal Rights Center, https://equalrightscenter.org/response-drive-lawsuits/ (accessed Dec. 11, 2018).

51. *See* "An Update on ADA Drive-by Lawsuits," ADA National Network, Nov. 15, 2017, https://adata.org/event/update-ada-drive-lawsuits.

52. *See* Daniel Axelrod, "Local Woman Sues 5 Businesses over ADA Violation Claims," *Times Herald-Record*, Apr. 9, 2017, www.recordonline.com/news /20170409/local-woman-sues-5-businesses-over-ada-violation-claims.

53. *See generally* Southeast ADA Center, "Disability Rights and Public Accommodations: State-by-State," Feb. 2011, https://adasoutheast.org/publications /ada/public_accommodations_disability_rights_state-by-state_Final.pdf. For example, California allows plaintiffs to obtain $4,000/violation plus punitive damages and attorney's fees. *See* Unruh Civil Rights Act, California Civil Code, § 52(a) and (b).

54. See H.R. 620, ADA Education and Reform Act of 2017, 115th Congress (2017–2018), https://www.congress.gov/bill/115th-congress/house-bill/620.

55. *See* J. Colin Knisely, "House Passes Changes to Title III of the ADA," *Duane Morris Banking Law* (blog), Feb. 22, 2018, https://blogs.duanemorris .com/bankinglaw/2018/02/22/house-passes-changes-to-title-iii-of-the-ada/.

56. *See* H.R. 620. ADA Education and Reform Act of 2017, 115th Congress (passed House by a vote of 225 to 192 on Feb. 15, 2018), www.congress.gov/bill /115th-congress/house-bill/620/all-actions?overview=closed&q=%7B%22roll-call -vote%22%3A%22all%22%7D.

57. Tyler Ray, "Congress Wants to Change the Americans with Disabilities Act and Undermine the Civil Rights of People with Disabilities," ACLU, Sept. 6, 2017, www.aclu.org/blog/disability-rights/congress-wants-change-americans -disabilities-act-and-undermine-civil-rights.

58. *See* Tammy Duckworth, "Congress Wants to Make Americans with Disabilities Second-Class Citizens," *Wash. Post*, Oct. 17, 2017, www.washingtonpost .com/opinions/congress-is-on-the-offensive-against-americans-with-disabilities /2017/10/17/f508069c-b359-11e7-9e58-e6288544af98_story.html?utm_term= .6b7f9d30f328.

59. *Id.*

60. *See* Mike DeBonis, "House Passes Changes to Americans with Disabilities Act over Activists' Objections," *Wash. Post*, Feb. 15, 2018, www.washingtonpost

.com/powerpost/house-passes-changes-to-americans-with-disabilities-act
-over-activists-objections/2018/02/15/c812c9ea-125b-11e8-9065-e55346f6de81
_story.html?utm_term=.06335b1e142c.

61. *See, e.g.,* Schutts v. Bently Nevada Corp., 966 F. Supp. 1549 (D. Nev. 1997);
Seawright v. Charter Furniture Rental, Inc., 39 F. Supp.2d 795 (N.D. Tex. 1999);
Bergeron v. Northwest Publications, Inc., 165 F.R.D. 518 (D. Minn. 1996); Foot-
man v. Cheung, 341 F. Supp.2d 1218 (M.D. Fla. 2004) (granting motion by defendant for Rule 11 sanctions and attorney's fees); Montoyo-Rivera v. Pall Life
Sciences PR, LLC, 245 F. Supp.3d 337 (D. Puerto Rico 2017) (imposing Rule
sanctions on plaintiff's lawyer for filing duplicative action).

62. Bagenstos, "The Perversity of Limited Civil Rights Remedies," at 18.

63. *Id.* at 23.

64. *See* Sharp v. Balboa Islands, 900 F. Supp.2d 1084 (S.D. Cal. 2012); Sharp
v. Islands Restaurant-Carlsbad, 900 F. Supp.2d 1114 (S.D. Cal. 2012); Sharp v.
Islands California Arizona LP, 900 F. Supp.2d 1101 (S.D. Cal. 2012); Sharp v.
Covenant Care, LLC, 288 F.R.D. 465 (S.D. Cal. 2012); Sharp v. Waterfront Restaurants, No. 99-CV-200 TW (AJB), 1999 WL 1095486 (S.D. Cal. Aug. 2, 1999).

65. *See* Sharp v. Balboa Islands LLC, 900 F. Supp.2d 1084, 1087 (S.D. Calif.
2012) (listing Gregory Francis Hurley as attorney of record for the defendants).

66. Defendants' Memorandum of Points and Authorities in Support of Their
Motion for Summary Judgment or, in the Alternative, Summary Adjudication,
Sharp v. Balboa Islands, No. 3:11-CV-00675-W-BLM, 2012 WL 13049198 (S.D.
Cal. Mar. 9, 2012).

67. Defendant's Opposition to Motion for Summary Judgment, Sharp v. Balboa Islands, No. 11-CV-675W(BLM), 2012 WL 13049202 at *2 (S.D. Cal. Apr. 9,
2012).

68. *See* Defendant's Memorandum of Points and Authorities in Support of
Defendant's Motion for Summary Judgment, Sharp v. Islands California Arizona
LP, Nos. 11CV-0671 W (BLM), 11 CV-0427 W (BLMx), 2012 WL 6865127 at *2
(S.D. Cal. Sept. 25, 2012).

69. Sharp, 900 F. Supp.2d at 1092.

70. *Id.* at 1092.

71. *See* Metz & Harrison, LLP, home page, www.metzharrison.com/attorneys
.html (accessed Apr. 11, 2019).

72. *See* Greenberg Traurig, "Firm History," www.gtlaw.com/en/general/our
-firm/firm-history (accessed Apr. 11, 2019).

73. *See, e.g.,* Access 4 All. v. BAMCO VI, No. 11-61007-CIV, 2012 WL 33163 at
* 5 (S.D. Fla. Jan. 6, 2012) (concluding that case is moot because "there is nothing in the record to suggest that Defendant's ADA non-compliance was a continuing and deliberate practice"); Kallen v. J.R. Eight, 775 F. Supp.2d 1374, 1379
(S.D. Fla. 2011) (it is untenable for plaintiff "to suggest that once the renovations

are completed they could be undone"); National Alliance for Accessibility v. Walgreen, No. 3:10-CV-780-J-32-TEM., 2011 WL 5975809 at *3 (M.D. Fla. Nov. 28, 2011) (finding "it is 'absolutely clear' that the ADA violations identified by Plaintiffs cannot 'reasonably be expected to recur.'")

74. 505 F.3d 1173 (11th Cir 2007).

75. *See* text associated with note 108.

76. National Alliance for Accessibility v. Walgreen, No. 3:10-CV-780-J-32-TEM., 2011 WL 5975809 (M.D. Fla. Nov. 28, 2011).

77. *Id.* at *1.

78. *Id.* at *1.

79. *Id.* at *3.

80. *Id.* at *2.

81. *Id.* at *3.

82. *Id.* at *3.

83. *Id.* at *3.

84. *See* Friends of the Earth v. Laidlaw Environmental Services, Inc., 528 U.S. 167, 190 (2000) ("As just noted, a defendant claiming that its voluntary compliance moots a case bears the formidable burden of showing that it is absolutely clear the allegedly wrongful behavior could not reasonably be expected to recur.").

85. 654 F.3d 903 (9th Cir. 2011).

86. *Id.* at 905.

87. *Id.* at 906.

88. *Id.* at 906 n.7.

89. *Id.* at 906.

90. *Id.* at 911.

91. *See* Appellee Ralphs Grocery Company's Answer Brief, 2010 WL 4316229 (9th Cir. Filed Mar. 5, 2010), in A.J. Oliver v. Ralphs Grocery Company, No. 09-56447 at *6 (9th Cir. 2010).

92. *Id.*

93. *Id.* (citing Peters v. Winco Foods, Inc., 320 F. Supp.2d 1035 (E.D. Calif. 2004)).

94. *See* Arthur R. Miller, "From Conley to Twombly to Iqbal: A Double Play on the Federal Rules of Civil Procedure," 60 *Duke L. J.* 1 (2010) (criticizing how recent decisions have made it exceedingly difficult for a plaintiff to have a meaningful day in court).

95. *See* Buckhannon Board and Care Home, Inc. v. West Virginia Department of Health and Human Resources, 532 U.S. 598 (2001).

96. Coleman v. Chin Ju Pritchett d.b.a. New Star Restaurant, No. 5:05-cv-0040-RS-MD (N.D. Fla. Apr. 14, 2006).

97. *Id.* at *6.

98. *See, e.g.,* Access for America, Inc. v. Associated Out-Door Clubs, Inc., 188 Fed. Appx. 818, 2006 WL 1746890 at **1–2 (11th Cir. 2006) (affirming dismissal based on lack of standing for not demonstrating "any reasonable chance of his revisiting the Track, other than 'someday'"; dissent criticizing majority of requiring too specific an intention to return especially in light of plaintiff's assertion that he "traveled to the Track six or eight times per year for the last three years"); Defendant's Motion to Dismiss and Memorandum of Law in Support Thereof, Access for America, Inc. v. Associated Out-Door Clubs, Inc, No. 8:04CV-650-T-17-EAJ, 2004 WL 2742009 (M.D. Fla. May 10, 2004) (arguing that this "case is yet another example of the 'cottage industry' into which ADA-related litigation has evolved"; describing plaintiff as a "serial plaintiff"); Defendant's Memorandum of Law in Support of Its Motion to Dismiss Plaintiffs' Complaint for Lack of Subject Matter of Jurisdiction, 2004 WL 2742208, No. 8:04CV653-T-24TBM (M.D. Fla. 2004) (successful motion to dismiss in which defendant argued that plaintiff has no plan to return to defendant's hotel because he has filed numerous lawsuits, lives about one hundred miles away from this property, and has limited income selling "pencils in front of grocery stores and post offices").

99. 254 F. Supp.2d 1250, 1252 (M.D. Fla. 2003).

100. *Id.* at 1253.

101. Steven Brother v. Tiger Partner, LLC, 3331 F. Supp.2d 1368, 1371 (M.D. Fla. 2004).

102. *Id.* at 1369.

103. *Id.* at 1375.

104. *See, e.g.,* Brothers v. Rossmore Tampa Limited Partnership, 2004 WL 3609350 at *4 (M.D. Fla. Aug. 19, 2004) ("Plaintiff's professed intent to return to Defendant-hotel lacks credibility"); Brother v. CPL Investments, Inc., 317 F. Supp.2d 1358 (S.D. Fla. 2004) (judgment for hotel owner, dismissing suit); D'Lil v. Best Western Encina Lodge & Suites, 2006 WL 197142 (C.D. Cal. Jan. 12, 2006) (dismissing on standing grounds); Access 4 All, Inc. v. Wintergreen Commercial Partnership Ltd., 2005 WL 2989307 (N.D. Tex. Nov. 7, 2005 (dismissing on standing grounds); Molski v. Mandarin Touch Restaurant, 385 F. Supp.2d 1042 (C.D. Calif. 2005) (dismissing on standing grounds).

105. No. 11-60274-CIV, 2011 WL 4389894 (S.D. Fla. Sept. 21, 2011).

106. No. 11-61010-CIV, 2012 WL 602603 (S.D. Fla. Feb. 23, 2012).

107. *Id.* at * 6.

108. No. CV 07-841 PA (FFMx), 2007 WL 7543254 (C.D. Cal. Oct. 25, 2007).

109. *Id.* at *5.

110. *Id.* at *5.

111. *Id.* at *4.

112. *See* Friends of the Earth v. Laidlaw Environmental Services, Inc., 528 U.S. 167, 190 (2000) ("As just noted, a defendant claiming that its voluntary

compliance moots a case bears the formidable burden of showing that it is absolutely clear the allegedly wrongful behavior could not reasonably be expected to recur.").

113. Pereira v. Ralphs Grocery Company, 329 Fed. Appx. 134, 2009 WL 2039121 (9th Cir. 2009) (before Chief Judge Kozinski, Circuit Judge Pregerson, and District Judge Quist).

114. *Id.* at **1.

115. *See, e.g.,* Access 4 All. v. BAMCO VI, No. 11-61007-CIV, 2012 WL 33163 at * 5 (S.D. Fla. Jan. 6, 2012) (concluding that case is moot because "there is nothing in the record to suggest that Defendant's ADA non-compliance was a continuing and deliberate practice"); Kallen v. J.R. Eight, 775 Supp.2d 1374, 1379 (it is untenable for plaintiff "to suggest that once the renovations are completed they could be undone"); National Alliance for Accessibility v. Walgreen, No. 3:10-CV-780-J-32-TEM., 2011 WL 5975809 at *3 (finding "it is 'absolutely clear' that the ADA violations identified by Plaintiffs cannot 'reasonably be expected to recur'").

116. No. SACV 12-0128 AG (MLGx), 2013 WL 5509129 (C.D. Cal. Sept. 20, 2013).

117. *See* Complaint for Injunctive Relief and Damages, Rudder v. Fresh & Easy Neighborhood Market, Inc., No. SACV11-1884-JST (MlGx), 2011 WL 9372542 (C.D. Cal. Dec. 7, 2011).

118. *See* Rudder v. Costco Wholesale Corp., No. SACV 12-0128 (MLGx), 2013 WL 550919 (C.D. Cal. Sept. 20, 2013).

119. *See* Rudder v. Marmalade Café, Verdict for Plaintiff, 2011 WL 5055013, No. 10CV08498(GW) (C.D. Calif. June 2, 2011).

120. *See* Opposition to Demurrer, Rudder v. Hampton Inn, No. 30-2015-00793966-CU-MC-CJC, 2016 WL 10616477 (Cal. Super. Nov. 4, 2016); Minute Order, Rudder v. Pansuria, No. 30-2015-00793966-CU-MC-CJC, 2016 WL 10599575 (Cal. Super. Aug. 11, 2016).

121. *See* Rudder v. Los Angeles County Metro Transportation Authority, 114 S. Ct. 447 (1993) (denying writ of cert.)

122. *See* Complaint for Injunctive Relief and Damages, Rudder v. Costco Wholesale Corp. et al., No. SACV12-128-CJC, 2013 WL 550919 (C.D. Cal. Jan. 26, 2012).

123. Defendant's Memorandum in Support of Defendant's Motion to Dismiss, Rudder v. Costco, No. 8:12-CV-00128 at *3 (C.D. Cal. 2013).

124. Defendant's Memorandum in Opposition of Plaintiff's Motion for Summary Judgement, at 3, Rudder v. Costco, No. 8:12-cv-00128 (C.D. Cal. 2013).

125. Rudder v. Costco Wholesale Corp. et al., No. SACV 12-0128 AG (MLGx), 2013 WL 5509129 (C.D. Cal. 2013).

126. Doran, v. 7-Eleven, 524 F.3d 1034, 1042 (9th Cir. 2008).

127. 993 F. Supp.2d 1109 (C.D. Calif. 2012).

128. When he learned that there were no accessible seats in the Club level, the defendant allegedly offered to carry him to his seat, which he considered to be "humiliating and insensitive." Charlebois v. Angels Baseball, LP., No. SACV 10-0853 DOC (ANx), 2011 WL 2610122, at *1 (C.D. Cal. June 30, 2011).

129. The general requirements that need to be met are (1) ascertainability, (2) numerosity, (3) commonality, (4) typicality, and (5) adequacy of representation. *See id.* at *3–*11.

130. *Id.* at *9.

131. 993 F. Supp.2d at 1120.

132. *Id.* at 1121.

133. *Id.* at 1123.

134. *Id.* at 1124.

135. *Id.* at 1124.

136. *Id.* at 1125.

137. *Id.* at 1125.

138. *Id.* at 1116.

139. *Id.* at 1114.

140. *See* Benham v. S & J Security and Investigation, Inc., No. B207420, 2010 WL 761586 (LA Superior Court Mar. 8, 2010) (case involving false imprisonment, negligence, assault and battery, intentional infliction of emotional distress, and violations of California's civil rights laws regarding the actions of security officers during an improper accusation of shoplifting).

141. *See* Amy Robertson, "ADA Defense Lawyers Prolong Litigation and Postpone Access: A Case Study of Litigation Abuse," Civil Rights Education and Enforcement Center, Feb. 27, 2018, https://creeclaw.org/ada-defense-abuse-a-case-study/.

142. *See* Brief of *Amici Curiae* National Association of Convenience Stores, National Grocers Association, and Food Marketing Institute in Support of Appellant-Defendant and Reversal in Steak 'N Shake v. Mielo & Heinzl, No. 17-2678, 2017 WL 5759712 (3rd Cir. Nov. 20, 2017).

143. *See* Heinzl v. Cracker Barrel Old Country Stores, Inc., No. 2:14-cv-1455, 2016 WL 2347367 (W.D. Pa. Jan. 27, 2016).

144. Brief of *Amici Curiae* National Association of Convenience Stores, National Grocers Association, and Food Marketing Institute in Support of Appellant-Defendant and Reversal in Steak 'N Shake v. Mielo & Heinzl, No. 17-2678, 2017 WL 5759712 (3rd Cir. Nov. 20, 2017), at *9.

145. *See* Heinzl v. Cracker Barrel Old Country Stores, Inc., No. 2:14-cv-1455, 2016 WL 2347367 (W.D. Pa. Jan. 27, 2016).

146. Robertson, "ADA Defense Lawyers Prolong Litigation and Postpone Access."

147. Brief of *Amici Curiae* National Association of Convenience Stores, National Grocers Association, and Food Marketing Institute in Support of Appellant-Defendant and Reversal in Steak 'N Shake v. Mielo & Heinzl, No. 17-2678, 2017 WL 5759712 (3rd Cir. Nov. 20, 2017), at *10.

148. The brief was listed as being on behalf of the "National Association of Convenience Stores, National Grocers Association, and Food Marketing Institute." *Id.* at *i.

149. *Id.* at *8.

150. Their effort was successful in the Third Circuit case in which the industry group filed this amicus brief. *See* Mielo v. Steak 'N Shake Operations, 897 F.3d 467 (3rd Cir. 2018) (reversing class certification decision by district court).

151. *See* John Nichols, "Disability Rights Activists Are the Real Heroes of the Health-Care Fight," *The Nation*, July 28, 2017, www.thenation.com/article /archive/disability-rights-activists-are-the-real-heroes-of-the-health-care -fight/.

152. *See* Robert Pear and Thomas Kaplan, "Senate Rejects Slimmed-Down Obamacare Repeal as McCain Votes No," *N.Y. Times*, July 27, 2017, www.nytimes .com/2017/07/27/us/politics/obamacare-partial-repeal-senate-republicans -revolt.html.

153. *See* Emmarie Huetteman, "McCain Hated Obamacare: He Also Saved It," *NBC News*, Aug. 27, 2018, www.nbcnews.com/health/obamacare/mccain -hated-obamacare-he-also-saved-it-n904106.

154. *See* Michelle Alexander, *The New Jim Crow: Mass Incarceration in the Age of Colorblindness* (2010).

155. Media Impact Project, "*The New Jim Crow: Mass Incarceration in the Age of Colorblindness*"; A Case Study on the Role of Books in Leveraging Social Change," Nov. 2014, http://mediaimpactfunders.org/wp-content/uploads/2014 /12/The-New-Press-NJC-Case-Study-Nov20141.pdf. ("Media Impact Project").

156. The Media Impact Project describes the activism that was influenced by her book as including: "Students Against Mass Incarceration; standing-room-only events at churches around the country (including an 800-plus audience at Abyssinian Baptist Church in Harlem); marches organized by the Campaign to End the New Jim Crow; and sponsored events featuring Michelle Alexander in partnership with a range of nonprofit organizations, including the ACLU, the Drug Policy Alliance, Demos, the NAACP, and The Sentencing Project. These events provided an opportunity to reach individuals at the front lines of advocating for policy reform." *Id.*.

157. The Media Impact Project includes the following events as being influenced by Alexander's work: "In addition to events, The New Jim Crow also played an instrumental role in the Center for Constitutional Rights' legal preparation in advance of the seminal case, Floyd, et al. v. City of New York, et al.—a class action

lawsuit that challenged the New York Police Department's practices of racial profiling and stop-and-frisks, with Judge Shira Scheindlin citing The New Jim Crow twice in her decision." *Id.*

158. *See* Beth Avery & Phil Hernandez, "Ban the Box: U.S. Cities, Counties, and States Adopt Fair Hiring Policies," National Employment Law Project, Sept. 25, 2018, www.nelp.org/publication/ban-the-box-fair-chance-hiring-state-and-local -guide/ (33 states and over 150 cities and counties have adopted employment practices that ban questions about conviction histories on job applications).

159. *See* Jeffery C. Mays, "500 Women and Teenagers to Be Bailed Out from Rikers by Human Rights Group," *N.Y. Times*, Sept. 19, 2018, www.nytimes.com /2018/09/19/nyregion/rikers-island-inmate-population.html?module=inline (bail effort led by Robert F. Kennedy Human Rights group).

160. *See* Lisa W. Foderaro, "New Jersey Alters Its Bail System and Upends Legal Landscape," *N.Y. Times*, Feb. 6, 2017, www.nytimes.com/2017/02/06 /nyregion/new-jersey-bail-system.html?module=inline (defendants only required to post bail if they are a flight risk or are a threat to public safety).

161. *See* Frances Robles, "1.4. Million Floridians with Felonies Win Long-Denied Right to Vote," *N.Y. Times*, Nov. 7, 2018, www.nytimes.com/2018/11/07 /us/florida-felon-voting-rights.html (restoring voting rights for convicted felons who have served their sentences and were not convicted of murder or sexual abuse).

162. *See* Dara Lind, "The President Pulled an 'All Lives Matter' on DREAM-ers," *Vox*, Jan. 31, 2018, www.vox.com/2018/1/30/16953714/trump-state-union -immigration-dream-daca; Black Lives Matter, "In response to the State of the Union," https://blacklivesmatter.com/pressroom/responsesate-of-the-union/ (documenting Trump using the phrase "All Lives Matter" to undermine the Black Lives Matter movement).

163. *See* Michelle Alexander, "The Newest Jim Crow: Recent Criminal Justice Reforms Contain the Seeds of a Frightening System of 'E-carceration,'" *N.Y. Times*, Nov. 8, 2018, www.nytimes.com/2018/11/08/opinion/sunday/criminal -justice-reforms-race-technology.html?action=click&module=Opinion&pgtype =Homepage (arguing that risk assessment algorithms are based on factors that highly correlate with race and class).

164. *See* Carla Herreria, "Eric Holder Revises Michelle Obama Quote: 'When They Go Low, We Kick Them,'" *HuffPost*, Oct. 11, 2018, www.huffingtonpost.com /entry/eric-holder-amends-michelle-obama-mantra_us_5bbe767ce4b054d7 ddef4a8d.

165. Ruth Colker, "ADA Title III: A Fragile Compromise," 21 *Berkeley J. Emp. & Lab. L.* 377 (2000).

166. *See* Peter W. Stevenson, "The Iconic Thumbs-Down Vote That Summed Up John McCain's Career," *Wash. Post*, Aug. 27, 2017, www.washingtonpost.com

/politics/2018/08/27/iconic-thumbs-down-vote-that-summed-up-john-mccains
-career/?utm_term=.bfacae62e67c.

CHAPTER 4. IMMIGRANTS AS MURDERERS
AND RAPISTS

1. Ronald Takaki, *A Different Mirror: A History of Multicultural America*
159 (1993).
2. *See* David P. Oppenheimer, Swati Prakash & Rachel Burns, "Playing the
Trump Card: The Enduring Legacy of Racism in Immigration Law," 26 *Berkeley
La Raza L.J.* 1 (2016).
3. *Id.* at 7.
4. *Id.* at 7.
5. *Id.* at 7.
6. *Id.* at 14.
7. *Id.* at 8.
8. *Id.* at 8.
9. *Id.* at 9.
10. *Id.* at 15.
11. Noel Ignatiev, *How the Irish Became White* 96 (1995).
12. Kerby A. Miller, *Emigrants and Exiles: Ireland and the Irish Exodus to
North America* 329 (1985).
13. *See* Jau Caspian King, "Noel Ignatiev's Long Fight against Whiteness,"
New Yorker, Nov. 15, 2019, www.newyorker.com/news/postscript/noel-ignatievs
-long-fight-against-whiteness.
14. Ignatiev, *How the Irish Became White*.
15. *See* Noel Ignatin & Ted Allen, "White Blindspot," www.marxists.org
/history/erol/ncm-1/whiteblindspot.pdf (accessed Apr. 15, 2021).
16. Oppenheimer et al., "Playing the Trump Card," at 12.
17. Irving Howe, *The World of Our Fathers: The Journey of the Eastern European Jews to America and the Life They Found and Made* 406 (1976).
18. *Id.* at 12.
19. *Id.* at 13.
20. *Id.* at 18.
21. *Id.* at 18.
22. *Id.* at 23.
23. *See* "America and the Holocaust," Facing History and Ourselves, www
.facinghistory.org/defying-nazis/america-and-holocaust (accessed June 7, 2019).
24. *Id.*
25. *See* "Ford's Anti-Semitism" *American Experience*, www.pbs.org/wgbh
/americanexperience/features/henryford-antisemitism/ (accessed Mar. 26, 2021).

26. *See* "America and the Holocaust."

27. John Higham, *Strangers in the Land: Patterns of American Nativism 1860–1925* 309 (1955).

28. "America and the Holocaust."

29. *Id.*

30. Oppenheimer et al., "Playing the Trump Card," at 13–14.

31. *See* "Audit of Anti-Semitic Incidents: Year in Review 2018," A Report from the Center on Extremism, www.adl.org/media/12857/download.

32. *Id.*

33. *Id.* at 16.

34. *Id.* at 26.

35. *See* Michael Edison Hayden, "Republican Senate Candidate Praises Hitler and Sparks Condemnation from California GOP," *Newsweek*, May, 2, 2018, www .newsweek.com/republican-senate-candidate-praise-hitler-907749.

36. Dave Goldiner, "Neo-Nazi Republican Patrick Little Gets 1.2% in California Senate Primary," *Fast Forward: Quick Reads Through a Jewish Lens*, June 6, 2018, https://forward.com/fast-forward/402550/neo-nazi-republican-patrick -little-gets-12-in-california-senate-primary/.

37. Emmaia Gelman, "The Anti-Defamation League Is Not What It Seems," *Boston Review*, May 23, 2019, http://bostonreview.net/politics/emmaia-gelman -anti-defamation-league-not-what-it-seems.

38. *See* "ADL Calls on House Leadership to Take Action after Rep. Omar's Anti-Semitic Tweets," ADL, Feb. 11, 2019, www.adl.org/news/press-releases/adl -calls-on-house-leadership-to-take-action-after-rep-omars-anti-semitic.

39. Gelman, "The Anti-Defamation League Is Not What It Seems."

40. *See* People v. Hall, 4 Cal. 399 (1854).

41. *Id.* at 399.

42. *Id.* at 405.

43. Oppenheimer et al., "Playing the Trump Card," at 20.

44. *See* The African American Policy Forum (AAPF), "Chinese Exclusion Act 101," http://aapf.org/chinese-exclusion-act (accessed June 3, 2019).

45. Keith Aoki, "The Yellow Pacific: Transnational Identities, Diasporic Racialization, and Myth(s) of the 'Asian Century,'" 44 *U.C. Davis. L. Rev.* 897, 913 (2011).

46. Chae Chan Ping v. United States, 130 U.S. 581, 595–96 (1889).

47. History.com staff, "Chinese Exclusion Act," Nov. 19, 2018, updated Sept. 13, 2019, www.history.com/topics/immigration/chinese-exclusion-act-1882.

48. *See* AAPF, "Chinese Exclusion Act 101."

49. *Id.* at 608.

50. 163 U.S. 537 (1896).

51. *Id.* at 559 (Harlan, J., dissenting).

52. *Id.* at 561 (Harlan, J., dissenting).

53. *Id.* at 563.

54. Aoki, "The Yellow Pacific."

55. *Id.*

56. Benedict Anderson, *Imagined Communities: Reflections on the Origin and Spread of Nationalism* 148–49 (1991).

57. *Id.*

58. Oppenheimer et al., "Playing the Trump Card," at 26.

59. *Id.* at 27.

60. Oppenheimer et al., "Playing the Trump Card," at 27.

61. Aoki, "The Yellow Pacific."

62. *Id.*

63. *Id.* at 926–27.

64. *Id.* at 926.

65. *See* Pearl Harbor Visitors Bureau, "Aftermath of Pearl Harbor: The Roberts Commission," https://visitpearlharbor.org/aftermath-pearl-harbor-roberts-commission/ (accessed June 4, 2019).

66. *See* Aoki, "The Yellow Pacific," at 930.

67. Korematsu v. United States, 323 U.S. 215 (1944).

68. *Id.* at 233 (Murphy, J., dissenting).

69. *Id.* at 236–37 (Murphy, J., dissenting).

70. *Id.* at 240 (Murphy, J., dissenting).

71. *Id.* at 216 (Black, J., delivering opinion of the Court).

72. *Id.* at 223.

73. Susan Kiyomi Serrano & Dale Minami, "Korematsu v. United States: A 'Constant Caution' In a Time of Crisis," 10 *Asian L.J.* 37, 37 (2003).

74. 584 F. Supp. 1406 (N.D. Calif. 1984).

75. *Id.* at 1413.

76. *Id.* at 1416–17.

77. *Id.* at 1417.

78. *Id.* at 1417.

79. *Id.* at 1420.

80. Shannon M. Harris, "10 Shameful Facts about Japanese-American Internment," ListVerse, Oct. 25, 2014, https://listverse.com/2014/10/25/10-shameful-truths-about-japanese-american-internment/.

81. *Id.*

82. Michael Scherer, "Exclusive: Donald Trump Says He Might Have Supported Japanese Internment," *Time*, Dec. 8, 2015, time.com/4140050/donald-trump-muslims-japanese-internment/.

83. *See* Dana Milbank, "Now Playing at the Supreme Court: How to Preserve White Power in Four Easy Steps," *Wash. Post*, Apr. 24, 2019.

84. *See* Dana Milbank, "Trump's Raison *d*'etre Is White Power," *Wash. Post*, May 31, 2019, www.washingtonpost.com/opinions/trumps-census-scheme -exposed-a-lie-to-increase-white-power/2019/05/31/b6f40ef6-83b3-11e9-95a9 -e2c830afe24f_story.html?utm_term=.d584f77e62fb.

85. *Id.*

86. *See* Letter from Dale E. Ho to Supreme Court of the United States, May 30, 2019, www.supremecourt.gov/DocketPDF/18/18-966/101439/20190530 142417722_2019.05.30%20NYIC%20Respondents%20Notice%20of%20Filing %20--%20Final.pdf.

87. *Id.*

88. *See* Amy Howe, "Opinion Analysis: Court Orders Do-Over on Citizen-ship Question in Census Case," *SCOTUSblog*, June 27, 2019, www.scotusblog .com/2019/06/opinion-analysis-court-orders-do-over-on-citizenship-question -in-census-case/.

89. Oppenheimer et al., "Playing the Trump Card," at 38.

90. Melissa Vargas Lopez, "The Supreme Court's Reinforcement of the Invisi-bility of Mexicans," 38 *U. La Verne L. Rev.* 272, 277–78 (2017).

91. Kevin R. Johnson, "Forgotten 'Repatriation' of Persons of Mexican Ances-try," 26 *Pace L. Rev.* 1, 4 (2005).

92. *Id.* at 6.

93. *Id.* at 10.

94. 457 U.S. 202 (1982).

95. *Id.* at 207.

96. *Id.* at 218–19.

97. *Id.* at 220.

98. *Id.* at 228.

99. *Id.* at 230.

100. *Id.* at 242.

101. *Id.* at 250 (Burger, C.J., dissenting).

102. *Id.* at 251 n.12. (Burger, C.J., dissenting).

103. *Id.* at 251 (Burger, C.J., dissenting).

104. Oppenheimer et al., "Playing the Trump Card," at 39.

105. *See* League of United Latin American Citizens v. Wilson, 997 F. Supp. 1244, 1249 (C.D. Calif. 1997).

106. Kevin R. Johnson, "A Handicapped, Not 'Sleeping,' Giant: The Devastat-ing Impact of the Initiative Process on Latina/o and Immigrant Communities," 96 *Cal. L. Rev.* 1259, 1285 (2008).

107. *See* Peter S. Goodman, "From Welfare Shift in '96, a Reminder for Clin-ton," *N.Y. Times*, Apr. 11, 2008, www.nytimes.com/2008/04/11/us/politics /11welfare.html.

108. Shawn Fremstad, "Immigrants and Welfare Reauthorization," Center on Budget and Policy Priorities, Feb. 4, 2002, www.cbpp.org/research/immigrants-and-welfare-reauthorization.

109. "Congress: Immigration, Welfare, Minimum Wages," *Migration News*, Aug. 1996, migration.ucdavis.edu/mn/more.php?id=1006.

110. *See* Josh Gerstein, "In 1996, Newt Gingrich Opposed Flexibility for Criminal Aliens," *Politico*, May 15, 2011, www.politico.com/blogs/under-the-radar/2011/05/in-1996-newt-gingrich-opposed-flexibility-for-criminal-aliens-035864.

111. 442 U.S.256 (1979).

112. *Id.* at 272.

113. Katie Reilly, "Here Are All the Times Donald Trump Insulted Mexico," *Time*, Aug. 31, 2016, time.com/4473972/donald-trump-mexico-meeting-insult/.

114. *Id.*

115. 82 Fed. Reg. 8977 (Jan. 27, 2017).

116. Washington v. Trump, No. C17-0141-JLR, 2017 WL 462040 (W.D. Wash. Feb. 3, 2017).

117. 847 F.3d 1151 (9th Cir. 2017).

118. *Id.* at 1164.

119. *Id.* at 1167.

120. *See* Rebecca Shabad, "Officials Announce Travel Ban," *CBS News*, Mar. 6, 2017, www.cbsnews.com/news/trumps-new-travel-ban-executive-order/.

121. State of Hawaii v. Trump, 245 F. Supp.3d 1227 (D. Hawaii 2017).

122. Hawaii v. Trump, 859 F.3d 741 (9th Cir. 2017).

123. 241 F. Supp.3d at 1136.

124. *Id.* at 1136–37.

125. *Id.* at 1137.

126. *See* Int'l Refugee Assistance Project v. Trump, 2017 WL 1018235 (D. Md. Mar. 16, 2017).

127. Trump v. Int'l Refuge Assistance Project, 137 S. Ct. 2080, 2088 (2017).

128. *Id.* at 2089.

129. White House, "Presidential Proclamation Enhancing Vetting Capabilities and Processes for Detecting Attempted Entry into the United States by Terrorists or Other Public-Safety Threats," Sept. 24, 2017, www.whitehouse.gov/presidential-actions/presidential-proclamation-enhancing-vetting-capabilities-processes-detecting-attempted-entry-united-states-terrorists-public-safety-threats/.

130. 138 S. Ct. at 2435 (Sotomayor, J., dissenting).

131. *See* Department of Homeland Security v. Regents of the University of California, 2020 WL 3271746 (June 18, 2020).

132. 138 S. Ct. 2392 (2018).

133. 138 S. Ct. 1719 (2018).

134. For an excellent discussion of the contrast, see Daniel P. Tokaji, "Denying Systemic Equality: The Last Words of the Kennedy Court," 13 *Harv. L. & Pol'y Rev.* 539 (2019).

135. 138 S. Ct. at 1724.

136. *See id.* at 1724–25.

137. *See id.* at 1726.

138. *See id.* at 1726.

139. *See* Craig v. Masterpiece Cakeshop, Inc., 370 P.3d 272 (2015). The Colorado Supreme Court declined to hear the case. *See Masterpiece Cakeshop*, 138 S. Ct. at 1727.

140. Masterpiece Cakeshop, Ltd. v. Colorado Civil Rights Comm'n, 138 S. Ct. 1719, 1729 (2018) (citing transcript at 11–12).

141. *Id.* at 1729.

142. 138 S .Ct. 2392 (2018).

143. *Id.* at 2435 (Sotomayor, J., dissenting).

144. *Id.* at 2438 (Sotomayor, J. dissenting).

145. Tokaji, "Denying Systemic Equality," at 544.

146. As Tokaji notes: "Although the Court has long applied heightened scrutiny to religious discrimination as well as racial discrimination, it applies only rational basis review to Proclamation 9645. The majority offers little explanation and no relevant precedent for its decision to apply this deferential standard." *Id.* at 575.

CHAPTER 5. PEDOPHILES OR WELCOME ENTRANTS
TO MARRIAGE

1. *See* Eli Rosenberg, "A Right-Wing YouTuber Hurled Racist, Homophobic Taunts at a Gay Reporter: The Company Did Nothing," *Wash. Post*, June 5, 2019, www.washingtonpost.com/technology/2019/06/05/right-wing-youtuber-hurled-racist-homophobic-taunts-gay-reporter-company-did-nothing/?utm_term=.c61c565180a7.

2. *See* Julie Euber, "American Medical Association: Transgender Deaths Are an Epidemic," *Northwestern University Online MS in Global Health*, Oct. 2, 2019, https://nonprofitquarterly.org/american-medical-association-transgender-deaths-are-an-epidemic/.

3. *See* Lauren Holt, "Thousands Show Up for Black Trans People in Nationwide Protests," *CNN*, June 15, 2020, www.cnn.com/2020/06/14/us/black-trans-protests/index.html.

4. *See* Paula Ettelbrick, "Since When Is Marriage a Path to Liberation?," *Out/Look*, reprinted in William B. Rubenstein, Carlos A. Ball & Jane S. Schacter, *Cases and Materials on Sexual Orientation and the Law* 678, 683 (3rd ed. 2008).

5. *See* Doe 2 v. Shanahan, 755 Fed. Appx. 19 (D.C. Cir. 2019). The Biden administration has reversed this policy. See The White House, "Executive Order on Enabling All Qualified Americans to Serve the Country in Uniform," Jan. 25, 2021, www.whitehouse.gov/briefing-room/presidential-actions/2021/01/25/executive-order-on-enabling-all-qualified-americans-to-serve-their-country-in-uniform/.

6. Jeremy W. Peters, "Olson and Boies, Legal Duo, Seek Role in 2 Cases on Gay Marriage," *N.Y. Times*, Feb. 3, 2014, www.nytimes.com/2014/02/04/us/legal-duo-seeks-role-in-2-cases-on-marriage.html.

7. Ga. Code Ann. § 16-6-2.

8. Michael J. Bowers, Attorney General of Georgia, Petitioner, v. Michael Hardwick, and John and Mary Doe, Respondents, 1985 WL 667939 (U.S.), 21–23.

9. *Id.* at 33.

10. *See* Chris Kirk and Hanna Rosin, "Does Gay Marriage Destroy Marriage?," *Slate*, May 23, 2012, www.slate.com/articles/double_x/doublex/2012/05/does_gay_marriage_affect_marriage_or_divorce_rates_.html.

11. Bowers v. Hardwick, 478 U.S. 186, 196 (1986).

12. *Id.* at 192.

13. William N. Eskridge Jr. & Nan D. Hunter, *Sexuality, Gender and the Law*, Appendix 3 (3rd ed. 2011) (emphasis in original).

14. 517 U.S. 620 (1996).

15. *Id.* at 634.

16. California General Election, "Prop 8 Eliminates Right of Same-Sex Couples to Marry: Initiative Constitutional Amendment," https://web.archive.org/web/20121118053915/http://voterguide.sos.ca.gov/past/2008/general/argu-rebut/argu-rebutt8.htm (accessed June 20, 2019).

17. Perry v. Schwarzenegger, 704 F.Supp.2d 921, 1003 (N.D. Cal. 2010).

18. *Id.*

19. *Id.*

20. Perry v. Brown, 671 F.3d 1052, 1093 (9th Cir. 2012).

21. *Id.* at 1095.

22. Mathew S. Nosanchuck, "Response: No Substitutions Please," 100 *Geo. L.J.* 1989, 1997 (2012).

23. *Id.* at 1997.

24. Keith Cunningham-Parmeter, "Marriage Equality, Workplace Inequality: The Next Gay Rights Battle," 67 *Fla. L. Rev.* 1099, 1107 (2015).

25. *See* Thomas Stoddard, "Why Gay People Should Seek the Right to Marry," *Out/Look*, Fall 1989; and Paula Ettelbrick, "Since When Is Marriage a Path to Liberation?," *Out/Look*, reprinted in Rubenstein, Ball & Schacter, *Cases and Materials on Sexual Orientation and the Law.*

26. Carlos Ball, "Symposium: Updating the LGBT Intracommunity Debate over Same-Sex Marriage," 61 *Rutgers L. Rev.* 493, 497 (2009).

27. David W. Dunlap, "Paula L. Ettelbrick, Legal Expert in Gay Rights Movement, Dies at 56," *N.Y. Times*, Oct. 8, 2011, www.nytimes.com/2011/10/09/nyregion /paula-l-ettelbrick-legal-expert-in-gay-rights-movement-dies-at-56.html.

28. *Id.*

29. Ettelbrick, "Since When Is Marriage a Path to Liberation?," at 684.

30. Cunningham-Parmeter, "Marriage Equality, Workplace Inequality," at 1115.

31. *See* William N. Eskridge Jr. & Darren R. Spedale, *Gay Marriage for Better or for Worse?* 241–45 (2006).

32. *Id.*

33. *See* Leonore F. Carpenter, "The Next Phase: Positioning the Post-Obergefell LGBT Rights Movement to Bridge the Gap Between Formal and Lived Equality," 13 *Stan. J. Civ. Rts. & Civ. Liberties* 255 (2017).

34. *See* Leonore F. Carpenter, "Getting Queer Priorities Straight: How Direct Legal Services Can Democratize Issue in the LGBT Rights Movement," 17 *Univ. of Pa. J. of L. & Soc. Change* 107, 115 (2014).

35. Dean Spade & Craig Willse, "Freedom in a Regulatory State?: Lawrence, Marriage and Biopolitics," 11 *Widener L. Rev.* 309, 327–28 (2005).

36. Eskridge & Spedale, *Gay Marriage for Better or for Worse?*, at 261.

37. Obergefell v. Hodges, 135 S. Ct. 2584, 2594, 2597, 2598, 2599, 2603 (2015).

38. *See, e.g.,* "Love Wins," Human Rights Campaign, https://hrc.org/blog /live-blog-lovewins (accessed June 24, 2019) (referring to "marriage equality"); and "Marriage, Relationships and Family Protection," Lambda Legal, www.lambdalegal.org/issues/marriage-relationships-and-family-protections (accessed June 24, 2019) (referring to "freedom to marry").

39. *See* Roberta Kaplan, "'It's All about Edie, Stupid': Lessons from Litigating United States v. Windsor," 29 *Colum. J. Gender & L.* 85 (2015).

40. *See* Jonathan Clements, "Getting Married Has Its Financial Benefits," *Wall St. J.*, May 25, 2014, www.wsj.com/articles/getting-married-has-its -financial-benefits-1400977300.

41. *Id.*

42. *See* Deboer v. Snyder, 973 F. Supp.2d 757 (E.D. Mich. 2014).

43. *See* Ben Free, "April DeBoer and Jayne Rowse Celebrate Supreme Court Gay Marriage Decision in Ann Arbor," *MLive*, June 26, 2015, www.mlive.com /news/ann-arbor/2015/06/april_deboer_and_jayne_rowse_c.html.

44. "DeBoer and Rowse Exchange Vows in 'Historic' Wedding," *Detroit News*, Aug. 23, 2015, www.detroitnews.com/story/news/local/oakland-county/2015/08/22/deboer-rowse-exchange-vows-historic-wedding/32212729/.

45. Kat Stafford, "DeBoer, Rowse Formally Adopt Their 5 Children," *Detroit Free Press*, Nov. 5, 2015, www.freep.com/story/news/local/michigan/oakland/2015/11/05/jayne-rowse-april-deboer-adoption-wedding/75208698/.

46. Melissa Murray, "Obergefell v. Hodges and Nonmarriage Inequality," 104 *Calif. L. Rev.* 1207, 1208 (2016).

47. *Id.* at 1215.

48. *Id.* at 1216–26.

49. *Id.* at 1213–14.

50. Dana Harrington Conner, "Financial Freedom: Women, Money, and Domestic Abuse," 20 *Wm. & Mary J. Women & L.* 339, 363 (2014).

51. *See* Mareen Baker & Vivenne Elizabeth, "A 'Brave Thing to Do' or a Normative Practice? Marriage after Long-Term Cohabitation," 50 *J. Soc.* 393 (2014).

52. *Obergefell*, 135 S. Ct. at 2594.

53. *See* Carlos A. Ball, *From the Closet to the Courtroom: Five LGBT Rights Lawsuits That Have Changed Our Nation* (2010).

54. *See* Chris Geidner, "The Court Cases That Changed L.G.B.T.Q Rights," *N.Y. Times*, June 19, 2019, www.nytimes.com/2019/06/19/us/legal-history-lgbtq-rights-timeline.html.

55. SPLC, "10 Anti-Gay Myths Debunked," www.splcenter.org/fighting-hate/intelligence-report/2011/10-anti-gay-myths-debunked (accessed June 25, 2019).

56. *See* Southern Poverty Law Center, "American College of Pediatricians," www.splcenter.org/fighting-hate/extremist-files/group/american-college-pediatricians (designated as a hate group).

57. *See* "Just the Facts about Sexual Orientation and Youth: A Primer for Principals, Educators, and School Personnel," 2008, https://web.archive.org/web/20150717111746/http:/www.apa.org/pi/lgbt/resources/just-the-facts.pdf.

58. *See* Beth Hawkins, "Critics Challenge Findings, Funding and Methodology of Controversial Gay-Parents Study," *MinnPost*, July 20, 2012, www.minnpost.com/politics-policy/2012/07/critics-challenge-findings-funding-and-methodology-controversial-gay-parents/.

59. Brandon Watson, "UT Distances from Regnerus," *Austin Chronicle*, Mar. 4, 2014, www.austinchronicle.com/daily/news/2014-03-04/ut-distances-from-regnerus/.

60. *See* "NARTH Becomes Main Source for Anti-Gay 'Junk Science,'" *Intelligence Report*, Mar. 1, 2012, www.splcenter.org/fighting-hate/intelligence-report/2012/narth-becomes-main-source-anti-gay-'junk-science'.

61. *See* Casey Sanchez, "Anti-Gay Conspiracy Theories Debunked by Christian Professor," *Hatewatch*, June 17, 2009, www.splcenter.org/hatewatch/2009/06/17/anti-gay-conspiracy-theories-debunked-christian-professor.

62. Waltor Olson, "William Bennett, Gays, and the Truth," *Slate*, Dec. 19, 1997, https://slate.com/news-and-politics/1997/12/william-bennett-gays-and -the-truth.html.

63. *See* Robert S. Hogg et al., "Gay Life Expectancy Revisited," *Oxford Int'l J. Epidemiology*, Dec. 1, 2001, https://academic.oup.com/ije/article/30/6/1499 /651821.

64. *See* Olson, "William Bennett, Gays, and the Truth."

65. *See* GLAD, "History," www.glad.org/about/history (accessed Mar. 29, 2021).

66. *See* "ACT UP Accomplishments—1987–2012," https://actupny.com /actions/. (accessed Mar. 29, 2021).

67. Phillip M. Ayoub, "How the Media Has Helped Change Public Views about Lesbian and Gay People," SSN Key Findings, May 24, 2018, https://scholars.org /brief/how-media-has-helped-change-public-views-about-lesbian-and-gay -people.

68. Perry v. Schwarzenegger, 704 F. Supp.2d 921, 930 (N.D. Cal. 2010).

69. *Id.* at 933.

70. *Id.* at 934.

71. *Id.* at 934.

72. *Id.* at 937.

73. *Id.* at 937.

74. *Id.* at 938.

75. *Id.* at 940.

76. *Id.* at 940.

77. *Id.* at 948.

78. *Id.* at 950.

79. *Id.* at 952.

80. *Id.* at 998.

81. *Id.* at 999.

82. *Id.* at 1000.

83. *Id.* at 1001.

84. *Id.* at 1001.

85. *Id.* at 1002.

86. *See* JamieAnn Myers, "Transgender Day of Remembrance 2011: Remembering Our Dead, Seeking Justice for Our Living," *HuffPost*, Feb. 2, 2016, www .huffpost.com/entry/transgender-day-of-remembrance-2011_b_1100830.

87. *See* Katy Kreitler, "Top 10 Myths about Transgender People," *Everyday Feminism*, Aug. 2, 2012, https://everydayfeminism.com/2012/08/myths-about -transgender-people/.

88. *See* Ruth Colker, *Sexual Orientation, Gender Identity, and the Law in a Nutshell* 266–76 (2017).

89. *See* EEOC v. R.G. & G.R. Harris Funeral Homes, Inc., 884 F.3d 560 (6th Cir. 2018).

90. *See* Ruth Colker, "Public Restrooms: Flipping the Default Rules," 78 *Ohio St. L. J.* (2017).

91. G.G. *ex rel.* Grimm v. Gloucester Cty. Sch. Bd., 822 F.3d 709, 716 (4th Cir. 2016).

92. 2020 WL 3146686 (June 15, 2020).

93. *Id.* at *17.

94. *See* Bostock oral argument transcript at 17, www.supremecourt.gov/oral _arguments/argument_transcripts/2019/17-1618_7k47.pdf.

95. *See* Zubik v. Burwell, 578 U.S. 1557 (2016).

96. *See* Espinoza v. Montana Department of Revenue, No. 18-1195 (U.S. June 22, 2020).

97. *Bostock*, at *18.

CHAPTER 6. ABORTION

1. *See* Reis Thebault and Emily Wax-Thibodeaux, "Missouri's Last Abortion Clinic Will Stay Open after Ruling Ends Contentious Year-Long Legal Battle," *Wash. Post*, May 29, 2020, www.washingtonpost.com/nation/2020/05/29 /ruling-saves-missouri-abortion-clinic/.

2. *See* Reis Thebault, "Explaining the Missouri Pre-abortion Exam Rachel Maddow Called 'State-Sanctioned Sexual Assault,'" *Wash. Post*, June 8, 2019, www .washingtonpost.com/health/2019/06/08/explaining-missouri-pre-abortion -exam-rachel-maddow-called-state-sanctioned-sexual-assault/.

3. Rosalind Pollack Petchesky, "Fetal Images: The Power of Visual Culture in the Politics of Reproduction," 13 *Feminist Studies* 263, 266 (1987).

4. *Id.* at 264.

5. *See* David C. Reardon, *Aborted Women: Silent No More* (1987).

6. *See* Joshua Prager, "Norma McCorvey: The Woman Who Became 'Roe'— Then Regretted It," *Politico*, Dec. 28, 2017, www.politico.com/magazine/story /2017/12/28/norma-mccorvey-obituary-216184.

7. *See* Ali Gostanian, Shamar Walters, and Chelsea Bailey, "Norma McCorvey, Who Was at Center of Roe v. Wade Abortion Rights Case, Dies at 69," *NBC News*, Feb. 18, 2017, www.nbcnews.com/news/us-news/norma-mccorvey-who-was -center-roe-v-wade-abortion-rights-n722826.

8. *See* McCorvey v. Hill, 385 F.3d 846 (5th Cir. 2004).

9. *Id.* at 850–51 (Edith H. Jones, Circuit judge, concurring).

10. *See* Dave Andrusko, "Some Fascinating Insight into Sandra Cano, the Plaintiff in Doe v. Bolton, Who Never Wanted an Abortion," *NRLS News Today*, Feb. 23, 2017, www.nationalrighttolifenews.org/2017/02/some-fascinating

-insight-into-sandra-cano-the-plaintiff-in-doe-v-bolton-who-never-wanted-an
-abortion/ (reprinting 1989 interview).

11. *See* Testimony of Sandra Cano, June 23, 2005, www.judiciary.senate.gov
/imo/media/doc/Cano%20Testimony%2062305.pdf.

12. *Id.*

13. *See* Linda H. Edwards, "Hearing Voices: Non-Party Stories in Abortion
and Gay Rights Advocacy," 2015 *Mich. St. L. Rev.* 1327 (2015).

14. 136 S. Ct. 2292 (2016).

15. *See* Linda H. Edwards, "Telling Stories in the Supreme Court: Voices Briefs
and the Role of Democracy in Constitutional Deliberation," 29 *Yale J. L & Feminism* 29 (2017).

16. *Id.* at 32.

17. Planned Parenthood of Southeastern Pennsylvania v. Casey, 505 U.S. 833,
852 (1992).

18. Gonzales v. Carhart, 550 U.S. 124, 159 (2007).

19. *See* Ruth Colker, "Feminist Litigation? An Oxymoron?," 13 *Harv. Women's
L.J.* 137 (1990).

20. *See* Box v. Planned Parenthood of Indiana and Kentucky, 139 S. Ct. 1780,
1784 (2019) (Thomas, J., concurring) (emphasizing the "potential for abortion to
become a tool of eugenic manipulation").

21. *See* Joshua Prager, "Women's Rights: Exclusive: Roe v. Wade's Secret Her-
oine Tells Her Story," *Vanity Fair*, Jan. 19, 2017, www.vanityfair.com/news/2017
/01/roe-v-wades-secret-heroine-tells-her-story.

22. *See* Jenny Gross and Aimee Ortiz, "Roe v. Wade Plaintiff Was Paid to Switch
Sides, Documentary Says," *N.Y. Times*, May 19, 2020, www.nytimes.com/2020/05
/19/us/roe-v-wade-mccorvey-documentary.html?searchResultPosition=10.

23. *See* Joshua Prager, "The Accidental Activist," *Vanity Fair*, Jan. 18, 2013,
www.vanityfair.com/news/politics/2013/02/norma-mccorvey-roe-v-wade
-abortion

24. *See* Gross & Ortiz, "Roe v. Wade Plaintiff Was Paid to Switch Sides."

25. Trevor Hughes, "Planned Parenthood Shooter 'Happy' with This Attack,"
USA Today, Apr. 11, 2016, www.usatoday.com/story/news/2016/04/11/planned
-parenthood-shooter-happy-his-attack/32579921/.

26. Yochi J. Dreazen, "Photos of Women Who Get Abortions Go up on Internet," *WSJ*, May 28, 2002, www.wsj.com/articles/SB1022539371607091560.

27. Lorna Collier, "Patient Photos on Internet Test the Courts," *Chicago
Tribune*, May 15, 2002, www.chicagotribune.com/news/ct-xpm-2002-05-15
-0205150027-story.html.

28. *Id.*

29. *Id.*

30. *See* Missionaries to the Preborn, home page, http://missionariestothe preborn.com (accessed July 23, 2020).

31. Ruth Graham, "Politics: The Man Behind the Aborted-Fetus Signs," *The Atlantic*, Oct. 16, 2015, www.theatlantic.com/politics/archive/2015/10/the-man -behind-the-dead-baby-signs/410845/.

32. Lori Hadacek Chaplin, "'Abortion Victim Photos' and Why the Pro-life Movement Needs Them," *celebrateLIFE*, Fall 2017, clmagazine.org/topic/pro -life-activism/abortion-victim-photos-and-why-the-pro-life-movement-needs -them/.

33. *See* "Breaking: Planned Parenthood Defunded from Title X Program," Aug. 19, 2019, www.plannedparenthood.org/planned-parenthood-indiana -kentucky/newsroom/breaking-planned-parenthood-defunded-from-the-title-x -program-5.

34. Graham, "Politics."

35. Jonathan Van Maren, "Ben Shapiro on Abortion Victim Pictures: 'If It's That Ugly, You Should Do Something about It,'" *LIFESIT*, July 31, 2019, thebridgehead.ca/2019/07/31/ben-shapiro-explains-the-best-way-to-change -someones-mind-about-abortion/.

36. *See* Frisby v. Schultz, 487 U.S. 474, 477 (1988).

37. *Id.* at 487.

38. *Id.* at 484 (remarking on the unique nature of the home as "the last citadel of the tired, the weary, and the sick").

39. *See* Operation Rescue v. Women's Health Center, 626 S.2d 664 (Fla. 1993).

40. *Id.* at 678 (Appendix).

41. *Id.* at 679–80 (Appendix).

42. *Id.* at 675.

43. Madsen v. Women's Health Center, Inc., 512 U.S. 753, 770 (1994).

44. *Id.* at 772.

45. *Id.* at 773.

46. *Id.* at 773.

47. *Id.* at 775.

48. Schenck v. Pro-Choice Network of Western New York, 519 U.S. 357, 378 (1997).

49. *Id.* at 378.

50. *Id.* at 380.

51. Colo. Rev. Stat. § 18-9-122(3).

52. Hill v. Colorado, 530 U.S. 703, 729 (2000).

53. *Id.* at 741–42 (Scalia, J., with whom Justice Thomas joins, dissenting).

54. 18 U.S.C. § 248.

55. 18 U.S.C. § 248(a)(1).

56. *See* Planned Parenthood of Columbia/Willamette, Inc v. Am. Coal. of Life Activists, 290 F.3d 1058 (9th Cir. 2002); United States v. Gregg, 226 F.3d 253 (3rd Cir. 2000); United States v. Soderna, 82 F.3d 1370 (7th Cir. 1996); United States v. Dinwiddie, 76 F.3d 913 (8th Cir. 1996); Am. Life League, Inc. v. Reno, 47 F.3d 642 (4th Cir. 1995); Cheffer v. Reno, 55 F.3d 1517 (11th Cir. 1995); United States v. Weslin, 156 F.3d 292 (2nd Cir. 1998).

57. American Life League v. Reno, 47 F.3d 642, 648 (4th Cir. 1995).

58. *See* Planned Parenthood of Columbia/Willamette, Inc v. Am. Coal. of Life Activists, 290 F.3d 1058 (9th Cir. 2002).

59. Petchesky, "Fetal Images," at 263–64.

60. *Id.* at 268.

61. *Id.* at 281.

62. Celeste Michelle Condit, *Decoding Abortion Rhetoric: Communicating Social Change* 79 (1990).

63. Crystal Lane Swift, "Abortion as African American Cultural Amnesia: An Examination of the Dayton Right to Life Brochures," 32 *Women & Language* 44, 48 (2009).

64. *See* Kirsty McLaren, "The Emotional Imperative of the Visual: Images of the Fetus in Contemporary Australian Pro-Life Politics," 35 *Res. in Soc. Movements, Conflicts & Change* 81, 85 (2013).

65. *Id.* at 99.

66. *Id.* at 99–100.

67. Linda Myrsiades, "Split at the Root: Narrative Collapse in Abortion Jurisprudence," 16 *Cultural Stud.* 365, 368 (2002).

68. *Id.* at 371.

69. *Id.* at 384.

70. *See* Mallary Allen, "Narrative Diversity and Sympathetic Abortion: What Online Storytelling Reveals about the Prescribed Norms of the Mainstream Movements," 38 *Symbolic Interaction* 42 (2014).

71. *Id.* at 44.

72. *Id.* at 44.

73. 505 U.S. 833 (1992).

74. *See, e.g.,* Jeffrey Roseberry, "Undue Burden and the Law of Abortion in Arizona," 44 *Ariz. L.J.* 391 (2012) (discussing cumulative effect of post-*Casey* restrictions on abortion rights in Arizona); Katherine Godich, "Iowa's Unconstitutional Ban on Tele-Medicine Abortions," 19 *J. Gender, Race & Just.* 351 (2016) (discussing application of *Casey* to telemedicine abortions); Jason Del Rosso, "It's a Trap: The Constitutional Dangers of Admitting Privileges for Both Women and Abortion Providers," 24 *B.U. Pub. Int. L.J.* 195 (2015) (discussing admitting privilege laws under *Casey*); and Cynthia D. Lockett, "The Beginning of the End:

The Diminished Abortion Right Following Carhart and Planned Parenthood," 11 J. *Gender, Race & Just.* 337 (2008) (anticipating the "death-knell" for legal abortion).

75. 505 U.S. at 883.

76. *See* Callie Beusman, "A State-by-State List of the Lies Abortion Doctors Are Forced to Tell Women," *Vice*, Aug. 18, 2016 (providing language of "informed consent" brochures in twenty-six states), www.vice.com/en/article/nz88gx/a -state-by-state-list-of-the-lies-abortion-doctors-are-forced-to-tell-women.

77. *See* table 1.

78. Both of those claims were made and rejected in Planned Parenthood v. Casey, 505 U.S. 833, 884 (1992) (rejecting invalidation of informed consent under the undue burden standard as well as under the First Amendment argument).

79. *See* Ala. Code 1975, §26-23A-5(C); the brochure can be found at http:// adph.org/HEALTHCAREFACILITIES/assets/DidYouKnowBooklet.pdf.

80. *See* the pamphlet at www.azdhs.gov/documents/prevention/womens -childrens-health/informed-consent/a-womans-right-to-know.pdf.

81. *See* the pamphlet at http://dph.georgia.gov/sites/dph.georgia.gov/files /related_files/site_page/wrtk_dph_2016_DRAFT.pdf.

82. *See* the pamphlet at www.in.gov/isdh/files/Abortion_Informed_Consent _Brochure.pdf.

83. *See* the pamphlet at www.womansrighttoknow.org/download/Handbook _English.pdf.

84. *See* the pamphlet at http://ldh.la.gov/assets/oph/Center-PHCH/Center -PH/familyplanning/WmnsRghtToKnow.pdf.

85. *See* the pamphlet at www.wrtk.ncdhhs.gov/library/doc/AWomansRightTo Know-Web.pdf.

86. The brochure is only available upon request atwww.ndhealth.gov /NutrPhyAct/InformationAboutPregnancyandAbortionOrderForm.aspx. (copy on file with author).

87. *See* the pamphlet at www.awomansright.org/pdf/AWRTK_Booklet -English-sm.pdf.

88. *See* the pamphlet at https://hhs.texas.gov/sites/default/files/documents /services/health/women-children/womans-right-to-know.pdf.

89. *See* the pamphlet at www.wvdhhr.org/wrtk/wrtkbooklet.pdf.

90. *See*the pamphlet at www.dhs.wisconsin.gov/publications/p4/p40074 .pdf.

91. States such as California and New York, which do not seek to coerce pregnant women into continuing with their pregnancies, do not have any brochures at all on their state websites. They presumably expect physicians to comply with general principles about informed consent before terminating a woman's pregnancy.

92. *See* the brochure at www.in.gov/isdh/files/Abortion_Informed_Consent_Brochure.pdf

93. IN ST 16-34-2-1.5 (effective July 2, 2018).

94. *Id*. at 1.

95. *See* the brochure at www.womansrighttoknow.org/download/Handbook_English.pdf.

96. KS ST 65-6708.

97. *See* the brochure at www.wrtk.ncdhhs.gov/library/doc/AWomansRightTo Know-Web.pdf.

98. N.C.G.S.A. § 90-21.83 (effective Oct. 1, 2013).

99. North Carolina Department of Health and Human Services, *A Woman's Right to Know*, Sept. 2015, www.wrtk.ncdhhs.gov/library/doc/AWomansRightTo Know-Web.pdf, at 18.

100. *See* Lisa Rapaport, "Few U.S. Women Have Serious Complications after Abortions," *Reuters*, July 11, 2018, www.reuters.com/article/us-health -abortion-safety/few-u-s-women-have-serious-complications-after-abortions -idUSKBN1K1300. *See also* Laura Kurtzman, "Major Complication Rate after Abortion Is Extremely Low, Study Shows," University of California San Francisco, Dec. 8, 2014, www.ucsf.edu/news/2014/12/121781/major-complication-rate-after -abortion-extremely-low-study-shows (reporting low rates of complications for women receiving abortions under state-funded Medicaid program).

101. North Carolina, *A Woman's Right to Know*, at 22.

102. *See* Li Ke, Weiyan Lin, Yangqi, Liu, Weilin Ou & Zhifeng Lin, "Associ- ation of Induced Abortion with Preterm Birth Risk in First-Time Mothers," 8 *Sci. Rep.* 5353 (2018), www.nature.com/articles/s41598-018-23695-7#citeas.

103. *See* Texas Health and Human Services, *A Woman's Right to Know*, 2016, https://hhs.texas.gov/sites/default/files/documents/services/health/women -children/womans-right-to-know.pdf.

104. *Id*. at 8.

105. *Id*. at 9.

106. *Id*. at 16 & 19.

107. *See* "Abortion Doctors in Texas Must Give Patients Medically Inaccurate Information," *Texas Tribune*, July 27, 2016, www.governing.com/topics/health -human-services/tt-texas-abortion-booklet.html.

108. *See* Helena Pozniak, "Time to Change Destiny: When Will We Stop Giv- ing Women Deadlines?," *The Telegraph*, Mar. 5, 2019 (reporting on interviews with four women who experienced pressure from family, friends, and society to get married and have children).

109. *See* "Child-Free Women Feel Intense Pressure to Have Kids, but Rarely Stress over It," *ScienceDaily*, Oct. 9, 2012, www.sciencedaily.com/releases/2012 /10/121009121807.htm.

110. *See* Ellen Walker, "Direct and Subtle Pressure to Have Children—How Can Childfree Wannabe Cope?," *Psychology Today*, Apr. 6, 2011, www.psychology today.com/us/blog/complete-without-kids/201104/direct-and-subtle-pressure -have-children-how-can-childfree-wanna-1.

111. *See* Mark Leach, "Delaware and Maryland Join Massachusetts and Kentucky in Enacting Laws to Provide Information with a Down Syndrome Test Result," Down Syndrome Prenatal Testing, May 12, 2014, www.downsyndrome prenataltesting.com/delaware-and-maryland-join-massachusetts-and-kentucky -in-enacting-laws-to-provide-information-with-a-down-syndrome-test-result/ ?utm_content=bufferf7dd3&utm_medium=social&utm_source=facebook.com& utm_campaign=buffer.

112. *See* National Down Syndrome Society, "Pro-Information Laws and Tool-kit," www.ndss.org/advocate/ndss-legislative-agenda/healthcare-research/pro -information-laws-toolkit/ (accessed January 18, 2020).

113. Nancy McCrea Iannone, "Guest Post—Keep Abortion Politics out of the Pro-Information Movement," *How Did We Get into This Mess?* (blog), June 21, 2014, www.thismess.net/2014/06/keep-abortion-politics-out-of-pro.html.

114. *See* Genevieve Plaster, "Ohio Passes Down Syndrome Bill Requiring Healthcare Professionals to Provide Support Information to Parents," Charlotte Lozier Institute, Dec. 23, 2014, https://lozierinstitute.org/ohio-passes -down-syndrome-bill-requiring-healthcare-professionals-to-provide-support -information-to-parents/.

115. *See* Senate Bill 164, www.legislature.ohio.gov/legislation/legislation -summary?id=GA132-SB-164 (accessed Jan. 28, 2020).

116. David M. Perry, "How Ohio Is Using Down Syndrome to Criminalize Abortion," *Pacific Standard*, Oct. 3, 2017, https://psmag.com/social-justice/gop -using-down-syndrome-as-cynical-wedge.

117. *See* "Timeline: Our Fight against Opportunistic Abortion Bans during the Covid-19 Pandemic," Planned Parenthood Action Fund, www.planned parenthoodaction.org/issues/abortion/timeline-our-fight-against-abortion -bans-during-covid19 (accessed July 8, 2020).

CHAPTER 7. ANITA HILL AND THE #METOO MOVEMENT

1. Stephanie Coontz, "Why 'Mad Men' Is TV's Most Feminist Show," *Wash. Post*, Oct. 2010, www.washingtonpost.com/wp-dyn/content/article/2010/10/08 /AR2010100802662.html.

2. *See* Catharine A. MacKinnon, *Sexual Harassment of Working Women: A Case of Sex Discrimination* (1979).

3. *See* Catharine A. MacKinnon, *Toward a Feminist Theory of the State* (1989).

4. MacKinnon, *Sexual Harassment of Working Women*, at 7.

5. *Id.* at 23.

6. *See* Elyse Shaw, Ariane Hegewisch, and Cynthia Hess, "Sexual Harassment and Assault at Work: Understanding the Costs," Institute for Women's Policy Research, Oct. 15, 2018, https://iwpr.org/publications/sexual-harassment-work -cost/.

7. *See* Lisa Desjardins, "All the Assault Allegations against Donald Trump, Recapped," *PBS NewsHour*, June 21, 2019, www.pbs.org/newshour/politics /assault-allegations-donald-trump-recapped.

8. *See* Sheila Weller, "Feminist Hero Mechelle Vinson on the Ford-Kavanaugh Hearings," *Next Tribe Age Boldly*, Oct. 19, 2018, https://nexttribe.com/mechelle -vinson/.

9. *See* Meritor Savings Bank v. Vinson, 477 U.S. 57 (1986).

10. *Id.* at 60.

11. DeNeen L. Brown, "She Said Her Boss Raped Her in a Bank Vault: Her Sexual Harassment Case Would Make Legal History," *Wash. Post*, Oct. 13, 2017, www.washingtonpost.com/news/retropolis/wp/2017/10/13/she-said-her-boss -raped-her-in-a-bank-vault-her-sexual-harassment-case-would-make-legal -history/?utm_term=.a4eaeddd99f1.

12. Meritor Savings Bank, 477 U.S. at 60.

13. *See* Brown, "She Said Her Boss Raped Her in a Bank Vault."

14. Meritor Savings Bank, 477 U.S. at 60-61.

15. *Id.* at 61.

16. *See* Linda Hirshman, "How the Supreme Court Made Sexual Harassment Cases More Difficult," *Wash. Post*, June 19, 2019, www.washingtonpost.com /outlook/2019/06/19/how-supreme-court-made-sexual-harassment-cases-more -difficult-win/?utm_term=.5bfa4da087c5.

17. *See* Burlington Industries v. Ellerth, 524 U.S. 742 (1998).

18. *See* Hirshman, "How the Supreme Court Made Sexual Harassment Cases More Difficult."

19. Meritor Savings Bank, 477 U.S. at 72.

20. *Id.* at 73.

21. *See* Tanya Kateri Hernández, "'What Not to Wear'—Race and Unwelcome-ness in Sexual Harassment Law: The Story of Meritor Savings Bank v. Vinson," in *Women and the Law Stories* 277, 292–93 (Elizabeth M. Schneider & Stepha-nie M. Wildman eds. 2011) (reporting that Vinson was "blacklisted in the bank-ing industry" after she filed her lawsuit).

22. *See* Deborah L. Brake, "Coworker Retaliation in the #MeToo Era," 49 *U. Balt. L. Rev.* 1 (2019).

23. Hirshman, "How the Supreme Court Made Sexual Harassment Cases More Difficult" (quoting Nancy Erika Smith).

24. Ronan Farrow, "From Aggressive Overtures to Sexual Assault: Harvey Weinstein's Accusers Tell Their Stories," *New Yorker*, Oct. 10, 2017, www .newyorker.com/news/news-desk/from-aggressive-overtures-to-sexual-assault -harvey-weinsteins-accusers-tell-their-stories.

25. *See* Julia Jacobs, "Anita Hill's Testimony and Other Key Moments from the Clarence Thomas Hearings," *N.Y. Times*, Sept. 20, 2018, www.nytimes.com/2018 /09/20/us/politics/anita-hill-testimony-clarence-thomas.html.

26. *Id.*

27. *Id.*

28. *Id.*

29. *See* "Majority of Public Believed Thomas over Hill after Hearings, Polls Showed," *The Hill*, Sept. 26, 2018, https://thehill.com/hilltv/what-americas -thinking/408595-majority-of-public-believed-thomas-over-hill-after-hearings.

30. *See* "How History Changed Anita Hill," *N.Y. Times*, June 17, 2019, www .nytimes.com/2019/06/17/us/anita-hill-women-power.html.

31. *Id.*

32. *See* Jodi Kantor & Megan Twohey, "Harvey Weinstein Paid Off Sexual Harassment Accusers for Decades," *N.Y. Times*, Oct. 5, 2017, www.nytimes.com /2017/10/05/us/harvey-weinstein-harassment-allegations.html.

33. *See* Ronan Farrow, "From Aggressive Overtures to Sexual Assault: Harvey Weinstein's Accusers Tell Their Stores," *New Yorker*, Oct. 10, 2017, www .newyorker.com/news/news-desk/from-aggressive-overtures-to-sexual-assault -harvey-weinsteins-accusers-tell-their-stories.

34. *See* Dan Mangan, "Harvey Weinstein Sentenced to 23 Years in Prison for Rape and Sex Assault in Case That Sparked 'MeToo' Movement," *CNBC*, Mar. 11, 2020, www.cnbc.com/2020/03/11/harvey-weinstein-sentenced-in-prison-for -sex-assault.html.

35. *See* "More Than 12M 'Me Too' Facebook Posts, Comments, Reactions in 24 Hours," *CBS News*, Oct. 17, 2017, www.cbsnews.com/news/metoo-more-than-12 -million-facebook-posts-comments-reactions-24-hours/.

36. *See* Jamillah Bowman Williams, Lisa Singh & Naomi Mezey, "#MeToo as Catalyst: A Glimpse into 21st Century Activism," 2019 *U. Chi. Legal F.* 371 (2019).

37. *See* Audrey Carlsen, Maya Salam, Claire Cain Miller, Denise Lu, Ash Ngu, Jugal K. Patel & Zach Wichter, "#MeToo Brought Down 201 Powerful Men: Nearly Half of Their Replacements Are Women," *N.Y. Times*, updated Oct. 29, 2018, nytimes.com/interactive/2018/10/23/us/metoo-replacements.html.

38. *Id.*

39. *See* me too, "Statistics," metoomvmt.org/about/ (accessed April 1, 2021).

40. *See* Emma Brockes, "#MeToo Founder Tarana Burke: 'You Have to Use Your Privilege to Serve Other People,'" *The Guardian*, Jan. 15, 2018, www

.theguardian.com/world/2018/jan/15/me-too-founder-tarana-burke-women -sexual-assault.

41. *Id.*

42. *Id.*

43. *Id.*

44. *See* Hernández, "'What Not to Wear'—Race and Unwelcomeness in Sexual Harassment Law."

45. *Id.* at 301.

46. *Id.* at 303.

47. *Id.* at 58.

48. Tara Golshan, "Study Finds 75 Percent of Workplace Harassment Victims Experienced Retaliation When They Spoke Up," *Vox*, Oct. 15, 2017, www.vox.com /identities/2017/10/15/16438750/weinstein-sexual-harassment-facts.

49. Michael Z. Green, "A New #MeToo Result: Rejecting Notions of Romantic Consent with Executives," 23 *Employee Rts. & Emp. Pol'y J.* 115, 148 (2019).

50. Deborah L. Brake, "Coworker Retaliation in the #MeToo Era," 49 *U. Balt. L. Rev.* 1, 56 (2019).

51. Sheryl Sandberg & Adam Grant, "Women at Work: Speaking While Female," *N.Y. Times*, Jan. 12, 2015, www.nytimes.com/2015/01/11/opinion /sunday/speaking-while-female.html.

52. Green, "A New #MeToo Result," 147.

53. Jean R. Sternlight, "Mandatory Arbitration Stymies Progress towards Justice in Employment Law: Where to, #MeToo?," 54 *Harv. C.R.–C.L. Rev.* 155, 159 (2019).

54. *See* Charlotts S. Alexander, "#MeToo and the Litigation Funnel," 23 *Employee Rts. & Emp. Pol'y J.* 17, 19 (2019) (reporting an increase of more than 12 percent in sexual harassment charges filed in the reporting period ending in Oct. 2018).

55. *See* Jamillah Bowman Williams, Lisa Singh & Naomi Mezey, "#MeToo as Catalyst: A Glimpse into 21st Century Activism," 2019 *U. Chi. Legal F.* 371 (2019).

56. *Id.* at 392.

57. *See* Iravedra v. Municipality of Guaynabo, No. 3:16-cv-01585-RAM (D. Puerto Rico Nov. 13, 2019).

58. Jelú Iravedra v. Municipality of Guaynabo, No. 16-1585-ADC, *8 (D. Puerto Rico Oct. 15, 2018).

59. *Id.* at *4.

60. *Id.* at *5.

61. *See* Theresa M. Beiner, "Let the Jury Decide: The Gap Between What Judges and Reasonable People Believe Is Sexually Harassing," 75 *S. Cal. L. Rev.* 791 (2002).

62. Iravedra v. Municipality of Guaynabo, No. 3:16-cv-01585-RAM (D. Puerto Rico Nov. 13, 2019).

63. *See* Zhou v. Intergraph Corp., 353 F. Supp.3d 1220 (N.D. Ala. 2019).

64. Zhou v. Intergraph Corporation, No. 5:17-CV-01033-AKK (N.D. Ala. Mar. 19, 2019).

65. 353 F. Supp.3d at 1230.

66. *Id.* at 1227.

67. *Id.* at 1231.

68. Corbin v. Steak N Shake, 2019 WL 3944430 at *1 (S.D. Ohio 2019).

69. *Id.* at *1.

70. *Id.* at *2.

71. *See* EEOC v. Pacific Fun Enterprises LLC d/b/a Snapper Sports Bar and Grill, 2020 WL 406681 (D. Hawaii Jan. 7, 2020).

72. *Id.* at *5.

73. *Id.* at *2.

74. *Id.* at *3.

75. *See* "Court Orders Waikiki Sports Bar to Pay Over $250,000 for Sexual Harassment," EEOC, Oct, 4, 2019, www.eeoc.gov/newsroom/court-orders-waikiki-sports-bar-pay-over-250000-sexual-harassment.

76. *See* Bennett and Meads v. Luigi's Italian Restaurant, 2020 WL 1503472 (D. Kansas Mar. 30, 2020).

77. *Id.* at *7.

78. *Id.*

79. *See* Lauren Kaori Gurley, "Why Sexual Harassment Rates Are So High in the Restaurant Industry," *Bloomberg City Lab*, Nov. 21, 2017, www.bloomberg.com/news/articles/2017-11-21/a-living-wage-could-curb-sexual-harassment-for-tipped-wage-workers.

80. *Id.*

81. *See* U.S. Department of Labor, "Minimum Wages for Tipped Employees," Jan. 1, 2021, www.dol.gov/agencies/whd/state/minimum-wage/tipped.

82. Gurley, "Why Sexual Harassment Rates Are So High in the Restaurant Industry."

83. *See* Anna Claire Vollers, "Gadsen Locals Say Moore's Predatory Behavior at Mall, Restaurants Not a Secret," *AL*, Nov. 13, 2017, www.al.com/news/index.ssf/2017/11/gadsden_residents_say_moores_b.html.

84. *See* Vaughn Hillyard & Dartunorro Clark, "Roy Moore, Who Lost Alabama Senate Race after Allegations of Sexual Misconduct, Announced Another Run for the Seat," *CBS News*, June 20, 2019, www.nbcnews.com/politics/politics-news/roy-moore-who-lost-alabama-senate-race-after-allegations-sexual-n1019681.

85. Greg Price, "Child Molestation Claims Destroyed Roy Moore in Alabama," *Newsweek*, Dec. 13, 2017, www.newsweek.com/metoo-alabama-women-vote-jones-746591.

CHAPTER 8. BLACK LIVES MATTER

1. For an excellent discussion of this problem, see Dorothy Roberts, "The Supreme Court 2018 Term: Foreword, Abolition Constitutionalism," 133 *Harv. L. Rev.* 1 (2018).

2. *See* Sally E. Hadden, *Slave Patrols: Law and Violence in Virginia and the Carolinas* 18–24 (2001).

3. David W. Blight, *Frederick Douglass: Prophet of Freedom* 26 (2018).

4. Roberts, "The Supreme Court 2018 Term."

5. Stuart Banner, *The Death Penalty: An American History* 99–100 (2002).

6. Roberts, "The Supreme Court 2018 Term," at 29.

7. *Id.* at 30.

8. *Id.* at 31.

9. Blight, *Frederick* Douglass, at 743.

10. Roberts, "The Supreme Court 2018 Term."

11. *Id.* at 41.

12. *Id.*

13. *See* Jason Hanna, "3 Recordings, 3 Cries of 'I Can't Breathe', 3 Black Men Dead after Interactions with Police," *CNN*, June 10, 2020, www.cnn.com/2020 /06/10/us/cant-breathe-deaths-javier-ambler-george-floyd-manuel-ellis/index .html.

14. *See* Larry Buchanan, Quoctrung Bui & Jugal K. Patel, "Black Lives Matter May Be the Largest Movement in U.S. History," *N.Y. Times*, July 3, 2020, www .nytimes.com/interactive/2020/07/03/us/george-floyd-protests-crowd-size .html?action=click&module=Top%20Stories&pgtype=Homepage.

15. *See* Amna Akbar, "The Movement for Black Lives Offers an Abolitionist Approach to Police Reform," LPE Project, Jan. 23, 2018, lpeblog.org/2018 /01/23/the-movement-for-black-lives-offers-an-abolitionist-approach-to-police -reform/.

16. "The Supreme Court 2018 Term," at 9.

17. *Id.* at 10.

18. Kori Rumore & Chad Yoder, "Minute by Minute: How Jason Van Dyke Shot Laquan McDonald," *Chicago Tribune*, Jan 18, 2019, www.chicagotribune .com/news/laquan-McDonald/ct-jason-vandyke-laquan-McDonald-timeline -htmlstory.html.

19. "Laquon McDonald Police Reports Differ Dramatically from Video," *Chicago Tribune*, Dec. 5, 2015, www.chicagotribune.com/news/ct-laquan-McDonald -chicago-police-reports-met-20151204-story.html.

20. *See* Allison V. Hall, Erika V. Hall & Jamie Perry, "Black and Blue: Exploring Racial Bias and Law Enforcement in the Killings of Unarmed Black Male Civilians," 73 *Am. Psychologist* 175–86 (2016).

21. "Laquon McDonald Police Reports Differ Dramatically from Video."

22. *See* Nausheen Husain, "Laquon McDonald Timeline: The Shooting, the Video, the Verdict and the Sentencing," *Chicago Tribune*, Jan. 18, 2019, www .chicagotribune.com/news/laquan-McDonald/ct-graphics-laquan-McDonald -officers-fired-timeline-htmlstory.html.

23. Nick Blumberg, "Police Union President Defends Van Dyke, Vows Appeal," *WTTW*, Oct. 5, 2018, news.wttw.com/2018/10/05/police-union-president -defends-van-dyke-vows-appeal.

24. Husain, "Laquon McDonald Timeline."

25. *Id.*

26. *Id.*

27. *See* "Anita Alvaraz Comes Out Swinging as Protestors Call for Her Res-ignation," *ABC7 Chicago*, Dec. 3, 2015, abc7chicago.com/anita-alvarez-cook -county-state's-attorney-laquan-mconald/1107905/.

28. *See* Stephanie Lulay & Erica Demarest, "Anita Alvarez Loses, Concedes State's Attorney's Race to Kim Foxx," *DNAinfo*, Mar. 15, 2016, www.dnainfo.com /chicago/20160315/little-village/anita-alvarez-faces-tough-primary-fight-from -kim-foxx-after-laquan-shooting/.

29. *See* Carol Felsenthal, "Kim Foxx Wants to Tell You a Story," *Chicago Mag-azine*, Dec. 10, 2018, www.chicagomag.com/Chicago-Magazine/January-2019 /Kim-Foxx-Wants-to-Tell-You-a-Story/.

30. *See* Camila Domonoske & David Schaper, "Chicago Mayor Rahm Eman-uel Not Seeking Re-Election," *NPR*, Sept. 4, 2018, www.npr.org/2018/09/04 /644553271/chicago-mayor-rahm-emanuel-not-seeking-reelection.

31. Aya Gruber, *The Feminist War on Crime: The Unexpected Role of Women's Liberation in Mass Incarceration* 5 (2020).

32. Bill Hutchinson, "Former Chicago Police Officer Jason Van Dyke Beaten by Inmates in Prison," *ABC News*, Feb. 14, 2019, https://abcnews.go.com/US /chicago-police-officer-jason-van-dyke-beaten-inmates/story?id=61072762.

33. Felsenthal, "Kim Foxx Wants to Tell You a Story."

34. *Id.*

35. *Id.*

36. *Id.*

37. *See* Ray Sanchez, "Chicago Prosecutor Kim Foxx Wins Primary Despite Criticism over Smollett Case," *CNN*, Mar. 18, 2020, www.cnn.com/2020/03/18 /us/chicago-kim-foxx-states-attorney-primary/index.html.

38. Felsenthal, "Kim Foxx Wants to Tell You a Story."

39. *Id.*

40. *See* Richard Fausset, "What We Know about the Shooting Death of Ahmaud Arbery," *N.Y. Times*, May 22, 2020, www.nytimes.com/article/ahmaud -arbery-shooting-georgia.html.

41. Elliot C. McLaughlin, "What We Know about Ahmaud Arbery's Killing," *CNN*, May 12, 2020, www.cnn.com/2020/05/11/us/ahmaud-arbery-mcmichael -what-we-know/index.html.

42. Barnini Chakraborty, "Ahmadu Arbery's Mother Says Georgia Officials Would Have 'Covered Up' Son's Murder," *Fox News*, May 22, 2020, www.foxnews .com/us/ahmaud-arbery-mother-georgia-officials-would-have-covered-up -murder.

43. Fausset, "What We Know about the Shooting Death of Ahmaud Arbery."

44. *Id.*

45. Tim Stelloh & Minyvonne Burke, "Man Who Filmed Shooting Death of Ahmaud Arbery Used Vehicle to 'Detain' Him, Warrant Says," *NBC News*, May 22, 2020, www.nbcnews.com/news/us-news/man-who-recorded-ahmaud -arbery-s-shooting-death-video-arrested-n1212496.

46. Eugene Scott, "There's Anger about Ahmaud Arbery's Shooting across the Political Spectrum," *Wash. Post*, May 8, 2020, www.washingtonpost.com /politics/2020/05/07/why-outrage-about-amaud-arberys-shooting-came-all -corners-political-spectrum-quickly/.

47. Darcy Costello & Tessa Duvall, "Minute by Minute: What Happened the Night Louisville Police Fatally Shot Breonna Taylor," *Louisville Courier Journal*, May 15, 2020, www.usatoday.com/story/news/nation/2020/05/15/minute -minute-account-breonna-taylor-fatal-shooting-louisville-police/5196867002/.

48. Richard A. Oppel Jr. & Derrick Bryson Taylor, "Here's What You Need to Know about Breonna Taylor's Death," *N.Y. Times*, June 5, 2020, www.nytimes .com/article/breonna-taylor-police.html.

49. Kay Jones, Carma Hassan & Leah Asmelash, "A Kentucky EMT Was Shot and Killed during a Police Raid of Her Home: The Family Is Suing for Wrongful Death," *CNN*, May 13, 2020, www.cnn.com/2020/05/13/us/louisville-police-emt -killed-trnd/index.html.

50. *Id.* at 2.

51. Emily Taguchi, Deborah Kim, Kristofer Rios & Anthony Rivas, "Breonna Taylor's Mom Seeking Answers in Her Death: 'I Haven't Had Time to . . . Grieve,'" *ABC News*, June 10, 2020, https://abcnews.go.com/US/breonna-taylors -mom-seeking-answers-death-time-grieve/story?id=71184205.

52. *Id.*

53. Jones, Hassan & Asmelash, "A Kentucky EMT Was Shot and Killed during a Police Raid of Her Home."

54. Amina Elahi & Eleanor Klibanoff, "Support for Louisville May Greg Fischer Wanes as Protests Continue," *WFPL*, June 11, 2020, wfpl.org/support-for -louisville-mayor-greg-fischer-wanes-as-protests-continue/.

55. "#SayHerName: Resisting Police Brutality against Black Women," African American Policy Forum, www.aapf.org/sayhername (accessed April 2, 2021).

56. Alisha Haridasani Gupta, "Birthday for Breonna: A Campaign to Mourn and Honor," *N.Y. Times*, June 6, 2020, www.nytimes.com/2020/06/06/us/birthday -breonna-taylor-black-lives-matter.html.

57. "Metro Council Discusses 'Breonna's Law,' Which Calls for Changes to No-Knock Warrants," *WLKY*, June 8, 2020, www.wlky.com/article/metro-council -discussing-breonnas-law-which-calls-for-changes-to-no-knock-warrants /32801571.

58. Paul Kane & John Wagner, "Democrats Unveil Broad Police Reform Bill as Floyd's Death Sparks Protests Nationwide," *Wash. Post*, June 9, 2020, www .washingtonpost.com/powerpost/democrats-unveil-broad-police-reform-bill -pledge-to-transform-law-enforcement/2020/06/08/1ed07d7a-a992-11ea-94d2 -d7bc43b26bf9_story.html.

59. *See* Elizabeth Joseph & Eric Levenson, "Black Birdwatcher in Central Park 911 Call Doesn't Want to Be Involved in Prosecution of Amy Cooper, NYT Reports," *CNN*, July 8, 2020, www.cnn.com/2020/07/08/us/christian-cooper -central-park/index.html.

60. *See* Sarah Maslin Nir, "White Woman Is Fired after Calling Police on Black Man in Central Park," *N.Y. Times*, May 26, 2020, www.nytimes.com/2020 /05/26/nyregion/amy-cooper-dog-central-park.html.

61. *See* Scott Stump, "Woman Speaks Out after Viral Central Park Confrontation with Man Sparks Outrage," *NBC Today*, May 26, 2020, www.today.com /news/amy-cooper-woman-viral-central-park-confrontation-video-apologizes -t182412.

62. Catherine Kim, "Poll: Americans Are More Concerned about Police Violence Than Violence at Protests," *Vox*, June 7, 2020, www.vox.com/2020/6/7 /21283239/poll-americans-more-concerned-police-violence-than-violence-at -protests.

63. *See* Joseph & Levenson, "Black Birdwatcher in Central Park 911 Call Doesn't Want to Be Involved in Prosecution of Amy Cooper."

64. Evan Hill, Ainara Tiefenthäler, Christiaan Triebert, Drew Jordan, Haley Willis & Robin Stein, "8 Minutes and 46 Seconds: How George Floyd Was Killed in Police Custody," *N.Y Times*, May 31, 2020, www.nytimes.com/2020/05/31/us /george-floyd-investigation.html.

65. "George Floyd: What Happened in the Final Moments of His Life," *BBC News*, July 16, 2020, www.bbc.com/news/world-us-canada-52861726.

66. *Id.*

67. *Id.*

68. Derrick Bryson Taylor, "George Floyd Protests: A Timeline," *N.Y Times*, June 3, 2020, www.nytimes.com/article/george-floyd-protests-timeline.html.

69. Josh Campbell, Sara Sidner & Eric Levenson, "All Four Former Officers Involved in George Floyd's Killing Now Face Charges," *CNN*, June 4, 2020, www .cnn.com/2020/06/03/us/george-floyd-officers-charges/index.html.

70. Catherine Kim, "Images of Police Using Violence against Peaceful Protesters Are Going Viral," *Vox*, May 31, 2020, www.vox.com/2020/5/31/21275994/police-violence-peaceful-protesters-images; and Jen Kirby, "The Disturbing History of How Tear Gas Became the Weapon of Choice against Protesters," *Vox*, June 3, 2020, www.vox.com/2020/6/3/21277995/police-tear-gas-protests-history-effects-violence.

71. *Id.* at 5.

72. Catherine E. Shoichet, "Police Brutality Prompted the Protests: In Some Cities, the Police Response Only Proved the Protesters' Point," *CNN*, June 2, 2020, www.cnn.com/2020/06/02/us/police-protests-use-of-force/index.html.

73. Candace Owens, "Confession," Twitter, June 3, 2020, https://twitter.com/RealCandaceO/status/1268280610818101248?s=20.

74. Daniel Politi, "Trump Retweets Interview Trashing George Floyd's Character as He Breaks Own Twitter Record," *Slate*, June 6, 2020, slate.com/news-and-politics/2020/06/trump-interview-trashing-george-floyd-breaks-twitter-record.html.

75. Tony Romm & Allyson Chiu, "Twitter Flags Trump, White House for 'Glorifying Violence' after Tweeting Minneapolis Looting Will Lead to 'Shooting,'" *Wash. Post*, May 29, 2020, www.washingtonpost.com/nation/2020/05/29/trump-minneapolis-twitter-protest/.

76. German Lopez, "The Sneaky Language Today's Politicians Use to Get Away with Racism and Sexism," *Vox*, Feb. 1, 2016, www.vox.com/2016/2/1/10889138/coded-language-thug-bossy.

77. *Id.* at 11.

78. Paul Kane & Mike Debonis, "Cotton Urges Deployment of Military in Response to Violence; Other Republicans Empathize with Peaceful Protesters, Floyd Family," *Wash. Post*, June 1, 2020, www.washingtonpost.com/powerpost/cotton-urges-deployment-of-military-in-response-to-violence-other-republicans-empathize-with-peaceful-protesters-floyd-family/2020/06/01/4d0a8710-a412-11ea-bb20-ebf0921f3bbd_story.html.

79. *Id.* at 14.

80. *See* Emily Badger, "How Trump's Use of Federal Forces in Cities Differs from Past Presidents," *N.Y. Times*, July 23, 2020, www.nytimes.com/2020/07/23/upshot/trump-portland.html.

81. Michael M. Grynbaum, Annie Karni & Jeremy W. Peters, "What Top Conservatives Are Saying about George Floyd and Police Brutality," *N.Y. Times*, May 30, 2020, www.nytimes.com/2020/05/30/us/politics/george-floyd-tucker-carlson-rush-limbaugh.html.

82. Neil MacFarquhar, "Many Claim Extremists Are Sparking Protest Violence: But Which Extremists?," *N.Y Times*, May 31, 2020, www.nytimes.com/2020/05/31/us/george-floyd-protests-white-supremacists-antifa.html.

83. *Id.* at 8.

84. *See* Luis Ferre-Sadurni & Jesse McKinley, "New York Bans Chokeholds and Approves Other Measures to Restrict Police," *N.Y. Times*, June 12, 2020, www.nytimes.com/2020/06/12/nyregion/50a-repeal-police-floyd.html?action= click&module=Top%20Stories&pgtype=Homepage.

85. Ibram X. Kendi, *Stamped from the Beginning* (2016).

86. Donald Trump, Twitter, n.d., twitter.com/realDonaldTrump /status/1270018789250400257?ref_src=twsrc%5Egoogle%7Ctwcamp%5Eserp %7Ctwgr%5Etweet (account suspended).

87. Gruber, *The Feminist War on Crime*, at 17.

88. Jasmine Harris, "Taking Publicity Public," 169 *Penn. L. Rev.* (forthcoming 2021).

89. *Id.*

90. Eric Noll, "Person of the Week: Marcellinos Celebrate Signing of Rosa's Law," *ABC News*, Oct. 8, 2010, abcnews.go.com/WN/person-week-marcellinos -celebrate-signing-rosas-law/story?id=11823803.

91. *Id.* at 6.

92. Sarah Jasmine Montgomery, "Kim Kardashian Apologizes for Using the R-Word after Receiving Backlash," *Complex Magazine*, Nov. 1, 2018, www .complex.com/pop-culture/2018/11/kim-kardashian-apologizes-for-using-the-r -word-on-halloween.

93. Chuck Schilken, "Janoris Jenkins Released by Giants after Using Slur on Social Media," *LA Times*, Dec. 13, 2019, www.latimes.com/sports/story/2019-12 -13/janoris-jenkins-cut-by-giants-offensive-word.

94. Aris Folley, "GOP Senator Apologizes for Tweet Calling Pelosi 'Retarded,' Blames Autocorrect," *The Hill*, Mar. 25, 2020, thehill.com/homenews/senate /489486-gop-senator-apologizes-for-tweet-calling-pelosi-retarded-blames -autocorrect.

95. *See Crip Camp: A Disability Revolution*, Netflix, www.netflix.com/title /81001496.

96. *See* Doron Dorfman, "Fear of the Disability Con: Perceptions of Fraud and Special Rights Discourse," 53 *L. & Soc. Rev.* 1051 (2019).

97. *See* Colby Itkowitz, "Rep. Ted Yoho Removed from Board of Christian Charity over His Comments about Rep. Alexandria Ocasio-Cortez," *Wash. Post*, July 25, 2020, www.washingtonpost.com/politics/rep-ted-yoho-removed-from -board-of-christian-charity-over-his-comments-about-rep-alexandria-ocasio -cortez/2020/07/25/31037546-ceaa-11ea-91f1-28aca4d833a0_story.html.

98. *See* Jack Hutton, *User Clip: Rep Alexandria Ocasio-Cortez Addressing Rep Ted Yoho's Abusive Comments*, C-SPAN, July 23, 2020, www.c-span.org /video/?c4894472/user-clip-rep-alexandria-ocasio-cortez-addressing-rep-ted -yohos-abusive-comments.

Index

Founded in 1893,
UNIVERSITY OF CALIFORNIA PRESS
publishes bold, progressive books and journals
on topics in the arts, humanities, social sciences,
and natural sciences—with a focus on social
justice issues—that inspire thought and action
among readers worldwide.

The UC PRESS FOUNDATION
raises funds to uphold the press's vital role
as an independent, nonprofit publisher, and
receives philanthropic support from a wide
range of individuals and institutions—and from
committed readers like you. To learn more, visit
ucpress.edu/supportus.